skin deep

PENTECOSTALISM, RACISM AND THE CHURCH

ESSAYS BY SCHOLARS IN THE CHURCH OF GOD (CLEVELAND, TN)

Clifton R. Clarke
Wayne C. Solomon
Editors

Seymour Press SP

Skin Deep: Pentecostalism, Racism and the Church

Essays by Scholars in the Church of God (Cleveland, TN)

ISBN: 978-1-938373-52-7
LCCN: 2021936573

Cover Design by: ben Nkrumah
Printed in the United States of America

© Seymour Press
 Lanham, MD 2021

Table of Contents

Dedication
in Memory of
Bishop Harcourt Garfield Poitier, Sr.

This "Quiet Giant," was recognized as a bridge-builder in ministry and community affairs. H. G. Poitier was driven by the belief that, as Scripture records Peter's revelation, "that God is not one to show partiality, but in every nation, the man who fears Him and does what is right is welcome to Him." (Acts 10:34-35, NASB). He knew that a "church divided against itself cannot stand." AND THAT the church must become one in spirit, one in power, one in faith; and must demonstrate this in word and practicality. Even prior to being appointed by the Church of God to serve as Representative of Black Affairs, Bishop Poitier traveled extensively on behalf of the denomination to promote unity.

After experiencing salvation and the baptism in the Holy Ghost in 1924, he was one of nine charter members of the Deerfield Beach (Florida) Church of God (now Cathedral Church of God). Sensing the call of God, the spark of evangelism struck his soul and he began ministering. Well-versed in Scripture, he shared the importance of studying the Bible with fellow ministers as he encouraged them to take advantage of the ministerial enrichment programs offered at Lee College (now Lee University).

Following his 1945 ordination, Poitier organized twelve churches and served twelve pastorates. He also served as Secretary/Treasurer of the Church of God Colored Work and Overseer of black churches in Alabama, Mississippi, Georgia, and Florida, Director of Ministerial & Lay Enrichment, and Representative of Black Affairs to the Church of God Executive Offices.

Having confidence in the Word of God and his call to ministry, Poitier diligently pursued his bridge-building objectives despite negative criticism and repercussions by some of the more militant-minded ministers in the Colored Work. But he also faced the demeaning and condescending actions and racist attitudes of others. Yet, in spite of tremendous adversity, he remained focused on his mission and persevered because he understood the importance of the greater purpose to be achieved by becoming one.

"Daddy" to nine daughters and eight sons, he and his wife, Celestine Tynes Poitier, left a legacy that extends to the third, fourth, and fifth-generation family. In the midst of full-time ministry, often pastoring more than one church separated by several miles, Poitier took the time to "pastor" his own family. Among the children are four credentialed ministers, pastors wives, church musicians, and career professionals.

Foreword

Skin Deep provokes the reader to look introspectively into the historical mirror and reflect on the challenges, contributions, and sacrifices that men and women of color have endured to foster legacies this generation can emulate. Our existence was predestined by God's handy work who eyed our worth beyond the stereotypes associated with our skin color and conveyed the clarity of a heritage that provides contributions that empowers the minds of many. These writers' forward-thinking challenges the reader to explore the character, and conversation commitment, of black people within the Church of God (Cleveland, TN) before casting assumptions that will cause us to miss the effervescent beauty of God's entire Creation (Psalms 139:14). What if we allowed ourselves time to explore the accomplishments, giftings, faith, and dedication of people of color before allowing years of judgment to sway the true worth of individuals and give way to a system that has mandated years of misrepresentation?

We have witnessed one presidential campaign platform that champions "CHANGE" and another desiring to draw us backward to accept past voices that endeavor to re-enslave our minds because of fear. Fearful misconceptions have caused some to cut off the collaboration that would allow us to explore and undertake the changes necessary to bring about genuine unity. Yet, a concerted effort can make us stronger as ONE rather than keep our denomination divided and separated. "All things are possible," and we are people of multiple hues who can overcome the challenges we face as a nation and, most importantly, as a church. We can silence the voices of hostility that speak from history and become acquainted with one another in ways that change our thinking and bring positive resolution.

Black and white members of the Church of God owe a debt of gratitude to a great cloud of witnesses who chartered a course of greatness and left a legacy for people of color that allows us to look beyond enforced labels and assert our spiritual giftedness and intellectual ability. We have endured racial challenges that proven our allegiance to our resolve to, "Remain Faithful"! This proven faithfulness has survived the challenges of "CHANGE." Yet, men and women of color are becoming inspired to seek equality and demand recognition. These writers help us see that we no longer will accept a hand-out, but seek to make a lasting impact within our denomination and insist on the opportunity to be empowered to serve at every level. They speak of a desire for the chance to show our gifting and have the privilege to sit at the decision-making table to offer significant input. Our younger generations want greater opportunity for service and the elimination of labels that allow fear to conquer, rather than empower, all people to excel. When we stop placing people in stereotypical boxes, but allow us to blend our gifts into a well-knitted quilt of many colors and fabrics, we provide the privilege of letting each be recognized without allowing any pigmentation to have dominance! As you read this book, I hope you will see a different reflection of yourself in the mirror, conscientiously becoming a part of the solution, helping create racial harmony, and allowing yourself to fully appreciate the diversity in God's Creation!

Bishop Kenneth Hill, Administrative Bishop
Church of God – Southern New England Region

Preface

The struggle against racism in the church is part of a broader battle of eradicating racism in our world. The issue in the church—and our focus on the Pentecostal tradition—is particularly egregious because racial discrimination and violence is antithetical to everything that pertains to Christ as Savior, Sanctifier, Healer, Baptizer and Coming Lord.[1] The plague of racism within the Pentecostal church challenges our commitment to these historical foundation stones.

As Savior, Christ died to tear down walls of division between God and us, as well as eliminate oppressive cultural hegemonies such as white supremacy and institutional racial discrimination. As people, we are all born in sin, have been shaped in iniquity, and stand equally in need of a savior (Is. 51: 5-6). As Sanctifier, Christ prayed in John 17: 19, *'that we might also be sanctified through the truth.'* The ideas of white superiority, white normativity, and the inferiority of people of African descent are mendacious lies that quench the process of sanctification in the believer. The Pentecostal church's active and passive complicity with these lies must be a point of confession, repentance, and institutional transformation.[2] As Healer, Christ took our infirmities and bore our sicknesses (Matt. 8:17). Racism is a historical cultural sickness that needs to be healed. As well, as Kameron Carter and Willie Jennings point out in their brilliant texts, racism is a theological

---

[1] Donald W. Dayton, *Theological Roots of Pentecostalism* (Peabody: Hendrickson, 1987). Early uses of the fivefold pattern may be detectible outside North America as well. See Mark J. Cartledge, "The Early Pentecostal Theology of *Confidence* Magazine (1908–1926): A Version of the Five-Fold Gospel?" *The Journal of the European Pentecostal Theological Association* 28, no. 2 (2008): 117–30. See also, Steven J. Land, *Pentecostal Spirituality: A Passion for the Kingdom* (Sheffield: Sheffield, 1993), 183.

[2] See Jamal Tisby, *The Color of Compromise* (Grand Rapids: Zondervan, 2020).

sickness of the imagination and western historical biblical interpretation.[3]

In addition to violating these foundational Christological truths, racism and white supremacy are blasphemous misrepresentations of biblical truth according to Ephesians 4: 5, which asserts that there is, *'one body, and one Spirit, just as you were called in one hope of your calling; one Lord, one faith, one baptism; one God and Father of all, who is above all, and through all, and in you all.'* The church's overt, implicit, and ecclesialized racism therefore poisons the sacred truth that it is one body built up of diverse members who are equally valuable to it. William Padilla insightfully argues that idolatry is at the heart of social injustice and the eventual downfall of a nation[4]. The attempt to rise above others through racial injustice, is akin to coveting "god-status"—trying to make oneself a god and receive the devotion of those who are subjugated. The demise of racial injustice is critical to the survival of humanity. Its perpetuation is a formula for genocide. The prophet Amos understood that when he wrote, *'... let justice roll down like a river, righteousness like a never-failing stream.'* (Amos 5: 24 version)

Finally, the idea of Christ as soon coming King is based on the belief that Christ is returning for one united Church composed of people who have been transformed by the blood of Christ, which secured our access to eternal life. The struggle to defeat racism is an ongoing battle to remove its disruptive influence from the structures of our church and our world. To this end, Pentecostal scholars add a

---

[3] See, Willie James Jennings, *The Christian Imagination: Theology and the Origins of Race* (New Haven, CT: Yale University Press, 2011), and *After Whiteness: An Education in Belonging.* (Grand Rapids, MI: Wm. B. Eerdmans Publishing Co., 2020) and J. Kameron Carter, *Race: A Theological Account*, 1st edition. (New York: Oxford University Press, 2008).

[4] Padilla in Villafane, The Liberating Spirit, William B. Eerdmans Publishing Co., (Grand Rapids, MI, 1993

critical tool for deconstructing ideologies, institutions, and behaviors that tarnish the testimony of the unity of Christ's Church in the world.

The Motivation Behind this Volume

The brutal killing of George Floyd in May 2020 has caused Christians to revisit the issue of the evils of racism across the world. The, what can only be described as, public lynching of Floyd, sent shockwaves across the globe and reminded us how far we still have to go to eradicate the evil of institutional racism and state-sanctioned racialized violence in the world. One of the encouraging signs of the recent outbreak of protest was the mantra calling for the end of white silence. The coalition of demonstrations across the world awoke a global consciousness that recognized that the virus of racism infects us all, and we all have a role to play in its eradication. This volume brings together the diverse voices of Church of God scholars to speak into the challenge of racism in our churches and our communities. These Pentecostal scholars bring their education and the erudition given to us by the Holy Spirit for the service of the body of Christ and the world. With these, they tackle issues that have often been ignored or touched on only lightly. (1 Cor. 12:7).

Historically, in spite of the strident gains Pentecostal scholarship has made in establishing itself as a reputable tradition, too often it has been culpable in the collective white silence that has not brought its full weight to the task of eradicating racism in the church. Though some Pentecostal scholars have engaged race and justice in their work, these offerings have mostly been directed to the academy and rarely receive serious attention beyond that sphere.

Further, the relationship between church administrators and academia has often been tenacious. Senior administrators are rightly concerned with doctrinal loyalty and church unity, and these sometimes appear to be at odds with academic freedom. So, while it is often easier for the academy and church administrators to behave as if each other do not exist, creative tension between the church and the academy is healthy for both. The task of eliminating racism from our theological and ecclesiological structures is a colossal challenge that requires a joint effort that draws on all the resources that God has placed at our disposal.

The essays in this volume cover a range of topics that variously engages Pentecostalism, racism and the church and seek to help is do just that. They speak to these issues from the vantage points of biblical studies, theology, history, critical race studies and sociology. We surrender these essays with the hope that they will stimulate dialogue, and discussion as they provide edification for leaders and members in the Church of God, in particular, and the body of Christ, in general.

Clifton R. Clarke and Wayne Solomon

Black Thought Matters: The Miseducation and Delegitimization of Black Intellectual Thought in the Western Religious Academy

Clifton Clarke

Within the Western world, Pentecostal and Evangelical educational institutions of higher education have been tainted by the legacies of slavery, scientific racism, and racial stereotyping.[1] The American educational system, writ large, is built on the warped foundation of white superiority. Historically, this Eurocentric foundation has maliciously suppressed the contribution of people of color to world civilization.[2] To be black in America is therefore to be caught in a psycho-structural web of deception and miseducation vis-à-vis the significance of the black contribution to world development. To justify what Abraham Lincoln called "that peculiar institution" for ongoing economic exploitation, the white majority was forced to scientifically "demonstrate" that black people were not only inferior in their physical and emotional endowment but had not evolved to the intellectual level of the white race.

Scientists such as Carl Linnaeus, Samuel George Morton, and Johann Friedrich Blumenbach concocted racialized biological and social theories to legitimize the dogma of the inferiority of black or brown-skinned people.[3] In more recent times, the legacy of these scientific charlatans survived through William Shockley's theories that

---

[1] For a detailed summary of the influence of race on Evangelical churches and institutions, see chapter 2 of Michael Emerson and Christian Smith, *Divided by Faith* (New York: Oxford University Press, 2000).

[2] The New York Times bestseller, *Savage Inequalities* written by Jonathan Kozol provides a chilling study of the ongoing inequalities within the American school system. See Jonathan Kozol, *Savage Inequalities: Children in American Schools* (New York: Broadway Paperback, 1991); see also Elaine A. Robinson, *Race and Theology* (Nashville: Abingdon, 2012) for a more specific discussion on race and theological education.

[3] A good summary text of their views can be found in chapter 5 of Nicholas Wade, *A Troublesome Inheritance: Genes, Race, and Human History* (New York: Penguin Books, 2014).

black people belong to a lower species of the human race. He suggested mass sterilization of black men and women as a remedy.[4]

The notion of black inferiority, however, was not merely the opinion of a few white extremists. From the nation's founding, it was enshrined in the American legal system through the Constitution and intoned within its cultural fabric through the national anthem.[5] In a groundbreaking book, *Black Resistance/White Law: A History of Constitutional Racism in America*, Mary Frances Berry demonstrates that, "the government has weaponized the Constitution to deny black Americans their legal rights to the pursuit of happiness.[6]

Within the institution of slavery, it was not only illegal for blacks to own books or learn to read, but education was also deemed a waste for people considered having the intellectual level of the beast of the field. The perception of black people as too listless to appreciate "pearls of knowledge" still rests in the collective white educational psyche. Studies show that, from kindergarten to graduate school, white teachers hold low expectations of black students,[7] and that this attitude leads to a critical lack of appreciation of the contribution of African Americans to the advancement of life in all spheres, including religion and theology.

Racial Stereotyping

Racial stereotyping is linked to the idea of intellectual inferiority. The practice has a long history in America, stemming from images and caricatures of the sambo, Aunt Jemimah, and others in the public arena. Movies, for example, have been a powerful media for transmitting racialized stereotypes about people of color, and fueling

---

[4] See Roger Pearson, *Shockley on Eugenics and Race* (Washington, DC: Scott Townsend Publishers, 1992), 23.

[5] An example of this was the three-fifths compromise between northern and southern states in 1787.

[6] Mary Frances Berry, *Black Resistance/White Law A History of Constitutional Racism in America* (New York: Penguin Books, 1994).

[7] Marvin Lynn and Adrienne Dixon, *Handbook on Critical Race Theory in Education*, 2nd ed. (New York: Routledge, 2015).

implicit bias. The early twentieth century silent black and white film craze considered a breakthrough in cinematography, portrayed blacks extremely pejoratively, producing films such as *The Wooing and Wedding of a Coon*, *The Slave*, *The Nigger*, and the *Sambo* series.[8]

The image of the black male moved from the listless, Sambo to a "savage" needing to be tamed. Movies such as *Birth of a Nation* (1915), directed and co-produced by D. W. Griffith, promoted the idea that the Ku Klux Klan was formed because black males were dangerous savages that could only be contained through lynching.[9] Although such images have since evolved to more human depictions, this violent untamable savage image possibly runs deepest in the white male psyche. Imagery such as this was subliminally, though dramatically, portrayed in the movie *King Kong*, in which a giant black gorilla captures an innocent, vulnerable white woman. The ape—a symbol for black men—is big and robust, unspoken cues of sexual violation are palpable, and a compelling case of white identification of the black, untamed, savage male continues. In this long-running series, which recently resurfaced on the big screen, the white male figure, in a latent Freudian twist, seeks to impose his whiteness upon the deep dark jungle and replaces the ape image as the king of the jungle. Today the caricaturing of black bodies is more subtle, and messages are often more subliminal.[10]

On rereading Carter G. Woodson's, *The Mis-Education of the Negro*, reflecting on my role as an educator at a time of increasing unrest, and witnessing black students' failure to thrive within theological

---

[8] For a good discussion on black images in the media, see Jan Nederveen Pieterse, *White in Black: Images of African and Blacks in Western Popular Culture* (New Haven and London: Yale University Press, 1992).

[9] The original name of the 1915 silent movie *The Birth of a Nation* was adapted from the Thomas F. Dixon Jr. novel *The Clansman*. The movie was directed and co-produced by D. W. Griffith and starred Lillian Gish. In 2016, Nate Parker directed and re-released the film under the same title.

[10] For an example of the media criticism concerning the racial politics of *The Blind Side*, see http://www.thinkingpoker.net/2010/01/the-racial-politics-of-the-blind-side/, accessed September 19, 2018.

educational institutions that systemically disadvantage their intellectual development, I question how these institutions can be structurally revamped to foster black students' intellectual development and self-awareness. Ignoring the black intellectual life inspired and nurtured through our contribution to human advancement stymies advancement of black empowerment.

W. E. B. Du Bois and Booker T, Washington

The eminent black sociologist, William Edward Burghardt Du Bois, sought doggedly to debunk the perception of black intellectual inferiority. In his powerful collection of essays, *The Souls of Black Folk*,[11] he wrestled with the theme of education as the center of his theory of racial uplift. In this literary masterpiece, Du Bois brilliantly dismantles widely held beliefs that black people's ignorance results from their inferior intellect while white people's superior intelligence results from their natural ability. He argues forcefully, on the contrary, that the lack of black intellectual attainment can be attributed to the vicious legacy of slavery and the discriminatory conditions that remained in the South after its demise.[12] In this work, he opposes Booker T. Washington's thesis that black people should settle for trade occupations and focus on training that engages their hands and not a life of the mind.

Du Bois' position reminds us that black thriving is not just about the fact of receiving education, but also about the mode, means, and level of the education provided. In many educational institutions today, black people are steered toward the practical aspect of learning. In theology, for example, black students are often encouraged to pursue ministry-focused learning such as preaching, evangelism, pastoral care,

---

[11] W. E. B. Du Bois, *The Souls of Black Folk* (Chicago: A.C. McClurg & Co), 1903.

[12] For other texts that makes the same case, see Carter C. G. Woodson, The Education of Negroes Prior to 1861 (New York: Arno Press, 1968); Rosetta Austin Moore, The Impact of Slavery on the Education of Blacks in Orange County, North Carolina: 1619–1970 (Lulu Publishing Services, 2015).

and other service-orientated areas, while white students are nurtured in the more abstract and conceptual areas such as biblical literature, languages, textual criticism, and systematic theology.

After recognizing Washington's rise to prominence as "the most striking thing" in African American history since 1876,[13] Du Bois chides him for rendering blacks a permanent underclass by signing the Atlanta Compromise. This document essentially, agreed that Southern Blacks would cease their struggle for equality, integration, and social justice and submit to white political rule in exchange for white funding of basic academic programs and providing fairer treatment for blacks in the legal system.[14] For Du Bois, Washington's signing of the Compromise signaled taking the wind out of the sails of civil reform when it was most necessary. In his comprehensive critique of Washington's approach, Du Bois lifts seven paradoxes. At the core is the singular contradiction that, on one hand, Washington advocates dignity and self-reliance, while on the other, he renders the foundation upon which dignity and self-reliance rest (equality, integration, access to education) unattainable.[15]

Although Du Bois' approach to education carries an air of elitism and pomposity, his critique of Washington's approach hits the bull's eye. It must not go unnoticed that Du Bois' public critique of Washington was not without risk. Washington's approach received massive public support and endorsements from the rank and file of both black and white southern leaders. In his stinging rebuke, however, Du Bois leaves a lasting salutary lesson: even when black people hold positions of power, it is not always wielded for betterment of the community. He teaches us that when people of color misappropriate

---

[13] Du Bois, *Souls of Black Folk*, 28
[14] Signed in 1895 between Booker T. Washington, president of the Tuskegee Institute, other black leaders along with Southern White leaders.
[15] Du Bois, Souls of Black Folk, 29.

power, it should be resisted with the same ferocity as when perpetrated by white supremacists.

The New Evangelical/Pentecostal Compromise

Within contemporary white Pentecostal/Evangelical educational institutions, there often exists a compromise similar to that signed in Atlanta in 1895. Although not formally or publicly displayed, there is often a tradeoff between what Cornel West calls "race-effacing black leaders"[16] and white Pentecostal/Evangelical institutional leaders who seek to forge a more rainbow leadership image. This compromise assumes that black leaders will agree to work within white structures without demanding the required change to bring about equality, equity, and inclusion.

For this, black leaders are offered positions in the line of fire where resistance will probably show up. They are usually asked to serve as diversity, inclusion, or equal opportunity officers. Even when black leaders do not officially occupy these positions, they are expected to keep black agitation in check and show blind loyalty to the institution. Such race-effacing leadership is the greatest weapon for the maintaining of the status quo.

Black people want black leaders to achieve as they serve as a point of pride for the community, especially as there are few black leaders in such positions. Yet some of these leaders stand in the way of change when they become co-conspirators with white educational establishments. While differences of opinion exist among black leaders regarding how to be agents of change, these need to be expressed with the same degree of tenderness and respect that we observed in Du Bois' critique of Washington.

---

[16] Cornel West, in *Race Matters,* groups three types of black leadership in American political life: the race-effacing managerial leaders, the race-identifying protest leader, and race-transcending prophetic leader. See Cornel. West, *Race Matters*, Boston: Beacon Press, 1993, 58-59.

Hermeneutic of Suspicion

The American educational system has been weaponized to bring about black nihilism[17] so what Paul Ricoeur calls, a "hermeneutic of suspicion" must be applied to efforts of educational tutelage of blacks within the context of white Evangelical institutional hegemony.[18] In the context of black learning, this hermeneutic of suspicion does not simply question the particularism of the subject matter, but questions the very epistemic and ideological foundations upon which assumptions are made about black people.

This multivalent analysis of religion's origins foregrounds the notion of concealment as a form of deconstruction. It sees this hermeneutic as a critical tool for black students' academic inquiry within white Evangelical institutions. For to deny the contribution of any people to the advancement of the human race is to deny their very existence. Conversely, to value the contribution of a people to global advancement engenders self-respect and a sense of, what Martin Luther King called, "somebodiness."[19] All of this is at stake in black students' fight to include engagement of black thought, history, culture, and religious life in their educational experience.

A Personal Journey

As a student and professor of theology for over thirty years, purging internalized white theological normativity has been an ongoing intellectual struggle. Educated in white institutions by white professors and teaching in a context dominated by whiteness, I am continually assessing, reexamining, and problematizing my theological assumptions and conclusions because of presuppositions and conceptualizations imbibed from that context. Being schooled in white normative theological traditions informed me that white thinking is

---

[17] See Lewis Brogdon, *Hope on the Brink: Understanding the Emergence of Nihilism in Black America* (Eugene OR: Wipf and Stock Publishers, 2013.

[18] Paul Ricoeur, *Freud and Philosophy: An Essay on Interpretation* (New Haven: Yale University Press, 1970), 27.

[19] Martin Luther King, Jr., 'Life's Blueprint,'

right thinking, and suggested that my black theological education is abnormal, disruptive, and even—dare I say—unnatural.

As a student introduced to "giants" of Western thought of the likes of Thomas Aquinas, John Calvin, John Wesley, Dietrich Bonhoeffer, Reinhold Niebuhr, Paul Tillich, and Karl Barth, the metaphysical, rationalistic, and scientific playground of their theological inquiry became mine. Their quest for the historical Jesus to satisfy the expectation of an increasingly post-Christian age also became mine. In the fields of theological study, from biblical languages to hermeneutics, it was made clear that white people, particularly white men, were the standard bearers of orthodoxy.

My still evolving theological decolonization came gradually and three key experiences in my reshaping and remaking deserve mentioning. The first came twenty years ago by way of reading James H. Cone's *Black Theology and Black Power*.[20] In it, for the first time, I saw that a white Eurocentric theological approach was an optional and, in many ways, flawed reading of the biblical text and Christian history. From that point, reading all I could lay my hands on by Cone, such as his seminal, *God of the Oppressed*,[21] taught me about theology and location. The second experience came through reading John Mbiti's *African Religions and Philosophy*[22] and teaching and pastoring in Ghana for a decade. The theological questions to which I had devoted much of my academic studies up until that point were not being asked in this West African context.

Then, as the pastor of a predominately African American church in the United States, I had the third experience. Immersing myself in African American literature, I became familiar with the work of towering black authors such as Du Bois, James Baldwin, Carter G.

---

[20] James H. Cone, *Black Theology and Black Power* (New York: Seabury Press, 1969).

[21] James H. Cone, *The God of the Oppressed* (Maryknoll, NY: Orbis Books, 2012).

[22] John Mbiti, *African Religion and Philosophy* (New York: Anchor Books, 1970).

Woodson, Langston Hughes, Maya Angelou, Martin Luther King Jr., Malcolm X, Zora Neale Hurston, Angela Davis, Henry Louis Gates, Cornel West, and Michael Eric Dyson and many other black intellectual writers. This reading, along with my involvement as a pastor and a social justice activist against police brutality and mass incarceration of blacks, gained me a profound understanding of the dilemma of race in America.

The Queen of the Sciences

My turn to an examination of the of study systematic theology required a sharp, but necessary turn into a narrower road that provides an example of how white Pentecostal/Evangelical educational hegemony bears upon Christian theology. During the late medieval period when the idea of a university education was taking shape, schools were separated into classical liberal arts, grammar (which included subjects like logic and rhetoric), mathematics and astronomy, and theology which was considered the "queen of the sciences." The Bible was held as the standard for all knowledge and the source of all truth. To be a theology student, therefore, was to be a student of the "queen of the sciences." The "queen," however, was white and so was her science. This state of affairs has carried over to the contemporary situation. Yet, while this generalization may seem hyperbolic, the white normative anchorage of theological education in white Pentecostalism and Evangelicalism in America is well established.[23]

In the academy, *Systematic Theology* is the discipline of ordering key theological themes into a coherent system. The task of systematic theology is to link *biblical theology*; the branch associated with tradition, *historical theology*; and the branch associated with what moderns considered the highest form of thoughtful and expansive knowing known as *philosophical theology*. Systematic theology unites these

---

[23] A compelling argument for this case is made by Michael Emerson and Christian Smith in *Divided by Faith: Evangelical Religion and the Problem of Race in America* (Oxford, UK: Oxford University Press, 2001).

branches and their respective sources.[24] Standard texts in guiding this inquiry include such titles as Wayne Grudem's *Systematic Theology*, Louis Berkhof's *Systematic Theology*, Richard Plantinga and colleagues' *An Introduction to Christian Theology*, Stanley Grenz's *Theology for the Community of God*, and Paul Tillich's *Systematic Theology*. [25] In spite of any misgivings one might have with these texts, such substantial volumes unquestionably demonstrate the highest level of scholarship and research. There are, however, three general assumptions that I would like to point out.

The first concerns the assumption of universal appeal that has a matter-of-fact quality about it. The purveyors of this theology make little attempt to address the author's personal, subjective suppositions as interpreters of the field of inquiry. They exhibit a degree of sureness which they assume their postulations have universal applicability. Their assumptions often show up in the title itself. "Systematic" or "Christian" theology gives the reader no clue as to the perspectival location of the hermeneutic. Second, there is often no mention of how culture and racial biases shaped the finished product. Racial neutrality and an impartial cultural objectivity that extricate the writer from inevitable human biases and prejudice are presumed. Third, there is an assumption of "finality"—a sense of utmost certitude in theological and philosophical determinations and conclusions.

Lifting the Hegemonic Lid

Little or no place is given to black contributions in the theological classroom. If addressed at all, they are treated like trailers at the end of a blockbuster movie. Yet black thought has been part of the marrow of Christian teaching since the inception of the church. The "whiteout" of the black theological and philosophical contribution to

---

[24] Richard J. Plantinga, *An Introduction to Christian Theology* (Cambridge: Cambridge University Press, 2010), 15–16.

[25] Wayne Grudem, *Systematic Theology* (Grand Rapids, MI: Zondervan, 1994); Louis Berkhof, *Systematic Theology* [reprint 1995] (New York: GHL Publishing, 2017); Stanley Grenz, *Theology for the Community of God* (Grand Rapids, MI: William B. Eerdmans Publishing Co., 2000).

the Christian faith is not merely the result of a collective white amnesia, but part of a broader conspiracy of black exclusion, since the genesis of the European Enlightenment racial project is to portray black scholarship as intellectually inferior. Lifting the white hegemonic theological lid and incorporating thoughts, resources, and questions representative of the entire story of Christian theology will nurture a more wholesome and inclusive experience for students of color as well as for instructors.

Standard systematic texts usually begin with St. Anselm's definition of theology as the act of "faith seeking understanding." The term "theology" is etymologically derived from the Greek *theos-logos*—God talk. The student's introduction to Greek philosophy, especially Plato and Aristotle, forms the epistemic foundation to the works of St Augustine and Thomas Aquinas. Aquinas's breathtaking *Summa Theologiaca*[26] is silently highlighted as the undisputed systematic heavyweight champion as systematic texts go. Calvin's *Institutes of the Christian Religion* comes in second. In more recent times the fourteen-volume magnum opus of Swiss Protestant theologian Karl Barth is the gauntlet thrown down to seal the place of European systematic theological supremacy. Other scholars such as Wolfhart Pannenberg, Paul Tillich, Jürgen Moltmann, Dietrich Bonhoeffer—other white men— continue to dominate the field. Once these foundation stones are firmly in place and the preeminence of white theological thought established beyond doubt, black and other contextual theologies are scraped from the bottom of the barrel. Unlike the theologies of these Western "giants," these contextual responses to the particularities of human culture appear less important.

Black Theology and the Enlightenment

Certainly, the Western theological tradition provides insight for our knowledge of the Christian faith. Yet, to privilege this tradition as

---

[26] Thomas Aquinas, *Summa Theologica*, trans. Fathers of the English Dominican Province (New York: Benziger Brothers, 1911–1925).

the sole, unassailable authority, is untenable, and calls for a number of cautions. To start with, the notion that the white Western intellectual tradition, based upon Greek philosophy, is the foundation for enlightenment thought must be questioned. Millennia before Athenian philosophers such as Socrates, Plato, and Aristotle pondered the mysteries of the cosmos, Egyptian philosophers developed advanced systems of religion and morality, and carved these into their institutions of higher learning with profound insights into the natural world and the hereafter.[27] These earlier forms of religious knowledge drawn from ancient oral, mythological, and astrophysical sources provided the raw material for theology or *theos-logos* (God-talk). George James in his eye-opening book, *Stolen Legacy,* argues compellingly that the foundations of Greek philosophical thought were stolen from the temples of ancient Egypt.[28] According to James:

> From the sixth century B.C. to the death of Aristotle, (322 B.C) the Greeks made the best of their chance to learn all they could about Egyptian culture; most students received instructions directly from the Egyptian Priest but after the invasion of Alexander the Great, the Royal temples and libraries were plundered and pillaged, and Aristotle's school converted the library at Alexandria into a research center. There is no wonder then, that the production of the unusually large number of books ascribed to Aristotle has proved a physical impossibility, for any single man within a lifetime.[29]

---

[27] See Molefi Kete Asante, *The Egyptian Philosophers: Ancient African Voices From Imhotep to Akhenaten* (Chicago: African American Images, 2000); James Henry Breasted, *Development of Religion and Thought in Ancient Egypt* (Philadelphia PA: Pennsylvania University Press, 1972.)

[28] George G.M. James, *Stolen Legacy: Greek Philosophy Is Stolen Egyptians Philosophy* (Trenton, NJ: Africa World Press, 1992), 1.

[29] Ibid.

Students are fortunate if Egyptian philosophy, as a system of salvific thought and practice, makes the footnotes of any required texts on philosophy, theology, or world religious thought. The practice of delegitimizing and erasing black thought in Western institutions is the most egregious racism within higher education. The expunging of historical black thought is so enshrined within the educational culture that professors—black and white—are often not aware of their part in one of the greatest coverups in history. Two examples within the most prized period of Western historical thought—the enlightenment—highlight this situation.

As eighteenth-century Europe emerged out of the Dark Ages—inspired by classical Greek and Roman culture that sparked a renaissance, the enlightenment beckoned a new day. The enslavement of African people based upon their alleged inferiority provided a compelling reason for Europeans to deepen their resolve to erase any evidence of the black contribution to human progress. Yet, European and American criminalization of blackness, with the penalty of enslavement, could not stop black intellectual thought from rising from the quicksand of white supremacy. This ingenuity is seldom recognized by professors who are bent on maintaining the status quo philosophical and theological tradition. Despite institutional intent to blot out eighteenth-century black intellectual thought, the brilliance of black intellectualism shines through the darkness of whiteness through men like Zera Yacob and Anton Wilhelm Amo.

Ethiopian philosopher, Zera Yacob[30] was born in 1599, near the city of Axum (the world's first Christian Kingdom). After years of studying theology, rhetoric, poetry, and critical thinking, Yacob taught in one of the distinguished universities in Axum before running into trouble because of his views on religious subjectivity and the pluralism of religious thought. To avoid the accusation of heresy, Yacob fled and spent two years as a hermit in a cave along the banks of the Tekeze River in Ethiopia. Armed with only a few pieces of gold to purchase

---

[30] Also spelled, Zarä Yaqob

food at a nearby market and the book of Psalms, Yacob wrote some of the most insightful rationalist philosophy that rivaled or surpassed that of some of Europe's finest rationalist such as John Locke, Immanuel Kant, René Descartes, Isaac Newton, David Hume, and Voltaire. Yacob's groundbreaking work, *Hatäta* (Inquiry), provides some of the most brilliant rationalist-based thought against slavery and on religion, methodology, and epistemology.

In an essay entitled, *The African Enlightenment*, the Norwegian historian Dag Herbjørnsrud notes that in Yacob, "many of the highest ideals of the later European Enlightenment had been conceived and summarized."[31] Yet, the Western academic philosophical world has shown little to no interest in this non-European rationalist philosopher's work. More than 353 years after his work was published it is still, largely unknown by Western scholars[32] as part of an ongoing legacy of delegitimization and malicious erasure of the contribution of critical black thought from world history.

Anton Wilhelm Amo was a former house slave of Duke Anton Ulrich of Braunschweig-Wolfenbüttel. Seeing Amo's intellectual potential, his master permitted him to pursue academic studies. Amo completed his doctoral studies at the University of Halle in Saxon with a thesis entitled, "On the Impassivity of the Human Mind."[33] Wolfenbüttel was so impressed with the work that he placed it alongside Immanuel Kant's groundbreaking *Critique of Pure Reason*,[34]

---

[31] Dag Herbjørnsrud. The African Enlightenment. AEON. Dec. 13, 2017. https://aeon.co/essays/yacob-and-amo-africas-precursors-to-locke-hume-and-kant. Accessed August 30, 2020.

[32] The book was translated into English as part of Clause Summer's five-volume work on Ethiopian Philosophy in 1976. It was however published with a small unknown printing house in Addis Ababa and is not available for purchase and very difficult to locate in academic libraries.

[33] Antonius Guilielmus Amo, "On the Apathy of the Human Mind Or the Absence of Sense and of the Faculty of Sensing in the Human Mind And the Presence of These in Our Organic and Living Body," University of Wittenburg, Schlomach, April 1734.

[34] Immanuel Kant, *Critique of Pure Reason* (Boston: Bedford; New York: St. Martin's Press, 1929, 1965).

and the rector of the University of Wittenberg, heaped great praise upon it. In *The Enlightenment's Race Problem and Ours,* Joseph E.H. Smith's notes:

> A dedicatory letter was appended from the rector of the University of Wittenberg, Johannes Gottfried Kraus, who praised "the natural genius" of Africa, its "appreciation for learning," and its "inestimable contribution to the knowledge of human affairs" and of "divine things." Kraus placed Amo in a lineage that includes many North African Latin authors of antiquity, such as Terence, Tertullian, and St. Augustine.[35]

The works of Yacob and Amo are just two examples of how the western educational hegemony perpetuates the erasure of black intellectual thought. We could add to this list the works of Ottobah Cugoano, Ignatius Sancho, Phillis Wheatley, Olaudah Equiano, and a host of other black intellectuals. The profound theological and anthropological insight earthed in the various genres of their writings is priceless. What these black writers have to teach us about God, the human heart, faith, hope and love should never be assessed by the lack of inclusion within the field of study to which they contributed or the comparative paucity of their literature.

Black Thought and Systematic Theology

A significant part of systematic theology courses centers on the formation of Christian doctrine in the classical era. Critical teachings about God (the Trinity), Christ (Christology), the Church (ecclesiology), the Spirit (pneumatology), and other essential doctrines

---

[35] Joseph E. H, Smith, "The Enlightenment's Race Problem and Ours. " *The New York Times*, February 10, 2013, https://opinionator.blogs.nytimes.com/2013/02/10/why-has-race-survived. Accessed August 30, 2020.

were fiercely debated by Church Fathers. A course in systematic theology is often the first-time students are introduced to these Fathers' vital roles in warding off heresy and establishing theological orthodoxy. Very few theological students are aware that several of the Fathers—Tertullian, Origen, Athanasius, Augustine, and other North African theological luminaries that are carefully studied today—were black. Nor does the white professor make them any wiser.

The impact of the rich North African culture from which much of their theological discourse was hewn is assumed to be of little or no consequence by white scholars. It is unfathomable that the cultural context of Alexandria, Egypt—the seat of the genesis of systematic theology under the African scholar Origen—could go unmentioned as an empowering moment for black students.

Addressing the key themes of Christian belief is part of the work of systematic theologians. Arguments concerning the being of God, the nature of Christ, the person of the Holy Spirit, the nature of the church, the question of human identity, the problem of evil, and other important topics all fall into this realm.[36] Though limited resources by black theologians include Frederick Ware's *African American Theology*, James Evans's *We Have Been Believers*, and Katie Cannon and Anthony Pinn's *The Oxford Handbook of African American Theology* exist, production of a one-volume substantive work that delineates an African American theology is yet to be done.[37]

The assumption of biblical support to corroborate various theories within the classic systematic texts developed from a white, Western perspective produces an air of objectivity, and nonwhite

---

[36] A recent text discussing the contribution of early African Christian scholarship Vince Bantu, *Gospel Haymanot: A Constructive Theology and Critical Reflection on African and Diasporic Christianity* (Downers Grove, IL: InterVarsity Press, 2020).

[37] Frederick Ware, *African American Theology: An Introduction* (Louisville, KY: Westminster John Knox, 2018), James Evans *We have Been Believers: An African American Systematic Theology* (Minneapolis, MN: Fortress, 2012); Katie Cannon and Anthony Pinn, *The Oxford Handbook of African American Theology* (Oxford, UK: Oxford University Press, 2014).

perspectives are often overlooked. Works that provide hermeneutical insights into Scripture from African American perspectives such as Cain Hope Felder's *Stony the Road We Trod: African American Biblical Interpretations* as well as his *Troubling Biblical Waters: Race, Class, and Family*; and Vincent Wimbush's *Theorizing Scriptures*; *Scripturalectics: The Management of Meaning*; and *Misreading America: Scriptures and Difference* are rarely consulted.[38] Theological deliberations over the nature of God by white educators do not, generally, invite to the table such works as Karen Baker-Fletcher's, *Dancing with God: The Trinity from a Womanist Perspective*; Major J. Jones', *The Color of God: The Concept of God in Afro-American Thought*; William Jones', *Is God a White Racist*; or Benjamin E. Mays', *The Negro's God as Reflected in His Literature*.[39]

Classic Christological texts such as St. Anselm's *Why God Became Man*, Athanasius's *On the Incarnation*, and Gustaf Aulen's *Christus Victor* must be read in conjunction with contemporary black voices. Kelly Brown Douglas's, *The Black Christ*, James Cone's, *The Cross and the Lynching Tree*, George Yancy's *Christology and Whiteness*, Joanne Marie Terrell's, *Power in the Blood: The Cross in the African American Experience*, Jacqueline Grant's, *White Women's Christ and Black Women Jesus*, and Edward J. Blum and Paul Harvey's, *The Color of Christ: The Son of God and the Saga of Race in America* are worth noting.[40]

---

[38] Cain Hope Felder, ed., *Stoney the Road We Trod: American Biblical Interpretations* (Minneapolis, MN: Augsburg Fortress *African*, 1991) and Cain Hope Felder, *Troubling Biblical Waters: Race, Class, and Family.* (Maryknoll, NY: Orbis Books, 1989); Vincent Wimbush, ed., *Theorizing Scriptures* (New Brunswick, NJ: Rutgers University Press, 2008). *Scripturalectics: The Management of Meaning.* (New York: Oxford University Press, 2017); *MisReading America: Scriptures and Difference.* (New Brunswick, NJ: Rutgers University Press, 2008).

[39] Karen Baker-Fletcher, *Dancing with God: The Trinity from a Womanist Perspective* (St Louis: Chalice Press, 2006); Major J. Jones, *The Color of God: The Concept of God in Afro-American Thought* (Macon, GA: Mercer University Press, 2000); William Jones, *Is God a White Racist?: A Preamble to Black Theology.* (Boston: Beacon Press, 1997); Benjamin E. Mays, *The Negro's God as Reflected in His Literature* (Eugene, OR: Wipf and Stock, 2010).

[40] Anselm, *Cur Deus Homo* (New York: Magisterium Press, 2015); Athanasius of Alexandria, *On the Incarnation* (Salt Lake City: Pantianos

It should not surprise us that the suffering of Christ is considered low-hanging fruit for black systematic theological reflection and is addressed by so many scholars within the black religious scholarly community. Yet, Cone asserts,

> The conspicuous absence of the lynching tree in American theological discourse and preaching is profoundly revealing, especially since the crucifixion was clearly a first-century lynching.[41]

According to Frederick Ware, African American theologians have addressed suffering both generally, as a predicament of human existence, and in particular, as the distresses stemming from or intensified by racism.[42] The issue of the redemptive suffering of Christ is deeply personal for the community and individual experience and so deserves to be read alongside the other atonement theories for them to have meaning.

The idea of the nature of human identity, another key theme within systematic theology, addresses the question of what it means to be the only living being created in the image and likeness of God. Reinhold Niebuhr's *The Nature and the Destiny of Man*, Friedrich

---

Classic, 1944); Gustaf Aulen, *Christus Victor* (London: SPC, 2010); Kelly Brown Douglas, *The Black Christ* (Maryknoll, NY: Orbis, 1993); James Cone, *The Cross and the Lynching* (Maryknoll, NY: Orbis, 2011; George Yancy, *Christology and Whiteness* (London: Routledge, 2012); JoAnne Marie Terrell, *Power in the Blood? The Cross in the African Experience* (Eugene, OR: Wipf & Stock, 1997); Jacquelyn Grant, *White Women's Christ and Black women's Jesus: Feminist Christology and Womanist Response* (Atlanta: Scholars Press, 2012); Edward J. Blum and Paul Harvey, *The Color of Christ: The Son of God and the Saga of Race in America* (Chapel Hill, NC: University of North Carolina Press, 2012).

[41] See, James Cone, *The Cross and the Lynching Tree* (Maryknoll, NY: Orbis Books, 2011).

[42] Frederick Ware, *African American Theology: An Introduction* (Louisville, KY: Westminster John Knox, 2018), 131.

Schleiermacher's *The Christian Faith*, Richard Middleton's *The Liberating Image: The Imago Dei in Genesis 1*, and Martin Buber's *I and Thou* engage this question within the white Western paradigm. [43] Yet, rarely are these discussions related to the situation of African Americans' dehumanization as slaves and second-class citizens. The contribution of civil rights leader and theologian, Martin Luther King Jr., in championing the inclusion of black and other disenfranchised people, as fully created in that image and likeness, is pertinent here. As Richard W. Wills argues, for King, the value of human dignity and worth is attributable to being created in that image.[44]

Charles Long's work, *Signification*, and Cecil Cone's *Identity Crisis*[45] discuss the idea of human freedom as part of identity and provide powerful African American religious insights on the meaning of freedom. Discussions concerning human ontology as a dichotomy (body and soul) or trichotomy (body, soul, and spirit) may be brought into dialogue with a focus on embodiment in the work of such black scholars as Stephanie Mitchem essay on "Embodiment" in *The Oxford*

---

[43] Reinhold Niebuhr, *The Nature and Destiny of Man* (Louisville: Westminster John Knox, 1996; Friedrich Schleiermacher (London: T&T Clark, 2003); Richard Middleton, *The Liberating Image: The Imago Dei in Genesis 1* (Grand Rapids, MI: Brazos Press, 2005), Martin Buber, *I and Thou* (Mahwah, NJ: Paulist Press, 2003).

[44] See Richard W. Wills, *Martin Luther King Jr. and the Image of God* (Oxford, UK: Oxford University Press, 2009), chapter 4.

[45] According to Charles Long, African Americans' rhetoric on freedom emerges from "soul-stuff." Long contends that freedom was revealed as the ultimate resolution to the deep moral, spiritual, and humanitarian crisis of slavery and its aftermath. See, Charles H. Long, "African American Religion in the United States of America: An Interpretative Essay," *Nova Religio: The Journal of Alternative and Emergent Religion* 7:1 (July 2003), 21. Cecil Cone argues, "The problem of identity in Black Theology, therefore, is located at two points: its identification with the academic structure of predominantly white seminaries and with the Black Power motif of black radicals... Black Theology... is rooted in the black religious experience; it is an analysis of black religion." See Cecil Cone, *The Identity Crisis in Black Theology* (New York: African Methodist Episcopalian, 1975), 18.

Handbook of African American Theology, and Anthony Pinn's *Terror and Triumph*.[46]

As a final topic of systematic theology, eschatology envisions events at the end of history including the second coming, the resurrection of the dead, and the final judgment.[47] While classics such as Augustine's *City of God*, Marjorie Reeves's *Joachim of Fiore and the Prophetic Future*, and Rudolph Bultmann's *Demythologization of Eschatology* provide a starting point for discussing the topic, *Theology of Hope* by Jürgen Moltmann can be a bridge to describe the experience of the African Americans. Yet black theological works such as A. Elaine Brown Crawford's *Hope in a Holler* provides an excellent womanist interpretation; Leonard I. Sweet's *Black Images of America, 1784–1870*, and Gayraud S. Wilmore's *Last Things which Ground Eschatology: Hope in the African American Experience* are texts that have much to add to eschatological discourse.[48]

Conclusion

In 1935, more than eighty years ago, Du Bois asserted:

... race prejudice in the United States today is such that most Negroes cannot receive proper education in white institutions... many public school systems in the North [exist] where Negroes are admitted and tolerated but they are not educated; they are crucified... [there are] certain Northern

---

[46] Stephanie Y. Mitchem, "Embodiment," in *The Oxford Handbook of African American Theology*, ed. By Katie Cannon and Anthony Pinn (Oxford, UK: Oxford University Press, 2014), 308–18; For Anthony Pinn the focus on the body may be a form of materialism, where the supernatural or supersensory are neither necessary for nor an ultimate explanation of human behavior. See Anthony Pinn, *Terror and Triumph* (Minneapolis, MN: Augsburg Fortress, 2003), 142.

[47] Plantinga, *Introduction to Christian Theology*, 386.

[48] A. Elaine Brown Crawford, *Hope in the Holler: A Womanist Theology* (Louisville: Westminster John Knox, 2002); Leonard L. Sweet, *Black Images of America, 1784–1870* (New York: Norton, 1976); Gayraud S. Wilmore, *Last Things First* (Louisville: John Knox Press, 1982).

universities where Negro students... cannot get fair recognition, either in [the] classroom or on the campus, in [the] dining hall or student activities, or in human common courtesy... at Harvard, Yale, and Columbia, Negroes are admitted but not welcomed; while in other institutions like Princeton, they cannot even enroll.[49]

Undoubtedly, we have come a long way since Brown v. Board of Education removed the legal sanction of Plessy v. Fergusson that barred black students from entering institutions of higher education. Still, more than one hundred eighty years after the first black student was admitted to seminary, the relationship between education and race in America is still deeply divisive. While black students are admitted to white Evangelical institutions, black thought is expected to be checked at the door. Yet since, black identity is inextricably tied to the raw materials of black thought, role models, and resources from which it is fashioned, no one is a fully integrated self when deprived of his or her history and culture.

White Evangelical institutions that admit black students must consider how these students might thrive within a culture historically wedded to their inferiority. They must question whether reluctance to validate black thought subliminally echoes assumptions of this intellectual inferiority. They must also question how students of color could flourish if curricula were re-imagined and revamped to mine insight from the rich deposit of black theological and intellectual thought. While we are exploring how this might be done in systematic theology, this pedagogical re-imagination and revamping must happen in every arena of the religious academy including church history, ethics, biblical studies, missiology, and pastoral theology. Moreover, to have a lasting impact, such re-imagination must include black role models such as senior administrators, faculty, and staff with input at every level

---

[49] W. E. B. DuBois, "Does the Negro Need Separate Schools?" *Journal of Negro Education* 4:3 (July 1935), 328–29.

so that black students can aspire to positions beyond the limited roles that have historically been allotted to them within these institutions.

Black Pain, God's Pain: A Black Pentecostal's Reading of Dorothee Sölle's Theology for Skeptics and Bonhoeffer's Black Jesus

Wayne C. Solomon

The vagaries of human living are constituted and characterized by jubilation, anxiety, sorrow, fear, hope, pleasure, and pain. If there is one note of tragedy that has been heard in this symphony of our sojourn in the last millennium, it is the mournful woe of the Black experience. This essay explains that this cry has not fallen on deaf ears but is accompanied by the tears of Almighty God who suffers alongside people of color. Further, statistical data identifies and connects Black pain with theological and historical theses that reveal God's active engagement as a co-sufferer with global communities of color, particularly within America.

Black America

In 2015, the African American population[1] stood at just over 41 million people or 13.0% of the U. S. population.[2] Nearly eighty-five percent of the black population age 25 and over had at least a high school education and 20.6% of black men and 24% of black women age 25 and older had a bachelor's degree or higher.[3] 1.9 million of those

---

[1] The Black Alone Population in the United States: 2015, United States Census Bureau, https://www.census.gov/data/tables/2015/demo/race/ppl-ba15.html.

[2] The black Population is projected to be 74.5 million or 17.9% by the year 2060. New York with almost 4 million African Americans has the largest black population of any state or equivalent, the District of Columbia has the highest percentage of African Americans at 50%, followed by Mississippi with 38.3% and Cook County, Ill has the highest percentage of African Americans of any county and Claiborne County, Miss., was the county with the highest percentage of blacks in the nation standing at a staggering 85.1 percent.[2]

[3] US Census Bureau, 2015 American Community Survey, Table S0201. https://www.census.gov/acs/www/ data/data-tables-and-tools/data-profiles/2015/. Accessed July 09, 2020,

in this age range had attained an advanced degree[4] and 2.8 million[5] were enrolled in undergraduate educational institutions.

Despite the impressive statistics of educational attainment, a closer look at most major social indicators for American blacks paints a picture that is less hopeful. Beginning with the economic status of the community, the disparity is obvious. While in 2014, 108,473 of registered businesses were black-owned, the annual median income of black households in 2015 was $36,544.00, compared to the nation's median income of $55,775.00.[6] The percentage of the black population below the poverty level that year was 25.4%, while nationally it was 14.7 percent.[7] In 2016 the US poverty threshold was $24,563.00 and the overall poverty rate was 12.7%, while the African American poverty rate was 22.0%. In the fourth quarter of 2017, the unemployment rate for African Americans was 7.0% compared to the national rate of 3.9%, 3.4% for whites, 2.8% for Asians, and 4.7% for Hispanics.[8] In 2019, the share of blacks in poverty was still 1.8 times greater than their share of the general population. Black people represented 13.2% of the total U.S. population, but 23.8% of those in poverty. John Creamer points out in the September 2020 Census Bureau Report that racial inequity persists in poverty in America.[9]

In a 2020 article titled, "Black Women Share Approaches To Tackling the Wage Gap," Airen Washington[10] points out that the wage

---

[4] Ibid., Table B15002B.

[5] Ibid., Table B14007B.

[6] Ibid., Table S1903.

[7] Ibid., Table S1701.

[8] Labor Force Statistics from the Current Population Survey, Modified April 02, 2021. https://www.bls.gov/web/empsit/cpsee_e16.htm. Accessed April 06, 2021.

[9] John Creamer, Inequalities Persist Despite Decline in Poverty: For All Major Race and Hispanic Origin Groups, Census Bureau, September 15, 2020. https://www.census.gov/library/ stories/2020/09/poverty-rates-for-blacks-and-hispanics-reached-historic-lows-in-2019.html, accessed November 12, 2020.

[10] Airen Washington, "Black Women Share Approaches To Tackling the Wage Gap" *Forbes Business*, August 2020, https://www.forbes.com/sites/forbestheculture/2020/08/18/black-women-share-approaches-to-tackling-the-wage-gap/?sh=4bb7ca0d22cc, accessed November 02, 2020.

disparity for black women, was even higher than for black males, since these women earned 62 cents for every dollar their white male counterparts made, while black men earned 72 cents per for every dollar white males earned.[11] In America regardless of gender, people of African descent are underpaid for performing the same jobs as their white male counterparts.

Black women have the highest fertility rate of all Americans, standing at 64 per 100,000.[12] Yet black women have lower abortion rates than white women so while, in 2016, 35.0% of the babies aborted in America are black this compared to 37.0% among whites and 19.0% among Hispanics.[13]

Inadequate prenatal care, however, means that black women exhibit higher rates of problem pregnancies, babies born with birth defects, and infant mortality. According to the World Health Organization, in 2013, the U.S. maternal mortality rate was significantly higher than any other country of the developed world, registering 28 per 100,000.[14] A study in the April 2020 Berkley Public Policy Journal highlights, however, that , when disaggregating the data, the racial disparity shows that the ratio of black maternal mortality compared to

---

[11]Eileen Patten, Racial, gender wage gaps persist in U.S. despite some progress, Pew Research Center, July 01, 2016. https://www.pewresearch.org/fact-tank/2016/07/01/racial-gender-wage-gaps-persist-in-u-s-despite-some-progress/, accessed October 12, 2020.

[12] Joyce A Martin et al., National Vital Statistics System Births: Final Data for 2015, U.S. Department of Health and Human Services, Centers for Disease Control and Prevention National Center for Health Statistics 66:1, January 5, 2017. https://www.cdc.gov/nchs/data/nvsr/nvsr66/nvsr66_01.pdf, accessed August 15, 2019.

[13] Mark Hodges, 35% of Aborted Babies are Black, Life Site, December 05, 2016, https://www.lifesitenews. com/news/cdc-statistics-indicate-abortion-rate-continues-to-be-higher-among-minorities.

[14] Priya Agrawal, Maternal mortality and morbidity in the United States of America, March 2015 Bulletin, https://www.who.int/bulletin/volumes/93/3/14-148627/en/, accessed September 02, 2020.

that of whites was three to one, or 42.4 to 13.0 deaths per 100,000 live births in 2016.[15]

Seventy-two percent of black children are raised in single parent families, while this is true for only 25% of all US children.[16] This affects several indicators of black wellness. While 23% of black families live below the poverty level, only 8% of black married couples live in poverty, while 37% of black families headed by single women live below the poverty line. The highest poverty rates (46%) are for black families with children headed by single black women, and, significantly, more than half (55%) of black families with children are headed by single women.

Black individuals are dually affected by the criminal justice system. Not only are they more likely to be victims, but they are more likely to be in the criminal justice system. By the age of 14, approximately 25% of African American children have experienced imprisonment of at least one parent.[17] For white children that statistic stands at 4%.[18]

---

[15] Angélica Pagán et al., "Mitigating Black Maternal Mortality" *The Berkeley Public Policy Journal* (Spring 2020) https://bppj.berkeley.edu/2020/04/13/spring-2020-journal-mitigating-black-maternal-mortality/.

[16] According to the 2014 U.S. Census Bureau ACS study 27% of all African American men, women and children live below the poverty level compared to just 11% of all Americans. An even higher percentage (38%) of Black children live in poverty compared to 22% of all children in America. The poverty rate for working-age Black women (26%) which consists of women ages 18 to 64 is higher than that of working-age Black men (21%). Poverty rates for black families vary based on the family type.

[17] An African American child is six times as likely than a white child to have had an incarcerated parent. These children do worse across cognitive and noncognitive outcome measures. They are more likely to drop out of school; develop learning disabilities; misbehave in school; suffer from migraines, asthma, high cholesterol, depression, anxiety, post-traumatic stress disorder and be homeless.

[18] Valerie Strauss, Mass incarceration of African Americans affects the racial achievement gap, The Washington Post, March 15, 2017. https://www.washingtonpost.com/news/ answer-sheet/wp/2017/03/15/mass-incarceration-of-african-americans-affects-the-racial-achievement-gap-report/, accessed September 12, 2020.

According to the Federal Bureau of Investigation (FBI), sentencing rates for African Americans in 2006 was 1 in 33 and 1 in 205 for whites. In 2018, "black *men* were especially likely to be imprisoned and there were 2,272 inmates per 100,000 black men compared with 1,018 inmates per 100,000 Hispanic men and 392 inmates per 100,000 white men."[19] Two years earlier, the U. S. Department of Justice[20] reported that the total of all state and federal incarcerated American males was 450 per 100,000 and 64 females per 100,000. However, for blacks it was 2,415 males per 100,000 and 96 females per 100,000.

Prisoners, of whom blacks are disproportionately represented, pay phone carriers $24.95 for 15 minutes calls. This exploitation of the incarcerated generates hundreds of millions of dollars annually for the phone networks. Prisoners are exploited to manufacture defense industry products, Law enforcement equipment, McDonald's uniforms, furniture for United States government agencies, Microsoft products, Honda car parts, Victoria Secrets lingerie, Dentures, J C Penney's blue jeans, Starbucks packaging, copious amounts of processed meat and other goods as well as offering Call Center Services.[21] They fight forest fires with minimal compensation in California. They are arrested unnecessarily, and held pending the payment of high bails, to fund the 1.6 billion dollars bail bondsman industry.

Though blacks were less than 14% of the United States population they accounted for 50% of homicide victims.[22] African Americans are

[19] John Gramlich, "Black Imprisonment Rate in the U.S. has Fallen by a Third since 2006"https://www.pewresearch.org/fact-tank/2020/05/06/black-imprisonment-rate-in-the-u-s-has-fallen-by-a-third-since-2006/.

[20] Ann E. Carson and Joseph Mulako-Wangota. Corrections Statistical Analysis Tool (CSAT)-Prisoners, https://www.bjs.gov/index.cfm?ty=nps.

[21] Joe McGauley, 13 Everyday Items You Never Knew Were Made By Prisoners, May 20, 2015, https://www.thrillist.com/gear/products-made-by-prisoners-clothing-furniture-electronics, accessed September 02, 2020,

[22] George Coppolo and Kevin McCarthy. "Crime Rate and Conviction Rates Broken Down by Race, January 18, 2008".

2.5 times as likely as white Americans to be killed by police officers.[23] While African Americans constitute roughly 12% of opioid and street drug users, they constitute 38% of those arrested for drug offenses.[24]

The 2011 U.S. Bureau of Justice, Statistics Special Report,[25] detailed the disproportionate rate of human trafficking of black Americans.[26] Cheryl Nelson Butler traces the racial roots of this form of exploitation to slavery. In her careful historical excavation, she examines the myths of black hyper-sexualization in the characterization of black females as Jezebels and exploitation of black males as slave breeders. Blacks were forcibly obtained through human trafficking for their presumed value for sexual pleasure and economic gain, and these are still the driving forces behind human trafficking in black communities.[27]

---

https://www.cga.ct.gov/2008/rpt/2008-R-0008.htm, accessed September 12, 2020.

[23] Atiba G. Phillip and Hilary Rau. "Predicting Bad Policing: Theorizing Burdensome and Racially Disparate Policing through the Lenses of Social Psychology and Routine Activities", First published February 13, 2020. Accessed September 12, 2020, https://doi.org/10.1177/0002716220901349.

[24] Jennifer Turner and Jamil Dakwar. Racial Disparities in Sentencing in the Justice System of the United States. Submitted to the Inter-American Commission on Human Rights153rd Session, pp1–15, October 27, 2014. https://www.aclu.org/sites/default/files/assets/141027_iachr_racial_disparities _aclu_submission_0.pdf, accessed September 12, 2020.

[25] Jade Keller Confronting the beast: Racism's Role in Human Trafficking, The Freedom Story, January 18, 2018 "… between 2008 and 2010, nonwhite children accounted for 358 of the 460 cases (or 77.8%) of child sex trafficking investigated by the U.S. Department of Justice, the majority of whom were black and Latino…" https://thefreedomstory.org/confronting-the-beast-racisms-role-in-human-trafficking/, accessed June 02, 2020.

[26]Duren Banks and Tracey Kyckelhahn., "Characteristics of Suspected Human Trafficking Incidents", *Bureau of Justice Statistics- Special Report.* April 2011, 2008-2010, https://www.bjs.gov/ content/pub/pdf/cshti0810.pdf, https://thefreedomstory.org /confronting-the-beast-racisms-role-in-human-trafficking/, accessed March 12, 2020.

[27] Cheryl N. Butler, "The Racial Roots of Human Trafficking", *UCLA Law Review,* 62:1464, September 01, 2015, https://www.uclalawreview. org/racial-roots-human-trafficking/, accessed August 12, 2020.

Physical health discrepancies including diabetes, hypertension, obesity, cardiovascular maladies, cancer and renal failure that result in lower life expectancies, are more prevalent than among white Americans, with black life expectancy being 74.9 years compared to 78.5 years for whites.[28]

The Center For Disease Control (CDC) reports that systemic health and social inequities place black Americans at increased risk of contracting Coronavirus (COVID-19) and non-Hispanic black persons experience higher rates of hospitalization or death from the disease than non-Hispanic white persons. In June 2020, CDC reported that this population had a rate approximately five times that of non-Hispanic white persons.[29] While these statistics obviously do not tell the whole story of the pathos and pain of people of African descent in the United States, they paint a gloomy picture.

The history of American emergency medicine is rife with stereotypical tropes of black women as being "hypersexualized" with illness or pain that was likely, somehow, self-inflicted. If black women in emergency rooms are loud in their reaction to pain, they are deemed hysterical, and if they are calm, they are told that nothing is wrong with them. Accordingly, emergency room staff regularly undertreat black individuals for pain. The American Medical system has historically functioned with the false notion that "black people's skin is thicker than white people's skin," "black people age more slowly than white people," and "white people have larger brains than black people."[30]

---

[28] Elizabeth Arias and Jiaquan Xu. Division of Vital Statistics, 68:7, June 24, 2019, Table A. Expectation of Life, by Age, Race, Hispanic Origin, Race for the non-Hispanic Population, and Sex: United States, 2017. https://www.cdc.gov/nchs/data/nvsr/nvsr68/nvsr68_07-508.pdf.

[29] Center For Disease Control, COVID-19 in Racial and Ethnic Minority Groups, https://www.cdc.gov/ coronavirus/2019-ncov/need-extra-precautions/racial-ethnic-minorities.html, accesses July 17, 2020.

[30] Kelly M. Hoffman et al., *Racial Bias in Pain Assessment and Treatment Recommendations, and False Beliefs about Biological Differences between Blacks and Whites:* Proceedings of the National Academy of Sciences, March

According to a 2019 article, those practitioners surveyed often held these erroneous beliefs. Further, black patients were less likely to receive analgesia (pain numbing medication) for acute pain:[31] Though the study demonstrated the presence of these disparities, black pain is real, not imagined or illusory. Black pain registers and resonates with God.

In her 2019 Dissertation, *Association Between Substandard Housing and Asthma in African American Children*, Sharmanita Davis, showed that there was a significant association between asthma and substandard housing among low-income African American children. [32] According to the CDC, Davis contends, that African-American children between the ages of 5-14 most frequently demonstrate poor respiratory health outcomes including asthma." Davis concurs with Cutts, et al that "housing has been consistently noted to affect the respiratory health of individuals, especially... children. As a result, the housing condition that a child lives in has been recognized as a significant social determinant of health."[33]

In terms of mental health, black Americans are 20% more likely to experience serious mental disorders than the general population."[34]

01, 2016, https://www.pnas.org/content/pnas/ 113/16/4296.full.pdf, accessed September 12, 2020.

[31] Paulyne Lee et al., "Racial and Ethnic Disparities in the Management of Acute Pain in US Emergency Departments: Meta-Analysis And Systematic Review" in the September 2019 issue of the American Journal of Medicine, American Journal of Emergency Medicine 37:9, September 1, 2019, 1770-1777. https://doi.org/10.1016/j.ajem.2019.06.014, accessed June 05, 2020.

[32] Sharmanita Davis, *Association Between Substandard Housing and Asthma in African American Children* Doctoral Dissertation, Walden University, August 02, 2019, https://academic.oup.com/ jpubhealth/article/40/4/e614/5035761, accessed June 05, 2020.

[33] Diana B. Cutts et al., "US Housing Insecurity and the Health of Very Young Children" *American Journal of Public Health* (August 2011), https://www.researchgate.net/publication/5, 1226508_US_Housing_ Insecurity_and_the_Health_of_Very_Young_Children, accessed August 12, 2020.

[34] ADAA Board of Directors Statement: ADAA Stands against Racism, https://adaa.org/finding-help/blackcommunitymentalhealth#Facts, 06/04/2020, accessed August 12, 2020.

Related to higher rates of mental illness, black Americans become homeless at disproportionately higher rate. They make up 40 percent of the homeless population despite only representing 13 percent of the general population.[35]

In summary, African Americans experience disproportionate rates of unemployment, poverty, infant mortality and birth defects, single-parenting, arrests for drug offenses, homicide, parental incarceration, substandard housing, mental and physical illness, and access to healthcare. We cannot ignore the historical roots that set the course for these tragic disparities. And, while this work focuses primarily on the United States of America, a cursory glance at the black world offers invaluable corroborating insight.

The Black World

The black world comprises individuals from 55 African countries, as well as African-descended peoples of the Caribbean, Latin America, the United States, Canada, Europe, Australia, and Asia. That the sons and daughters of Africa who inhabit this world incorporate anguish, suffering, despair, and pathologies within their daily existence is well-documented. Historically, such black pain can be traced to episodes of slavery, colonialism, and segregation whose outworking continues in contemporary economic exploitation. Five separate chapters of slave trading beginning in 300 CE, forced over 35 million Africans across and off the continent of Africa into Europe, the Middle East, Asia, and the Americas over nearly 1600 years. These included the Trans-Saharan Trade, Red Sea Trade, Trans-Indian Ocean Trade, Trans-Atlantic Trade, and Trans-Africa-Continental Trade. Black suffering in the twenty-first century; continues through human trafficking, forced poverty, the disparity in health care, and a variety of other types of exploitation.

---

[35] The National Alliance to End Homelessness, https://endhomelessness.org/homelessness-in-america/what-causes-homelessness/inequality/, accessed October 10, 2019.

The Theodicy Puzzle

Despite the disparity in levels of black suffering, eighty-three percent[36] of African descended Americans are Christians. The question rings from the corridors of history, in the caustic scoffing once leveled at the Psalmist, "Where is your God?"[37] This theodicy puzzle is the unraveling of the faith of many, yet others hold steadfast knowing that Omnipotence exists in synch with Omnipresence. They understand that God stands resolutely, permanently, and powerfully with His suffering ebony-progeny.

In his groundbreaking book, *Night*, Nobel Peace Prize winner and Holocaust survivor, Eliezer Wiesel describes the execution of two men and a young boy in a German Concentration Camp during World War II. Wiesel recounted that three gallows were set up. After the three chairs were tipped over, the two men died quickly, but the young boy who was too light, was still breathing and his body hanging in limbo for over half an hour, between life and death, his tongue still red and his eyes not yet extinguished. Wiesel heard one of the prisoners behind him ask: 'for God's sake, where is God?' Then Wiesel said he heard a voice from within him respond; "Where is He? This is where He is— hanging here from these gallows." [38]

This story parallels the death of Christ. Wiesel contends, "He is here hanging on the cross." For us, Wiesel further insists that the cross is not proof of God's absence but the sign of His redeeming presence and love.[39] The cross is the greatest and most powerful sign of God's Omnipotence. His Son cried out, "My God, My God, why have You forsaken Me?" In a dramatic demonstration of His all-powerful nature, God restrained Himself from releasing His Son from this awful fate.

---

[36] Pew Research Center's Forum on Religion & Public Life, 2007, http://blackdemographics.com/ culture/religion/, accessed November 01, 2019.

[37] "As a shattering of my bones, my adversaries revile me, while they say to me all day long, "Where is your God?" Psalm 42:10.

[38] Eliezer Wiesel, *Night* (New York: Bantam Books, 1986.)

[39] "Where is God? Reflecting on Elie Wiesel's "Night" *A Way With Words.*" https://writingforfoodinindy. wordpress.com /2013/02/06/where-is-god-reflecting-on-elie-wiesels-night/, Accessed September 02, 2020

The sin of all humanity past, present, and future was being imputed to Christ; He became sin for us and was forsaken by the Father so that we will never be forsaken or abandoned by God. He will always and forever be with us, suffering with us as we suffer, so our pain becomes His pain.

Dorothee Sölle's Theology for Skeptics

Dorothee Sölle, liberation theologian, political activist, and feminist enlightens us to further unravel this puzzle. Sölle explained Christianity in the context of socialism and pacifism. Her lawyer father, though being a Protestant, was not religious or politically engaged. Young Dorothee had a thirst for knowledge, a passionate interest in the Evangelical Church and theology. Her activism led her to speak out against nuclear proliferation, oppression in both the American South and South Africa, and the dangers of capitalism.[40]

Though much of her writing is political, her theological work facilitates my discourse. In her ground-breaking treatise, *Theology for Skeptics,* Sölle addresses the matter of God as *co-sufferer.* In a distinctive feminist tone, expressing her struggle against the ideology of patriarchal theology, she calls for the liberation of language[41] that is "too small for God." She sees our limitation of God's capabilities as a gross devaluation of omnipotent sovereignty, expressed in the jargon and concepts we associate with the all too patriarchal God. She also insisted that our articulation of Divinity is fettered by our limited knowledge of the Divine. We are mired in incomprehensibility, so we inch our way forward in paltry human attempts to know more about the Incomprehensible One.

In challenging accepted conceptualizations of God, Sölle contends that we have framed our theologies of Yahweh, in the

---

[40] "Dorothee Sölle," *Your Dictionary*, https://biography.yourdictionary.com dorothee-soelle, accessed September 02, 2020

[41] Dorothee Sölle, *Theology for Sceptics* (Minneapolis MN: Fortress Press, 1995), 39.

verbiage of patriarchal triumphalism and, therefore, are not always successful in communicating the Christian rubric within the contemporary context. We sometimes suffer and die. And when we do, it begs the question; "where is God?" We are thus tempted to ask, "Is Christ not with us?" Sölle continues, Christ also suffered and died. He endured the mockery of a trial and the humiliation and torture of Roman Crucifixion. So, in our suffering we are not alone, "He feels what we feel."[42] He has felt pain and insists on feeling our pain. Sölle therefore, postulates, He, Christ, is our *co-sufferer*. He is there with us, Emmanuel, God with us; [43] in the fire, the water, and the flood with us[44]. In Matthew 28:20, Jesus said, "Surely, I am with you always…"

Sölle emphasizes that suffering is a part of lives in which God is invested and interested. She argues that even suffering that has been forced or inflicted on us can be changed into voluntary suffering. Sölle quotes Meister Eckhart saying, "if my suffering is in God, and if God suffers with me, how then can my suffering be misfortune."[45] Pointing to two illuminating elements she identifies in the process of suffering: freedom and solidarity, Sölle exhorts us to offer our suffering up to Christ and be conscious that we are free, and God joins us in our suffering.[46]

As for black suffering, Sölle notes that Martin Luther King Jr. carried the sorrow of "the sense of shock, that could not be assuaged over the brutality of a system that wants to function but does not

---

[42] Hebrews 4:15 15 For we do not have a high priest who is unable to empathize with our weaknesses, but we have one who has been tempted in every way, just as we are-yet he did not sin.

[43] Matthew 1:23 Behold, a virgin shall be with child, and shall bring forth a son, and they shall call his name Emmanuel, which being interpreted is, God with us.

[44] Isaiah 43:2 (NIV) 2 When you pass through the waters, I will be with you; and when you pass through the rivers, they will not sweep over you. When you walk through the fire, you will not be burned; the flames will not set you ablaze.

[45] Sölle, *Theology for Sceptics,* 82.

[46] Ibid., 81.

participate in God's pain, and does not admit God's vulnerability."[47] King knew that black pain is God's pain and as Sölle admonished, we ought to allow God to draw our pain into His pain and let us experience it as labor pains.[48] In other words, God is giving birth to new life through the black pain we see in our world.

Again, Sölle contends that God is present not as something experienced[49] or the "God of religion administered by men.[50]" In fact she demands that we "free God from the Bible and liturgy... and get rid of the old "White Man" in heaven." [51] She warns us to avoid the trivialization of life and embark upon an honest interpretation of reality, that makes "the mystery of God, visible for us[52]or *pro nobis.*"

Finally, Sölle contends that, "all suffering people are in the presence of God."[53] But we are left to question whether that is so for the peoples of African descent, who were dragged across the Atlantic and marooned on these Western shores?

Sölle's *presentia Dei,* like Dietrich Bonhoeffer's Proletarian Jesus, is not the old *God* who isolates believers and *Himself* from catastrophes. Rather, the *presentia Dei* has "liberating qualities."[54] Her riveting question is, "does God occur among us?" or is as God-above us as a superhero who acts independently, untouched, and unscathed by human suffering? Sölle calls for a liberation theology that disentangles God from objectified and false transcendence. This is God who must be moved from being God-above-us to God-within-us, feeling what we feel, walking where we walk, and *co-suffering.*

Dietrich Bonhoeffer in Harlem

---

[47] Ibid., 74.
[48] Ibid., 80.
[49] Sölle, *Theology for Sceptics,* 40.
[50] Ibid.
[51] Ibid., 41.
[52] Ibid., 43.
[53] Ibid., 72.
[54] Ibid., 48.

35

Sölle's elaborately clear explication is a prescription for living out the truest lifestyle of Christianity as was done by her countryman, Dietrich Bonhoeffer in New York in the 1930s. The Lutheran theologian arrived in New York City, one year after the October 1929 stock market crash that initiated the Great Depression. He was brimming with German patriotism and the child of a society infused with *"Herrenvolk,"* or *Aryan Master Race* ideology, and German Nationalism.[55] Undertaking a one-year Sloane Fellowship in Theology at the prestigious Union Theological Seminary, he found the students and faculty there to be hesitant to speak about Jesus, sin and salvation. He later described Union's theological foundation as modern American liberalism,[56] which he saw as both inadequate and heretical.[57]

His disillusionment with the white churches he visited, mirrored his disillusionment with the Seminary and the German Church, for he saw them as social corporations,[58] that had forgotten the real point of Christianity. For him, the ethos of the American Christian enterprise was a "liberal theological worldview" that rendered whiteness as the apotheosis or elevation to divine status, of human social progress.[59]

Disappointed, but still searching for the religion of Christ — the *Stellvertretung, the agency or deputy of Jesus in the world,*[60] 24-year-old Dietrich encountered Harlem's African American Community and a tradition of Jesus, that became decisive for his continued theological development. These black people lived under the iron feet of Jim Crow oppression, enforced through white terrorism. Lynching and other atrocities, and hyperbolic narratives that included a white racist fiction

---

[55] Williams, 16.

[56] According to Richard Crockatt's Article in the Journal of American Studies Vol. 11:1 (Apr. 1977), 123-143 *American Liberalism and the Atlantic World, 1916—17,* Modern American Liberalism of the late 19th and early twentieth centuries referred to "freedom from prejudice, generosity of spirit and conducive to liberty." https://www.jstor.org/stable/i27553262, accessed August 11, 2020.

[57] Ibid.,17.

[58] Williams, 18.

[59] Ibid.

[60] Ibid., 11.

of black sub-humanity characterized their lot. Yet their faith provided both a social and theological *counter-meta-narrative* that aligned with Bonhoeffer's *Stellvertretung*, his Jesus agency.

His encounter came at the height of the Harlem Renaissance with its outpouring of black pride, artistic expression, music, literary genius, and intellectual prowess. The promise of black progress and empowerment was bolstered by a theology that did not portend staid intellectualism, but "the Hermeneutic of the black Jesus in the context of oppression.[61]"

The Great Migration, beginning after Reconstruction deposited a black working class to the North that had escaped Southern pogroms, re-enslavement, and segregation in an attempt to distance themselves from some of the pathos and pain. These refugees aided in making Harlem the Capital City of the black world. Billie Holliday, Duke Ellington, Josephine Baker, Louis Armstrong, Countee Cullen, James Weldon Johnson, Langston Hughes and Aaron Douglas were among those who contributed to Harlem's cultural acclaim. Marcus Mosiah Garvey, Alain Locke, W.E.B. DuBois, Zora Neal Hurston, and Claude McKay contributed to its intellectual atmosphere. But white patrons who visited its hot spots and intellectual dens ignored the suffering and sorrow of the dispossessed who lived in its slums. For many white patrons, Harlem was a place of experiencing the exotic while not accepting the children of Africa as equals. The naivete of Harlem Renaissance proponents, proved disappointing when the vision of equality on the ground of common intellectualism and artistry unraveled.

For Bonhoeffer, the Abyssinian Baptist Church led by Adam Clayton Powell, Sr. was the place of crucifixion that truly revealed *Stellvertretung, Jesus agency of the true church in the world*. Bonhoeffer concluded that he "finally became a Christian," in Harlem where he learned "a black tradition of Jesus that connected faithfulness to God, the recognition of suffering, and the presence of Christ as *co-sufferer*."

---

[61] Ibid., 27.

[62] His message exposed the stark heretical contrast between prevailing Christology and working-class representations[63] of Christ. For him, the "comingling of Jesus with capitalism and domination' made the church into a shrine to privilege led by the Bourgeois Jesus, removed from the historical context and co-opted as an oppressor's Jesus." Bonhoeffer saw this Jesus-plus-power mixture as "lethal for both the oppressed and the oppressor alike."[64]

Reggie Williams, in his celebrated work, *Bonhoeffer's Black Jesus*, notes that the African American tradition of the proletarian Jesus Bonhoeffer encountered, resisted ideologies of white supremacy that devalued or distorted black humanity.[65] This Jesus is very present in every moment and aspect, situation, and circumstance of the lives of all, including—and especially—the oppressed. As James Cone helps us see in his seminal work, *God of the Oppressed*, God does not ignore the oppressed.[66] His presence is not to be discounted as that of a *Cosmic bystander*, but to be understood as that of the engaged Divine *co-sufferer*.

They Could not Breathe

Where was God in those slave dungeons of Cape Coast and Elmina in Ghana, and others along the West African Coast that were destroyed by the Swiss, the Swedes, the Dutch, and the Danes to hide their sins? Was God with those captured by Arabs; bought and sold by Dutchmen, Americans, Englishmen, the French, and Spaniards when they "could not breathe?" Was God there as they were shackled to shelves, fastened to hulls, and packed to capacity on trans-Atlantic slavers' voyages, owned and operated by the Browns or the De Wolfes,

---

[62] Ibid.,107.
[63] Ibid.,117.
[64] Ibid.
[65] Ibid.
[66] Cone, James, God of the Oppressed, 13.

the Dutch East India Company or the Royal African Company? Was God there in the narrow bellies of slave ships that held our black ancestors in dehumanizing conditions: coughing incessantly, vomiting profusely, bleeding continually during mensural cycles, defecating and urinating where they lay, and unable to breathe? Where was God?

When blacks were deposited on the shores of the New World, ill-equipped to inhale the pungent, putrid stench of abuse and exploitation they would face, they "could not breathe." When the chains of slavery were closed around their physical, emotional, and mental beings, squeezing their throats, cutting off their air supply, they "could not breathe." As they were dragged to the auction block, as chattel and cattle to be sold like property, and still "could not breathe." Where was God?

On the plantations, as they mournfully thought of their homes and loved ones who had been vanquished and violated, "they still could not breathe." Waking up every morning to long rows of cotton and miles of sugarcane that they grew in the scorching, sweltering, humid heat of the Caribbean or the Mississippi Delta, "they could not breathe." And where was God, in the underground copper, silver, gold and diamond mines, hundreds of feet below the surface in the caverns of the earth's bowels where they stood barefoot in cold, bacteria-infested, dark shafts where the air was thin and toxic? Still "they could not breathe." So, where was God?

Where is God?

Where is God when poverty kills Africans in the villages and towns of Rwanda, Southern Sudan, South Africa, or South America? Where is God when former Namibian prisoners of war realize that

---

[67] Thomas De Wolfe, Inheriting the Trade: *A Northern Family Confronts Its Legacy as the Largest Slave-Trading Dynasty in U.S. History* by Thomas De Wolfe, outlines how his ancestors pillaged West Africa and enriched themselves, New England, America and the Western World. Reprint edition (Boston, MA: Beacon Press, 2009).

they were deliberately infected with the AIDS virus by their South African captors? Where is God when a black Cuban teenage girl or Dominican boy is raped by a friend of her/his father? Where is God when starvation shreds the intestines and shuts down the organs of a Liberian or Haitian child whose mother painfully watches her gasp for her last breath? Where is God when a mother sees her only son lying in his blood from a drive-by-shooting, on an inner-city street in Detroit?

"Where is God when innocent, unarmed black people are executed by police officers in the U.S. or elsewhere in the Western Hemisphere? Where was God when Trayvon Martin was stalked and gunned down by George Zimmerman on a bleak, rainy night in Sanford Florida? Where was God when twenty-five-year-old Ahmaud Arbery was killed near Brunswick in Glynn County, Georgia, while jogging on Holmes Road, by Travis McMichael and his father Gregory, who were armed and stalking him in a pickup truck? "Where was God" when 26-year-old Breonna Taylor, an Emergency Medical Technician, was fatally shot by Louisville Kentucky Police officers Jonathan Mattingly, Brett Hankison, and Myles Cosgrove on March 13, 2020?[68]

Each person of African descent killed by law-enforcement officers between 2014 and 2018 is someone who should be grieved. Though the list is not comprehensive, each individual is among all the lives and deaths that matter. "Where was God" when each African descended individual in this litany was killed by the police?

Dontre Hamilton – Apr 30, 2014
Eric Garner – Jul 17, 2014
John Crawford III – Aug 5, 2014
Michael Brown – Aug 9, 2014

---

[68] Dylan Lovan, "Experts: Obstacles to Charging Police in Breonna Taylor" *ABC News,* August 4, 2020, https://abcnews.go.com/US/wireStory/experts-obstacles-charging-police-breonna-taylor-case-72167563, accessed January 21, 2021.

Ezell Ford – Aug 11, 2014

Dante Parker – Aug 12, 2014

Tanisha Anderson – Nov 13, 2014

Akai Gurley – Nov 20, 2014

Tamir Rice – Nov 22, 2014

Rumain Brisbon – Dec 2, 2014

Eric Harris – Apr 2, 2015

Walter Scott – April 4, 2015

Freddie Gray – April 19, 2015

William Chapman II – Apr 22, 2015

Brendon Glenn – May 5, 2015

Sandra Bland – Jul 13, 2015

Sam DuBose – Jul 19, 2015

Jamar Clark – Nov 15, 2015

Greg Gunn- Feb 25, 2016

Akiel Denkins– Feb 29, 2016

Alton Sterling – Jul 5, 2016

Philando Casteel – Jul 6, 2016

Paul O'Neal – Jul 28, 2016

Terrence Crutcher – Sept 16, 2016

JR Williams, Jan 9, 2017

Darrion Barnhill, Jan 10, 2017

Nana Adomako, Feb 5, 2017

Chad Robertson, Feb 8, 2017

Raynard Burton, Feb 13, 2017

Alteria Woods, Mar 19, 2017

Jordan Edwards, Apr 29, 2017

Tashii Brown, May 14, 2017

Aaron Bailey, Jun 29, 2017

Dejuan Guillory, Jul 6, 2017

Brian Easley, Jul 7, 2017

Isaiah Tucker, Jul 31, 2017

Patrick Harmon, Aug 13, 2017

David Robinson, Aug 25, 2017

Anthony Antonio Ford, Aug 30, 2017

Dewboy Lister, Oct 19, 2017

Calvin Toney, Nov 13, 2017

Lawrence Hawkins, Nov 18, 2017

Keita O'Neil, Dec 1, 2017

Jean Pedro Pierre, Dec 6, 2017

Arther McAfee Jr, Jan 20, 2018

Ronnell Foster, Feb 13, 2018

Shermichael Ezeff, Mar 14, 2018

Cameron Hall, Mar 15, 2018

Stephon Clark, Mar 18, 2018

Danny Thomas, Mar 22, 2018

Juan Markee Jones, Apr 8, 2018

Marcus-David L. Peters, May 14, 2018

Robert Lawrence White, Jun 11, 2018

Antwon Rose, Jun 19, 2018

Anthony Marcell Green, Jun 20, 2018

Rashaun Washington, Jul 7, 2018

Cynthia Fields, Jul 27, 2018

Botham Jean, Sept 6, 2018[69]

The epidemic of police brutality in 2019 saw blacks killed by the Police at a rate of 31 per hundred thousand[70] while for Hispanics that number was 23, whites 13 and others 4. The total number of people

---

[69] For a more detailed list of names of all people killed by American law enforcement officers categorizes by state, age, gender, and race see "Police Shooting and Crime Database" *KBP News* https://killedbypolice.net or "Unarmed Black Americans Killed by Police in 2018" *Abagond* June 20, 2018, accessed January 23. 2021https://abagond.wordpress.com/2018/06/20/unarmed-black-americans-killed-by-police-in-2018.

[70] Julie Tate et al., Fatal Force Database, The Washington Post, April 07, 2020, https://www. washingtonpost.com/graphics/investigations/police-shootings-database/, accessed January 23, 2021.

of African descent killed by the police[71] in 2019 is 259 and by November 2020 was 188.[72] Their blood cries out from the ground for justice.

Where was God, when these black people's lives were snuffed out by police bullets, pepper spray, tasers and chokeholds? **Didn't these "Black Lives Matter to God?"** Yes, they did.

Here is God: *Presentia Dei*

Where was God, when George Floyd was pleading for his life, as Derek's Chauvin's knee pressed hard upon his neck cutting off his air supply for nine minutes and twenty-nine seconds, as he begged for mercy saying, "I can't breathe?" Where was God? He was right there on that pavement experiencing Floyd's agonizing pain. In that instant, he was occurring among us! Like Wiesel's inner voice response to his fellow inmate's angry questioning, "Where is God?" He was there right there on that pavement.

Pentecostals understand *paraclete* (consoler), but black Pentecostals have no choice but to understand *presentia,* and they are not essentially the same. Our job is to precipitate an accurate Pentecostal theology of *presentia Dei* that is liberated from the unacceptable, triumphalism rhetoric of contemporary pop-Pentecostal-theology. As former General Overseer of the Church of God, Lamar Vest contends, "in today's[73] pragmatic church, oftentimes, a person's grief, tears, suffering, and lament are forced underground" and, I will add, so is their God.

Where is God? He is not an aloof observer. Instead, he is grieving with the father and mother, brother and sister, child, girlfriend, and

---

[71] Number of People Killed by Police by Ethnicity U.S. 2013-2019, Statista Research Department, December 10, 2020, , https://www.statista.com/statistics/1124036/number-people-killed-police-ethnicity-us/.

[72] KBP News, Police Shooting and Crime Database, https://killedbypolice.net/kbp2020/, accessed January 22, 2021.

[73] Lamar Vest, *Faith to Stand When You Can't Understand: When Life Hurts and Answers Aren't Enough.* (Atlanta: MindShift Publishing, 2013), 47.

friend of George Floyd. "Where is God? He was experiencing the pain and the attendant horrors of Floyd's death. And God is agonizing with every person whose outrage over this blatant murder, and that of all others in every part of the world, that has taken them to social media platforms, the press and the streets to protest.[74] For as **Martin Luther King** explains:

> Rioting is the language of the unheard... America has failed to hear that the plight of the Negro poor has worsened, that "the promises of freedom and justice have not been met, that large segments of white society are more concerned about tranquility and the status quo than about justice, equality and humanity. And so, in a real sense our nation's summers of riots are caused by our nation's winters of delay. And as long as America postpones justice, we stand in the position of having these recurrences of violence and riots over and over again. Social justice and progress are the absolute guarantors of riot prevention.

There is God, *paraclete*, but also *presentia Dei*. Our pain is His pain. He is with us in the same way He was with Israel in Egypt, and Babylon, co-suffering as Sölle contends.

Conclusion

Terrence Fretheim[75] insists that God is suffering because of, for and with His creation. He contends that this contravenes prevailing theologies of God's omniscience. Fretheim claims though there are

---

[74] Joshua Bote, A Riot is the Language of the Unheard': MLK's Powerful Quote Resonates amid George Floyd's protests, https://www.usatoday.com/story/news/nation/2020/05/29/ minneapolis-protest-martin-luther-king-quote-riot-george-floyd/5282486002/, accessed August 20, 2020.

[75] Terrence Fretheim, The Suffering of God, Minneapolis MN: Fortress Press 1984, xx.

many questions, we are compelled to respond, 'yes' or 'no,' to the issue of God's suffering "Does He suffer with us?" Is Jesus truly with us? Is the God of the Pentecostals in general and black Pentecostals in particular more than *paraclete* but also *presentia Dei*? Is He *presentia Dei* for a hated, alienated, disenfranchised, dehumanized, brutalized, impoverished, oppressed, castigated, maligned, stalked race? And does he feel our pain? As a black Pentecostal, I answer "Yes, *presentia Dei!*"

Pentecostalism and Racism: Towards a Recovery Praxis

Carver Anderson

Introduction

Like me, many believe human beings were 'created' by God and reflect His likeness. In the words of Genesis 1:26, "... God said, Let us make man in our image, after our likeness." Based on this 'truth', all humans have value and worth, consequently, any attempt to degrade, oppress, or disregard another human being is contrary to the will of God.[1]

The contradictions between God's will and how individuals and groups express or fail to express care, love, racial justice, and compassion for each other, is both stark and complex and in the context of this chapter, relates to three issues, centered on the fragility of human life. The first is the emotional pain of seeing needless death from disease as well as violence against communities of color. The second is the diversity of responses to personal and institutional racism and oppression. The third is the church's specific responses (especially within the Pentecostal community) to the injustices of the institutionalized criminal justice systems and the disproportionate impact of the global COVID-19 pandemic on black families and other minority groups.

James Cone argues that churches that proclaim Christ are obliged to apply faith and action towards supporting those identified in Luke 4:18 and Isaiah1:17–18.[2] For Cone, God calls churches to seek justice,

---

[1] See, for example, Michael Griffin, and Jennie Block W. eds. *In The Company of The Poor: Conversations with Dr. Paul Farmer and Fr. Gustavo Gutierrez* (Maryknoll, NY: Orbis Books, 2013), 27-30; Anthony B. Pinn, *The Black Church in the Post–Civil Rights Era* (Maryknoll, NY: Orbis Books, 2002), 44-45; Dwight Hopkins, *Introducing Black Theology of Liberation* (Maryknoll, NY: Orbis Books, 1999), 4-5; and James Cone, *The Cross and The Lynching Tree* (Maryknoll, NY: Orbis, 2011), 2.

[2] James Cone, *Speaking the Truth – Ecumenism, Liberation, and Black Theology* (Grand Rapids, MI: William B. Eerdmans Publishing Co., 1986), 7-10.

support the oppressed and fatherless, empower widows, bring comfort and 'good news' to the poor, and minister to prisoners. He further explains,

> When Faith is understood as a commitment to an ultimate concern, then it is obvious that there can be no separation between faith and obedience, because obedience determines faith. I know your faith not by what you confess but only by what you do.[3]

With similar gravity, John Lewis, Civil Rights icon and a member of the United States congress insisted:

> When you see something that is not right, not fair, not just, you have a moral obligation to say something, to do something, stand up, speak up, speak out, no matter what part of the world you come from.[4]

The words of Cone and Lewis resonate with liberationist theologies, as a form of 'ideological criticism' that tackle social injustice and exclusion from a faith-based perspective.[5] As liberation and black theologies insist, Scripture supports the notion that God sides with the oppressed against the oppressors.[6] As with the Christian-based communities and the movements that inspired them, liberation theologians, rely on readings of biblical texts such as Exodus 3:7–9, Psalm 146:9, Isaiah 1:10–17, 58:6–9, Jeremiah 7:6, Job 29:13, 31:16, Luke 6:20, 7:21–22, Matthew 25:40, and Galatians 2:10 as a precedent

---

[3] Cone, *Speaking Truth*, 40.

[4] John. Lewis, "When You See Something That is Not Right, You Have to Speak Up." Boston University graduation speech. *Quartz*. May 23, 2018. Video, 2:56. https://www.youtube.com/watch?v=A7xggPgdi3s.

[5] Griffin and Block, *The Poor,* 35.

[6] Leonard Boff and Clodovis Boff, *Introducing Liberation Theology* (Tunbridge Wells, Kent: Burns & Oates, 1987),54-55.

for reflection and action aimed at framing God's preference for the marginalized, oppressed and poor. This preference, they argue, is key to strategies and practices that emerge from our Christian faith.

The Pain is Real for Us

During the COVID-19 lockdown period in the United Kingdom, the virus has disproportionately affected black (African and Caribbean heritage) and South Asian families. As I write this, I had lost a family member and twelve friends and associates. It has been a challenge to support families, as we grieved together, as well as alone. Safety restrictions meant we could not follow our cultural and spiritual traditions in burying our loved ones. Pastors had to find alternative ways to support families and friends through deep emotional pain. Though anecdotal, it is worth mentioning that no white clergy colleagues had lost any friends or family to the virus at this stage.

During discussions between black clergy and public health officials about racial inequalities and health determinants for people of African, Caribbean and South Asian heritage, key concerns were highlighted by black 'activist communities.' These concerns challenged leaders on issues of institutional racism, health disparities and recovery plans since studies show that experiencing discrimination and racism can have profound effects on people's health and welfare. According to Wayne Farah, the COVID-19 pandemic has amplified and compounded existing inequalities that further diminish the quality of life of these groups, causing multiple health challenges and more 'early' deaths.[7]

There are no easy or 'quick fixes' for our situation in these unprecedented times. Yet, pastors cannot remain silent or become complicit in exacerbating the crisis facing black families and communities. While the virus does not discriminate in its transmission, structural racism and discriminatory distribution of health services that

---

[7] Wayne Farah "New Right, Old Racism-The Battlefield of Covid-19," *Institute of Race Relations,* May 20, 2020, Outlandish production.

already kill, distort, and damage people of color influence its rate of propagation, diagnosis, and treatment.

The existing pain of dealing with lives negatively impacted by racialized inequalities in health care was made worse by watching a black life cut short by racist policing. The inexorable grief and anger that erupted as millions witnessed the merciless killing of George Floyd on Monday, May 25, 2020 in Minneapolis was made worse because professional police officers who were sworn to protect the individuals and communities they serve carried out the act. Though many could not grasp what unfolded before our eyes, we cried as we realized that we were witnessing a murder. Even now, there are tears, as we remember Mr. Floyd, grasping life and calling out for his mother. We still hear him pleading: 'I can't breathe.' 'Please let me stand.' We still see the officer taking a knee.

Though U. S. police officers had brutally killed hundreds of black brothers and sisters, Mr. Floyd's visible 'lynching' was the tipping point for inciting mass protests around the world, demanding change in racist policies, procedures, and attitudes in other countries as well. These culturally, racially, gender, and generationally diverse protestors have expanded their concerns to wider justice issues. Innumerable, people and communities have stood together to say, 'Enough!' At their best, these protests have embodied the message that racism, inequality, xenophobia, and oppression are unacceptable and called for ineffective and unjust structures, including criminal justice systems, to be redefined or dismantled.

Most of these protests were peaceful. Though they sought to bear witness to community solidarity and justice, some responses involved civil unrest and violence, often directed at the police as an 'occupying power.' Sometimes rage was directed at racist and nationalist groups that wanted to 'take back the streets' for white power. As Pentecostal Christians who do not condone such behavior, we must put forth biblically-based responses to both institutionalized racism and chaotic violence. One inspiration for this work could be Dr. Martin Luther

King's prophetic words uttered in 1967 that remind us of the causes of such civil unrest. He says:

> Certain conditions continue to exist in our society, which must be condemned as vigorously as we condemn riots. But, in the final analysis, a riot is the language of the unheard. And what is it that America has failed to hear? It has failed to hear that the plight of the Negro poor has worsened over the last few years. It has failed to hear that the promises of freedom and justice have not been met… And so, in a real sense our nation's summers of riots are caused by our nation's winters of delay. And as long as America postpones justice, we stand in the position of having these recurrences of violence and riots over and over again. Social justice and progress are the absolute guarantors of riot prevention.[8]

As King expressed, riots are 'the language of the unheard' that the government has 'failed to hear' for years. The best way to prevent riots is to condemn the conditions that limit 'social justice and progress.' Amid the global COVID-19 pandemic, Floyd's 'lynching' reminds us that we also have a 'global racist pandemic.' White racism, privilege, power, and violence are openly displayed on the world stage, disrupting lives from the streets to hospitals, board rooms and secular and ecclesial government offices. Its pernicious tentacles still influence institutional, communal and individual thinking in wider society, while those in power do not take the concerns and pleas of marginalized communities seriously. That changed when people took to the streets and demanded justice and peace under the banner of "Black Lives Matter." Issues of racism, oppression and inequalities are now on the

---

[8] Martin L King, Jr. "The Other America." Stanford University Lecture, April 14,1967. video, 47:50.https://shu.zoom.us/j/ 3422266183?pwd= MlJBTEY3VlVia2hobi8zS0Qxd3NBdz09.

agendas of the places of power and influence and, on the surface at least, seem to be taken seriously. Marches have been launched, statues have been pulled down, new ways of policing planned, and new communities formed, where once, the demands for justice were misrepresented and minimized. As in Dr King's America, we have a choice. We can condemn the violence of the unheard and mouth platitudes as the winters of delay deepen or we can be true to the God of Luke 4:18-32 and declare God's kingdom of justice, peace, and equality.

My Reality and Motivation

I arrived in the United Kingdom from Jamaica in 1967 to enter an educational system that labelled young black men as lazy, aggressive, troublesome, and lacking in academic ability. Teachers misunderstood and misrepresented me and those who looked like me. During this period, these issues started receiving national attention,[9] and studies continue to show that inequalities of treatment, experience and outcomes are an indictment on that education system.[10] That people have won through that system and been able to support themselves and their families is a testament to their determination and resilience.

Secondly, as the father of two young black men born in the United Kingdom, I have seen their lives negatively impacted by discrimination and racism from both students and teachers. In one instance, one of my sons was beaten-up by two white schoolmates. This was something different to the 'normal' playground fight or the 'normal' beatings taken at school. This beating traumatized him so much that after days of crying, he informed me that he wanted to be white because if he

---

[9] The wholesale labelling of the attitudes and behaviours of black boys, as 'dangerous', 'deficient' and 'deviant' is highlighted in Bernard Coard, *How the West Indian child is Made Educationally Sub-Normal in the British School System* (England: Beacon Press,1971), 26-30.

[10] Cheron Byfield, *Black Boys Can Make It: How They Overcome the Obstacles to University in the UK and USA* (Stoke on Trent: Trentam Books Limited, 2008), 10-18.

were white, this beating would not have happened to him. The pain we went through with him, as we reassured him of his worth and our love for him is still remembered and was recently triggered by the humiliating killing of Mr. Floyd.

As a New Testament Church of God[11] pastor and a social worker in deprived areas of Birmingham where incidents of gun and gang violence have occurred, I have worked with young black men, being an advocate of justice, peace and equality. This mission, along with my roles in the church and community, and my spiritual biography raises key questions about how church leaders can provide effective theological and practical responses to the socio-political challenges facing the black families that are over-represented in unemployment, mental health, school exclusions and criminal justice statistics:[12]

- What are my Christian responsibilities and obligations towards marginalized people and communities?
- What role should Pentecostal pastors and denominations play in supporting marginalized families such as those represented in Luke 4:18, who are unchurched and not connected to families from local congregations?
- How might the experiences and narratives of black and other minority groups shape Pentecostal leaders work towards a 'practical activist theology' that effectively responds to their needs and interests?
- Are the diverse Pentecostal communities in the United Kingdom and United States prepared to partner with

---

[11] The New Testament Church of God is part of the Church of God (Cleveland, TN).

[12] Martin Glynn, Black *Men, Invisibility, and Crime: Towards a Critical Race Theory of Desistance*. (London: Routledge, 2014),127-131.

Carver Anderson, "Towards a Practical Theology for Effective Responses to Black Young Men Associated with Crime for Black Majority Churches" (PhD Thesis, Birmingham University 2015), 120-148.

other groups to challenge and influence internal and external systems on racial justice concerns?

- What is there in the traditions, theologies and beliefs of Pentecostal denominations that supports or hinders their involvement with active anti-racist struggles?
- How might truth and reconciliation forums support a re-imagination of Pentecostalism as a spiritual, anti-racist and social justice change agent?

This is not an exhaustive list, but it highlights my concerns with the disconnect between the Pentecostal church and the needs and realities of 'the least of these' (Matthew 25:40). Wrestling with these questions, however, can be exhausting, requiring coping mechanisms and tenacity from me and my family just to keep bodies, souls, and spirits alive and well.

Interdisciplinary Approaches: Practical Theology and Public Health

My reflections on the questions raised regarding Pentecostalism, racism, the church, and 'recovery' and on my own experiences are reinforced by King and Lewis' thinking on individual and corporate responsibilities. Though these answers are informed by my experiences in family and community, my work as pastor, social worker, church leader and researcher, they are guided by the Spirit of the Lord. They are not the final words, but the start of a conversation, associated with hope, liberation, and recovery.

Here I offer a black Pentecostal response using the lenses of practical theology and public health to see and build the Kingdom of God. The discipline of practical theology is not without its challenges and there are debates around the theory and practice of public health. However, taken together, they allow the creative re-imaging of the work of justice and peace in the power of the Spirit. I use them to offer a 'recovery and intervention' framework for leaders who are serious about personal, communal, and institutional changes related to racial injustice, social inequalities, and health disparities.[13]

This framework uses two simple tools. The first is the pastoral cycle (PC), (Figure 1) and the second is an adapted public health framework (PHF) (Figure 2). Both the PC and the PHF allow for the use of perspectives and tools from other disciplines in the Enquiry, Analysis, and Intervention phases. This may include approaches from, criminology, sociology, psychology, anthropology, and epidemiology. Mark Cartledge's work on Charismatic perspectives on Practical Theology acknowledges the potential interplay between sociology and theology in considering Pentecostalism and its responses to racial inequalities and other socio-political concerns.[14] He makes it clear that the growing literature suggests that the field of Practical Theology is both evolving and open to interdisciplinary perspectives, as it empirically explores situations and issues of concern or interest. Critical conversations between people involved in theology and social science, medical science, and social ethics have allowed for collaboration on a number of key issues, such as poverty, HIV/AIDS, inner city deprivation, poverty, and black young men's over-representation in the criminal justice system and their deaths at each other's hands. There have been many studies and debates in the United States and the United Kingdom with responses and interventions that are numerous and varied.

The use of the PC and PHF offers the tools to critically engage Pentecostal denominations' and churches' response to the needs and interests of black and other marginalized groups impacted by racial oppression, discrimination, stereotyping, and multiple health determinants (factors influencing one's ability and capacity to live a

---

[13] Carver Anderson "Black Young Men: Problematisation, Humanisation and Effective Engagement" In *The Palgrave Handbook of Auto/Biography,* ed. Julie M. Parsons and Anne Chappell (Switzerland: Palgrave MacMillan, 2020), 577-598.

[14] Mark Cartledge, *Practical Theology: Charismatic and Empirical Perspectives* (Carlisle, Cumbria: Paternoster Press, 2003), 12-13.

healthy and productive life). Ballard and Pritchard (see Fig.1 below) argue for a 'doing theology from below' approach.

Figure 1: Ballard & Pritchard (2006) Adapted Pastoral Cycle

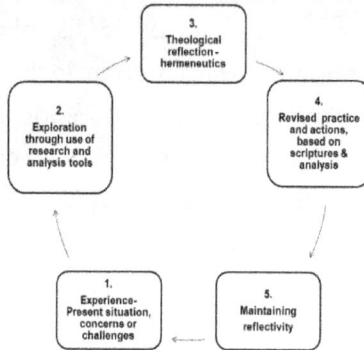

They suggest that this has two connotations that reflect the perspective of liberation and its insistence on praxis. First, the reference is to theology's starting point. The cycle starts as we have seen, with present experience, which becomes questioned by some event or crisis. It starts in the concrete reality of where people are.[15]

The PC offers the opportunity for social analysis to help us make sense of the experience of the black lives being cut short by racist policing and negligent health care systems. Theological reflection forms a crucial aspect of the process, providing a way for reflecting on the Word of God in our analysis as a means for revising our actions and redefining our practices. This is not an end within itself but an aspect of an ongoing process for continued theological and practical development, a way of 'doing' Luke 4:18 in community. This approach has the potential of helping churches grapple with anti-racist theologies and contribute to wider conversations regarding racial equality and

---

[15] Paul Ballard and John Pritchard, Practical Theology in Action: Christian Thinking in the Service of Church and Society,2nd end. (London: SPCK, 2006), 89.

discrimination. It offers a framework for working out effective means for addressing white supremacy and institutional racism, a means to discern the use of particular contributions to the debate.

For example, on May 27, 2020, following George Floyd's murder, Dr Timothy Hill, General Overseer of the Church of God, spoke on behalf of the International Executive Committee when he said:

> Racism is sin. God despises it. It is not a matter of 'we must do better.' Instead, it is a matter that all people are created equal. Brutality and murder must stop, whether from a citizen or those in authority. People of all races must be protected, respected and be able to live without fear.
>
> I unequivocally condemn racist acts against any and all people. Such actions are something that should never be tolerated by a God-fearing society. Every man, woman, boy, and girl were created in the image of God. Regardless of race, color, or national origin. Therefore, we are all His children.[16]

While Hill's statement is well intended, I am somewhat cautious at best and skeptical at worst about how he, heading up a white-dominated denomination will address the personal and institutional forms of racism that exist in 'church' and 'state.' Importantly, what actions to bring about increased protection of black communities does the executive committee have planned and how do they envision the Pentecostal church challenging a supposedly God-fearing, but racist American church and culture? My skepticism

---

[16] Timothy Hill, "Racism is Sin-God Despises It." *Church of God, Cleveland TN Faith News*, 27 May 2020, https://vacog.org/blog/hill-condemns-racist-acts.

echoes that of Cone's, in his landmark book, *The Cross and the Lynching Tree*. Cone challenges white church leadership, as well as others, who fail to connect the crucifixion of Jesus by Roman soldiers in Jerusalem with the brutal lynching of black folk by 'God-fearing' white people in America. He suggests:

> That the analogy between the cross and the lynching tree should have eluded the Christian agents of white supremacy is perhaps not surprising. But how do we understand the failure of even the most 'progressive' of American white theologians and religious thinkers to make this connection?[17]

His question is still pertinent, given the continued disconnect between white religious leaders and those black families and communities who have lost loved ones to racist brutality and neglect.

The acknowledgement of the presence of the 'lynching tree' challenges my denomination and others, to address the historical concerns associated with responses about race, inequalities, power-sharing, and validation of black ministers, who over the years have contributed much to the sustainability of the denomination. Furthermore, Cone's work emphasizes a theology of activism, towards addressing spiritual as well as socio-political issues, impacting *church* and *community*.

Public Health Framework

Like the PC, the Public Health Framework (Figure 2) offers tools to pastors and denominational leaders, to help wrestle with questions regarding race inequalities and help us to work in partnership with other agencies to address common concerns such as crime and gang

---

[17] Cone, *The Cross and the Lynching Tree*, 31-32.

violence.[18] The needs are simply too great or complex for a single agency response. This may challenge Pentecostal leaders who are more drawn to a 'divine command' paradigm. However, Thompson, et al. warn against 'treating the Bible as a literary pope that utters holy truth without regard for circumstance or context while closing issues that should be left open to the speaking of God.'[19]

Scripture should be used alongside other interdisciplinary perspectives, to address what Hill calls the 'sin of racism.' The PHF allows us to bring together our understanding of Scripture, practice of mission, and research and analysis to build God's kingdom. This evidence would also include experiences of discrimination and the psycho-social stressors that damage spiritual, physical, and mental health. Speaking as a public health professional, Julio Frenk, Dean of the Faculty at the Harvard School of Public Health, insists:

> Simply stated, racism is a public health problem that contributes to higher levels of stress, greater exposure to risk factors, reduced access to medical and social services, and ultimately to excess levels of disease, disability, and death. As leaders in the field of public health, these issues are of concern to us all. As a community dedicated to issues of public health, we must persist in our scholarly and professional work so that we can contribute to the amelioration of ongoing disparities and the improvement of health conditions.[20]

---

[18] James Marcy, et al, "Public Health Policy for Preventing Violence," Health Affairs,12, no 2(1993):7-29, http://content.healthaffairs.org/content/12/4/7.

[19] Judith Thompson, Stephen Pattison and Ross Thompson. *SCM Study Guide: Theological Reflection.* (London: SCM Press,2008), 79-79.

[20] Julio Frenk, "Racism and Public Health." *Harvard T.H. Chan School of Public Health News,* December 17, 2014. https://www.hsph.harvard.edu/news /features/racism-and-public-health-statement-from-dean-julio-frenk/.

Figure 2 : Mercy et al (1993) Adapted public health Framework

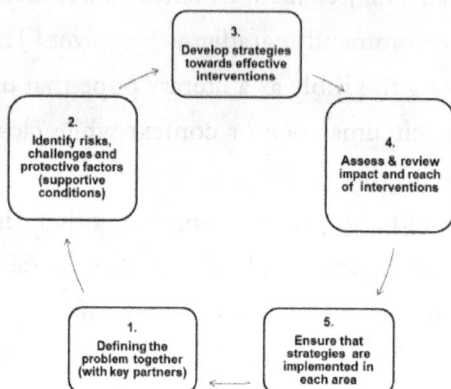

The PHF raises questions that directly apply to our Pentecostal explorations of issues associated with creating equalities amid institutional racism, discrimination and personal prejudices. These questions include the following:

- What problem do we agree is of concern/interest?
- When and where did the problem begin?
- Who is involved?
- Where is the problem?
- Which individuals or communities are impacted?
- How can we engage with the individuals causing or impacted by the problem?
- What are the causal factors relating to the problem?
- Who should be involved in addressing the problem?

My research and interventions relating to public health, community-led initiatives. and faith-based approaches around policing, 'gangs' and youth violence, continue to offer insights into these areas. As an aspect of my work in Birmingham and the West Midlands, I have produced a comprehensive report, the *'Commission on Gangs and*

Violence: United to Improve Safety.[21] It confirms that no single individual, group, agency, perspective, method, or approach can effectively address all concerns. Instead, it shows the need for sustainable interagency/multi-agency partnerships.[22] Such partnerships should have a key community-involvement component in developing effective responses to violence in local communities or neighborhoods. The public health framework and its key questions support the concept of partners collaborating to reduce spontaneous, intentional, or organized violence.

The report highlights some sad realities of such violence: people dying young, leaving families in pain, trauma, and fear; individuals and groups enraged and intent on revenge for friends or family members hurt or killed; and pained stories of both victims and preparators, individuals, families, and communities. The PHF approach showed that all lived in local communities and were crucial in any exploration of causes, influences and solutions associated with the violence.

While use of a PHF may be viewed with suspicion and caution by some Pentecostal scholars and pastors, increasingly, other scholars of practical theology, from diverse backgrounds are prepared to grasp opportunities for increased intersectional and interdisciplinary work. From a black theology context, Dwight Hopkins suggests that this work is driven by second-generation black scholars who want to place 'black religious scholarship into conversation with bodies of knowledge different from theology.'[23] From within a United Kingdom white theological perspective, Stephen Pattison's work, *The Challenges of Practical Theology*, offers suggestions for such partnership. He says:

---

[21] Carver Anderson, *Commission on Gangs and Violence: Uniting to Improve Safety*. (Birmingham: Office of West Midlands Police and Crime Commissioner, 2017), 3-5.

[22] Anderson, *United to Improve Safety*, 9.

[23] Hopkins, *Black Theology*, 110.

61

I would characterize my theology as universalist, liberal, inclusive, humanistic, non-metaphysical, interrogative (seeking to ask some of the right questions rather than to know all the answers), and dialogic with people and insights of many different disciplines and professions. It is based upon the belief that God takes humanity with absolute seriousness, to the extent of imaging Godself as material human being in history. For me, this implies that all humans should take all other humans seriously in their material bring and situation, too. God is to be found in all people and places and can be learned about best often at the edges of orthodox religious communities and thought systems.[24]

I have no contention with Pattison's theological 'positioning' which offers room for dialogue, partnership and reflection and is based on the notion that all human beings should be taken seriously within their respective context. It offers a practical template for interdisciplinary conversations and the co-production of fresh ideas and effective action. However, one might question how his principles would fare if applied to research into unfamiliar areas of concern or interest, such as those commonly associated with women or the black community.

With our interdisciplinary lens, it is necessary to remind ourselves of the basis of our Pentecostal spirituality, the great bursting forth from a prayer meeting of devout black Christians in Azusa Street in 1906 [25] This Pentecostal spirituality and resilience have been features of black British Pentecostalism form the outset.

Black Pentecostalism, Resilience, and Contemporary Situations

---

[24] Stephen Pattison, *The Challenges of Practical Theology: Selected Essays*. (London: Jessica Kingsley,2007), 18.

[25] Walter Hollenweger, *Pentecostalism: Origins and Developments Worldwide*. (Massachusetts: Hendrickson Publishers, 1997).

In developing a practical theological framework for black majority churches to respond effectively to young black men associated with crime, I consider how the theology, spirituality and experiences of black Christians in the United Kingdom shaped their responses to their challenges, concerns, and aspirations. The key factors that shaped the dynamics and ethos of black British Christianity are highlighted in several scholarly works.[26] It is now seventy-two years since 'The Empire Windrush' docked in England in 1948, beginning the post-war migration to Britain by citizens from the 'New Commonwealth.'[27] The arrival of these citizens from Africa, the Caribbean and the Indian sub-continent needs to be understood as a response to a post-war labor shortage.

Although the New Commonwealth immigrants were welcomed rarely and often feared, representatives of the British government and large companies actively encouraged them to support the reconstruction of the Motherland.[28] It was their labour that was needed and not their presence: they were met with blatant opposition and discrimination, with overt expressions of racism and oppressive practices that damaged black families seeking economic, social and educational stability and success.[29] Signs and notices proclaiming 'No

---

[26] See, for example Clifton Clarke R. *Pentecostalism: Insights from Africa and the African Diaspora.* (Eugene: Cascade Books, 2018),156-159 and *The Reason Why We Sing: Introducing Black Pentecostal Spirituality.* (Cambridge: Grove Books); Joe Aldred, *Respect: Understanding Caribbean British Christianity.* (Peterborough: Epworth Publication, 2005), 68-90; Valentina Alexander, "Breaking Every Fetter: To What Extent has the Black Led Church in Britain Developed a Theology of Liberation?" (PhD Thesis, University of Warwick,1996); and Mark Sturge, *Look What the Lord Has Done: An Exploration of Black Christian Faith in Britain,* Bletchley, (UK: Scripture Union, 2005), 81-112.

[27] Peter Fryer, *Staying Power: The History of Black People in Britain.* (London: Pluto Press,1984),67-69.

[28] Mike Phillips and Trevor Phillips, *Windrush: The Irresistible Rise of Multi-Racial Britain.* (London: HarperCollins, 1998), 215-223.

[29] Phillips, *Windrush,105.*

Coloured, No Children, No Dogs' were a common sight outside rooms to rent.[30] Similar views were expressed by local and national politicians such as Alderman Peter Griffiths, a Conservative candidate for the Smethwick constituency in the West Midlands, who endorsed the slogan: "If you want a nigger for a neighbour, vote Labour."[31] The view was that fewer immigrants meant better 'race relations.' In a 1968 speech in Walsall, Enoch Powell, Member of Parliament for Wolverhampton South West, offered a powerful defense of the popular 'halt immigration' position.[32] He was sacked from his government job, but British workers struck and marched in his support. British society defined New Commonwealth immigrants and their children—rather than its own institutionalized injustices and prejudiced culture —as the 'immigrant problem'.[33]

Within this context, Christians from the New Commonwealth entered British churches. There are stories of rejection from African, Asian and Middle Eastern Christians. I'm personally familiar with how people from Jamaica made attempts to engage with British churches to fellowship, share their skills and experiences and have their spiritual and material needs recognized and addressed[34]. For many, experiences

---

Richard Jenkins and John Solomos, *Racism and Equal Opportunity Policies in the 1980s*.2nd ed. (Cambridge: Cambridge University Press,1989), 30-38.

[30] Anderson, "Theology for Effective Responses to Black Young Men,*"* 210-223.

[31] Peter Ely and David Denny, *Social work in a Multi-Racial Society*, (Aldershot: Gower, 1987), 24.

[32] Kathleen Paul. *Whitewashing Britain: Race And Citizenship In The Post-War Era,* (New York: Cornell University Press,1997).

[33] Ely and Denny, *Multi -Racial Society,* 21-32 and Phillips, *Windrush, 90-94.*

[34] Babatunde Adedibu, *Coat of Many Colours: The Origin, Growth, Distinctiveness and Contributions of Black Majority Churches to British Christianity,* (Gloucester: Wisdom Summit,2012)19-23.

Oliver Lyseight, *Forward March: An Autobiography.* (Sedgley, West Midlands: George S Garwood, 1995). 28-33.

Aldred, *Caribbean British Christianity,* 80-90.

of rejection and isolation challenged the core of their spiritual beliefs.[35] According to Cappel's research, there were three broad responses to the hostility and rejection: retreat, innovation, and persistence.

The 'retreaters' were those whose faith and confidence were so shaken by their deep and negative experiences that they turned away from religion and the Christian faith altogether. It was not necessarily total abstinence from church attendance or interaction with black Christian folk. They would periodically attend for special occasions, like Christmas, Easter and for christenings and funerals.

The 'innovators', while equally disappointed with the racism, prejudice, and rejection from white churches and wider society, chose to subscribe to a greater sense of hope that transcended the reality of their situation. This hope, along with faith, trust, passion for fellowship and prayer motivated their quest to survive. Time was set aside to pray and fast for answers to challenging, uncertain, and hostile situations.[36] Like some pioneers associated with the historic black majority churches (BMC), they emphasized the significance of applying spiritual power and 'anointing' for their mission. Informed by Luke 10:19: "Behold, I give unto you power to tread on serpents and scorpions, and overall the power of the enemy: and nothing shall by any means hurt you," they understood that having God's power allowed them to survive by constructing 'spiritual strategies' and a 'survival theology' to sustain them.[37] They began meeting in 'spaces' with like-minded

---

[35] Cecilia Cappel, "From Whence Cometh My Help?"; Domestic Abuse and Black-Led Churches in Britain" (PhD thesis, University of Surrey, 2009), 28.

[36] Selwyn Arnold. *From Scepticism to Hope: One Black-Led Church's Response to Social Responsibility,* (Nottingham: Grove Books Ltd,1992), 17-19.

Ira Brooks, *Where do we go from here: a history of 25 years of the New Testament Church of God in the United Kingdom – 1955-1980,* (London: Charles Raper,1982), 13-16.

[37] Beckford, Robert. *Dread and Pentecostal: A Political Theology for the Black Church in Britain,* (London: SPCK, 2000), 44-50.

people to develop a safe and mutually trusting environment for sharing and worship.[38]

Despite the challenges, some 'persisters,' as they are appropriately named, imposed their presence on congregations, implying that they were there to stay. This group determined to worship in these churches, producing causalities with fractured relationships and mistrust. Their actions engendered responses resulting in, what Cappel categorized as, 'white flight'—the departure of white Christians from some inner-city churches to 'migrant free' spaces.[39]

At the same time, many black families were labelled negatively by statutory institutions (social services, police and health service) and were treated with hostility by the white British.[40] These experiences and their isolation and detachment from 'Back a Yard' realities (the familiarities and customs of their countries of origin) led folk to explore ways of engaging with others from their migrant communities. This approach was both to combat a sense of alienation and forge new relationships and solidarity. Migrants with spiritual lives and church affiliations and customs prior to entering Britain sought to bridge the gap in their social, spiritual, and economic needs by creating their own churches, 'safe spaces,' and communities.

Based on our tenacious journey and the intergenerational skills, insights and aspirations gained through it, Pentecostals and the wider church can offer responses to the challenges of institutional injustice and racism affecting the wellbeing of black families and other minority groups. In doing this we must consider the use of the pastoral cycle and public health framework to address these issues with an effective recovery praxis.

---

[38] Sydney Thompson, *Unfolding Destiny: An Autobiography,* (Birmingham: Majesty Design and Print, 2004),17-27.

[39] Cappel, *Black-led Churches in Britain,* 28-32.

[40] Anderson, *Towards a Practical Theology,* 208-223.

Pentecostalism Re-imagined: Towards an Effective Recovery Praxis

This discussion does not set out 'a one size fits all' Pentecostal plan but offers tools for use by leaders and churches who seek to follow God's preferential option for the poor to where the 'Cross meets the lynching tree.' Allan Anderson's study of Pentecostal and Charismatic churches worldwide gives us insight into the challenges faced by those who present a 'homogeneous Pentecostal' paradigm or perspective. For him, 'Pentecostals have defined themselves by so many paradigms that diversity itself has become a primary defining characteristic of Pentecostal and charismatic identity.'[41] Babatunde Adedibu is well worth quoting at length here, to represent the homogenous and heterogeneous dialogue:

> This heterogeneity has contributed to the shaping of the theologies and *leitmotifs* of these churches. The apparent influences of liberation theology – a product of the influence of James Cone's fusion of Martin Luther King's and Malcolm X's 'theologies' of social inequality and social justice in relation to the egalitarian status of blacks in America and the repudiation of colonialism – cannot be over-emphasized. Though there are diverse denominational strands amongst Black–Led Churches, the intriguing and challenging feature of these churches is the absence of generalized theologies common to all black-led denominations in Britain. There exist, however, points of convergence on various doctrinal ideals, such as prayer, the strong affirmation of literalism in biblical exegesis, works of the Holy Spirit and power evangelism.[42]

---

[41] Allan Anderson, *An Introduction to Pentecostalism: Global Charismatic Christianity,* (Cambridge: University Press, 2004), 10.

[42] Adedibu, *Distinctiveness and Contributions of Black Majority Churches,* 113.

While there are churches that are intentional about being contextually relevant, there are others that remain inward-looking, consequently, they are disconnected from the socio-political realities of local communities. Margaret Kane acknowledges this challenge and argues:

> The church is not geared to making God known to the world, but to its own survival. Though this fact should concern us, it should not cause us to despair. If God is in history, He is also in the history of the church; if there is hope for history, there is hope for the church.[43]

Her argument points to a need for serious reflection if Pentecostal churches are to be the manifestation of God's 'love' in caring for all humanity, including black families devastated by disproportionate losses during the COVID-19 pandemic and in responding to the causal factors that sparked the worldwide Black Lives Matter protests. Cone and Wilmore support the notion that churches should be relevant to and a part of the lives of people located in the poor neighborhoods in the heart of our communities, some are.[44] John Stott helps us see this, by suggesting that,

> It is exceedingly strange that any followers of Jesus Christ should ever need to ask whether social involvement was their concern, and that controversy should have blown up over the relationship between evangelism and social responsibility. For it is evident that in his public ministry Jesus both 'went about... teaching and preaching' (Matt. 4.23; 9.35, RSV) and 'doing good and healing' (Acts 10.38, RSV). In consequence,

---

[43] Margaret Kane, *What kind of God: reflections on working with people and church in North-East England,* (London: SCM Press, 1986), 102.

[44] Gayraud Wilmore and James H. Cone, *Black theology: A Documentary History 1966-1979,* (Maryknoll, NY: Orbis Books,1979), 15-16.

evangelism and social concern have been intimately related to one another throughout the history of the Church.[45]

Stott's 'obligatory theology' arguably connects to Cone and Wilmore's argument that the responsibility of black churches is to be both spiritually and socially relevant.[46] These two contend that black churches are located in areas of social deprivation, requiring their support and intervention. It is from this context that like-minded scholars urge black churches to seriously embrace their responsibility as social and spiritual ambassadors to communities, families, and individuals impacted by injustices. Pentecostals and charismatics have theologized around 'obligation and action' in the Spirit's work of bringing about God's kingdom and have begun dialogue about what it means to be a prophetic, relevant and reflective church.[47] While there is some way to go, there is steady growth in the number of black Pentecostal theologians who recognize the need for more critical thinking, conversations, and scholarship that relates faith in the crucified and resurrected Christ with activism that addresses socio-political issues and concerns.

Avery Dulles' work in *Models of the Church* helps us re-imagine a 'Pentecostalism' that can effectively and unapologetically engage with all people. In that work, he argues that:

God's gifts are not confined to people who employ biblical or Christian symbolism. The Church understands God as the loving Father of all men; it celebrates and preaches God's redemptive love extended to all. [48]

---

[45] John Stott, *Issues Facing Christians Today: A major appraisal of contemporary social and moral questions,* (Basingstoke: Marshalls, 1984) 2.

[46] Wilmore and Cone, *Black Theology,* 15-19.

[47] Robert Beckford, *God and the Gangs*, (London: Darton, Longman and Todd Ltd, 2004), 6-7.

[48] Avery Dulles, *Models of the Church,* (London: Image Books, 1991), 63.

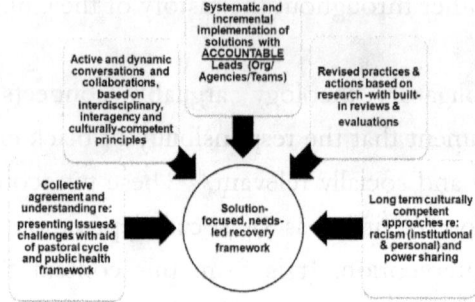

Figure 3 : Practical theology and public health Partnership (Anderson,2020)

There are movements towards building the capacities of Pentecostal denominations and wider church communities to respond to institutional racism and social injustice. This includes multi-agency planning and interdisciplinary recovery strategies related to the disproportionate impact of both COVID-19 and oppressive criminal justice systems on black people and other minority groups. In my work, the strategy outlined in Figure 3 above, along with the PHF and PC, helps me to pray, fast, reason, prioritize and strategize.

While not exhaustive, the six foundational principles have been useful tools in Birmingham's struggles, to grapple with the above issues. Each principle, which has links to the PC and PHF (represented in Figures 1 and 2 above) can help guide denominations and churches in addressing racism, discrimination, and white supremacy and promoting resistance, resourcefulness, resilience, and recovery in working toward the Kingdom of God where justice and peace *kiss*.

1) **Honest acknowledgment and appraisal of impact and reach**: Churches need to critically assess what type of contacts, relationships, interactions, knowledge, and information they have regarding race, racism, and discrimination. This acknowledgement is necessary before progressing to any further stages in the process (see PC1, PC2 and PHF 1. PHF2)

70

2) **Commence conversations (internal and external)**: Churches must involve themselves in reflective conversations, with 'insider' and 'outsider' groups around making racial justice a key issue for proactive work. This should include hearing specifically from black folk who have experienced racism and oppression (see PHF1 and PC2).

3) **Engage in Training associated with practical theology and public health:** Church leaders and staffs must engage in relevant training and develop seminars, conferences, and workshops focused on informed approaches to effectively grappling with issues and challenges associated with racism, inequality, and other community concerns.

4) **Exploring relevant research data and literature**: Church leaders, staff, and volunteers need to be actively involved in basic and advanced research that informs approaches and practices regarding racial justice, socio-political concerns, and community-involved partnerships.

5) **Developing outward-looking approaches**: Churches must be involved in strategic and intentional outreach and support programmes for unchurched individuals and families that may be impacted by crime, violence poverty, racism and other associated concerns. [49]

6) **Develop sustainable ecumenical and community links:** Churches must develop partnerships and linkages with credible organizations involved in community activism that supports black individuals and families. Furthermore, there should be intentional interdenominational partnerships geared towards addressing issues and concerns. These partners must

---

[49] Farmer and Gutierrez in Griffin and Block, *In the Company of the Poor,* 5-10.

understand Pentecostalism as representing the Spirit and anointing: they must see Luke 4:18, as pointing to an activism supporting a liberation trajectory for the poor, marginalized, oppressed, and imprisoned. [50]

Conclusion

I remain committed to contributing to conversations and activism, and formulating a Pentecostal theology that re-imagines a church that sides with 'the least of these.' Pentecostal and other Christians must commit to using an interdisciplinary framework in responding to the concerns and challenges of black families and communities. For, without such commitment from church leaders and denominational heads, this agenda will remain just words and the theologies and values that support white supremacy will remain in place.[51]

---

[50] (see PC 1, 2, 3, 4, and 5, and PHF 1, 2, 3, 4, and 5.)
[51] (Matthew 25:40).

The Bible and Racial Justice

Trevor Grizzle

Race, ethnicity, religion, and nationalism are among the pressing issues that bedevil our world today. Rabid racism has become a volatile and polarizing force in many nations. Unbridled anti-black violence in the United States catalyzed and unleashed a firestorm of protest in 2020 which gained global support and brought the virulent virus of racism to the attention of the world.

The value of a biblical worldview in addressing this problem can inform our understanding and help forge a way forward as we wrestle with racial and cultural challenges today. How did the people of the ancient world perceive and relate to each other? Upon what basis did they accept or reject people that were different from themselves? What does God's word have to say about racial justice?

The God of Justice

Justice is intrinsic to the very nature of God and is fundamentally important to all God does. The Psalmist attests that God's throne rests on the pillars of justice and right judgment: "Righteousness and justice are the foundation of your throne; love and faithfulness go before you" (Ps 89:14). God's divine administration is founded on justice, conforms to it, and is sustained by it. Inextricably tied to God's nature and just government is social, economic, and racial justice. Though often flouted by Israel's kings, the execution of justice was to be central to their role. Justice was a keynote of the message of the prophets of ancient Israel. The entreaty of the prophet Micah to Israel to "do justice" is a muffled echo of the remonstrations of many of its prophets:

He has told you, O man, what is good; and what does the Lord require of you but to do justice, and to love kindness, and to walk humbly with your God." (Mic 6:8).

Justice and Human Origin and Nature

Any adequate discussion of racial justice in the Bible must have its moorings and legitimacy in the justice of God and the biblical doctrine of human origin. The approach I adopt takes a dim view of the polygenetic theory of human origin which is foreign to the Bible. God made all humankind from one man—Adam. The biblical account states,

And God said, 'Let us make man in our image, according to our likeness; and let them have dominion over the fish of the sea, and over the birds of the air, and over all the wild animals of the earth, and over every creeping thing that creeps upon the earth'... God saw all that He had made, and it was very good. (Gen 1:26, 31 NIV).

Paul dittos this in insisting that all nations and peoples share a common ancestry in Adam:

From one man He made all the nations, that they should inhabit the whole earth; and He marked out their appointed times in history and the boundaries of their lands. (Act 17:26 NIV).

As bearer of the *imago Dei* (Gen 1:26), every human being is imbued with dignity, equality, and honor, and with the responsibility to rule, not be ruled; to conquer, not be conquered; to be free, not to be enslaved. Historically, however, concrete actualization of this truth has not been the case; the opposite, rather, seems to have been the rule.

74

Race and Racism

"Race" is not a moniker that is applicable to the three sons of Noah from whom it is believed all the peoples of the world descended. It is a concept that developed much later. Nor does the notion of race, as it is presently understood in the contemporary world, uniformly square with the way ancient peoples characterized, classified, and identified themselves. Present-day concepts in which skin color and discernible and distinguishable traits determine one's racial identity are alien to the ancient world. To be sure, ethnic prejudices were definite aspects of ancient life and thought. Negative stereotyping, cultural biases, caricatures, exclusion, and prejudice of one group toward another existed. Race and color were, however, not the basis for accepting or rejecting a person or the group they represented. The writings of Greek geographer and historian Strabo (64 or 63 BCE – c. CE 24), for example, acknowledged the physical features of Ethiopians but not in a pejorative way. He centered instead on their temperament and manner of life,[1] not on their color.

The notion of race as it is presently understood does not rest on biological or scientific evidence, but is a socio-political construct spawned in the era of European colonialism and Western imperialism. More precisely, it was based on a strategy whose purpose was to categorize and classify colonized peoples,[2] flaunt the superiority and supremacy of white people, and legitimize white control over the people they colonized. This is especially true of people of color.

The concept of "nation" is not defined or well-established—even in the Bible. Scripture commonly describes a "group of people with a cohesive system of political and military rule"[3] with power centralized in a king who was circumspectly selected and sanctioned by an elaborate religious system. The prophets of Israel denounced as

---

[1] Strabo, 3:8; 2-3.
[2] John Andrew Kirk, "Race, class, caste and the Bible" *Themelios*, 10:2 Jan 1985, 5. Benjamin Isaac, *The Invention of Racism in Classical Antiquity* (Princeton: Princeton University Press, 2004), 25-7, 515.
[3] Ibid., 6.

covenant disloyalty Israel's every effort to pattern its government on the basis of other nations. Furthermore, whereas people existed free from geographical boundaries prior to the 17th century C.E., with the creation of the racist ideology of "race" came geographical boundaries of nation states.

As Kathy Ehrenspreger has noted, "Whatever stereotyping of other peoples existed in antiquity - and it certainly did exist, operating with various images and prejudices - no such concept as the modem concept of 'race' can be found."[4] She further insists that "whatever negative stereotyping existed it did not lead to exclusivism in an absolute sense as is the case in the racist discourse of modernity."[5] In the ancient world, the concept of a white or black race did not exist. Notably, what did exist was prejudice of one group toward another, practices of group inclusion and exclusion on the basis of ethnic identity, cultural favoritism, and ethnocentrism.

Prejudice and racism are not the same thing. Prejudice is a preconception, a prejudgment of someone or something before the facts are examined. Racism is more than intolerance toward and exclusion of a person or group. It is the belief that members of one race are inferior to members of another, thus granting special rights, opportunities and privileges to the "superior" race while denying them to members of the "inferior" one.

But racism involves more! Racism uses power to exclude individuals from the privileged group by legalizing, institutionalizing, formalizing, and enforcing prejudice in all its multiform configurations and expressions. While it could take on racial overtones, ethnocentrism does not necessarily involve a negative perspective of the race of other people. Ethnocentrism is a "we"/"they" view of life in which a person may see his/her own culture as the only correct way of living. One's

---

[4] Kathy Ehrenspreger, Paul, his People and Racial Terminology, *Journal of Early Christian History,* 3:1 2013, 19.
[5] Ibid., 20.

ethnic group then becomes the center of gravity and axis of the world on which everything turns, is weighed and measured.

Race as contemporarily understood is an anachronism in the ancient world. This study of racial justice and the Bible, therefore, considers the social intercourse among the peoples of the world of the Bible, not from the framework of the modern characterization of persons' skin pigmentation and phenotypical features, but in terms of ethnic groups,[6] the ethnocentrism and internecine prejudices that governed their relationships leading to the inclusion of one group and the exclusion of another. There will be occasions, however, when race will be used with its present-day connotation for the sake of phenotypical demarcation.

Ethnic Diversity and the Ancient World

Ancient Israel, the chosen people of God, may serve as a microcosm of the larger world and a divine pilot project which comes to fulfillment in the Church universal. Israel was not a monolithic people or a uniform, undifferentiated, and pure-bloodied ethnic group. The Israelite people developed from the Asiatic/Semitic group of peoples and were "a mixed lot with no recognizable racial stock. In fact, they were an amalgamation of races. When they came out of Egypt, they might have been Afro-asiatic's. To refer to them as Semites would rather mean not a race but a family of languages—Hebrew, Akkadian, Arabic and Ethiopic."[7] Quite possibly, the "language of the 'burnt-face' Africans could have been equally Semitic as was that of the Jews and Arabs. This affirms the contention that theories of race and the phenomenon of racism with their discriminatory effects are by-products of the post-biblical era."[8]

---

[6] For the most part, individuals will represent the group.
[7] Arun Kumar Wesley, "Sacralisation and Secularisation: An Analysis of a Few Biblical Passages for Possible Racial Overtones and Ethnocentrism" *The Asia Journal of Theology*, 16:2 Oct 2002, 378.
[8] Ibid., 378.

Egypt's role in shaping world civilization is undeniable. A bird's-eye view into its ethnic composition and how its diverse peoples related to one another provide insights that may help racial relations today. The Nile River region served as a magnet, drawing people from all over; ancient Egypt was ethnically diverse, its peoples showing no preoccupation with skin color. Obedience to the king, speaking the language, and worshiping the gods qualified one to be an Egyptian. There was no prohibition on outsiders marrying Egyptians, and racial integration as presently conceived was well represented even in the aristocracy.[9] African blacks were assimilated into Egyptian society, powerful African kings becoming pharaohs of Egypt and building thriving empires that lasted for centuries. The 25th dynasty of Egypt (ca. 770-656 BCE), known as the Ethiopian Period of Ancient Egypt, witnessed a succession of Nubian pharaohs which conquered and dominated Egypt. These black pharaohs, the most notable of which was Shabaka, decisively shaped the culture and civilization of Egypt.[10] Statues and artifacts in museums and other places around the world bear eloquent witness to this fact.

Twice in Isaiah (chapters 18 and 30), the NIV Study Bible (2011 edition) makes reference to the 25th dynasty of Egypt and the role of "Shabako" in its founding and expansive geo-political influence: "In 715 BC a Cushite named Shabako gained control of Egypt and founded the Twenty-Fifth Dynasty."[11] The note on Isaiah 30:1 states, "After Shabako became pharaoh in 715 BC, the smaller nations in Aram (Syria) and Canaan sought his help against Assyria. Judah apparently joined them."[12]

---

[9] Ridley Scott's Exodus: Were Ancient Egyptians White, Black, or Brown? https://slate.com/technology/2014/12/ridley-scotts-exodus-were-ancient-egyptians-white-black-or-brown.html. Accessed 9/23/20.

[10] https://www.nationalgeographic.com/history/magazine/2016/11-12/ancient-egypt-nubian-kingdom-pyramids-sudan/

[11] Note Isaiah 18:1.

[12] Note Isaiah 30:1.

In his seminal research, "The Ethnicity of the Ancient Egyptians," Herbert Foster has given irrefragable proof that Egypt's pre-dynastic civilization was created by Negroid peoples and that a strong Negroid admixture was present in the pharaohs of the dynastic period.[13] As clinching proof of the diversity and multi-ethnic make-up of ancient Egypt, he appeals to Egyptian art works which show Mongoloids, Negroids, and Caucasoids held as slaves and concludes: "It would seem that they did not have the modern conception of race." He adds, "Their attitude toward people was based on cultural status, not color. Monuments and paintings show black, yellow, and white people in obeisance to their Egyptian conquerors."[14]

Significantly, ethnic diversity features quite early in the biblical story of human redemption. Abraham's first son, Ishmael, was born to an Egyptian wife (Gen 16:3, 15). Both his son Isaac and grandson Jacob married Aramean women, the succeeding generation marrying Canaanites (Judah, Gen 38:2; Simeon, Gen 46:10) and Egyptians (Joseph, Gen 41:50). Joseph's Egyptian wife bore him Manasseh and Ephraim (Gen 46:27; 48:1), who were the only two of Jacob's grandchildren to become independent tribes. It has been the widespread practice of Jews to bless their sons, "May God make you like Ephraim and Manasseh."

Referring to those who left Egypt with the Israelites during the exodus, Exodus 12:38 records that a "mixed multitude also went up with them, and very much livestock, both flocks and herds." Who constituted this mixed multitude? Some scholars suggest they were Egyptian slaves; others opine that they were the fruit of intermarriage between Israelites and Egyptians. There can be little doubt, however, that they were an ethnically diverse group who would later be brought into covenant relationship with God.

---

[13] Herbert J. Foster, "The Ethnicity of the Ancient Egyptians," *Journal of Black Studies* 5:2 (Dec. 1974): 188-190.

[14] Ibid., 187.

A strong injunction to Israel to love, deal justly with and take care of the foreigner who lived among them threads through the legal materials in the Hebrew Bible (Deut 10:17–19; Lev 19:33–34). One reason given is: "you were strangers in the land of Egypt" (Deut 10:19). Among these strangers were, indubitably, members of the mixed multitude. Not only is kindness and a compassionate disposition toward foreigners encouraged in these passages, but the people of Israel are expected to identify with them.

The Curse of Ham

After the creation narrative, Genesis 9:18-27—a passage greatly misinterpreted by some—is the first biblical text that brings the issue of "race" into debate, although Noah and his sons are not described in racial terms. The so-called "curse of Ham" unfortunately read into the text by some interpreters is exegetically flawed, but has been used by Judaism, Christianity, and Islam to derogate blacks who were believed to be the progeny of Ham. Christian and non-Christian Europeans alike received the text as biblical sanction for the enslavement of blacks.

In the Old Testament, Egypt is repeatedly referred to as the "Land of Ham" (Ps 78:51; 105:23, 27; 106:22; 1 Chron 4:40). "Ham" in both Hebrew and Egyptian means "hot," "burnt," or "black." Ham's four sons were Cush, Mizraim, Put, and Canaan (Gen 10:6). Cush was later given the name Ethiopia; Mizraim was renamed Egypt; Put took the name Libya, and Canaan became Israel.[15] To conclude that all of Ham's descendants were black and settled in Africa is skating on thin ice. That is inconsistent with ethnographic and ethnohistorical evidence and the geographic and migratory lines of Noah's descendants. Among the

---

[15]http://freepages.rootsweb.com/~sturnbo/folklore/files/oldest/Table%20of %20Nations%20and%20Genealogy%20of%20Mankind.htm.

descendants of Ham were the Assyrians, Babylonians, Phoenicians, Hittites, Canaanites, and the people of Philistia.

Fortunately, the belief that black people are under the curse pronounced on their "forefather Ham" has progressively lost credibility and traction notwithstanding the presence of obdurate contemporary mutations and new adaptations. The concept of the curse of Ham has nothing to commend it. First, nowhere does the text say that Ham was cursed. It clearly states, "Cursed be Canaan! The lowest of slaves will he be to his brothers" (Gen 9:25 NIV). Second, a curse is never retroactive; it is always prospective. That is, it does not reach back to preceding generations; it affects only future ones. Third, ethnographic evidence shows that Canaan's descendants were not a single monolithic ethnic group but consisted of a collection of tribes of varying ethnicities who lived in Phoenicia, modern-day Israel, Palestine, Lebanon, Syria, and Jordan. Finally, many scholars believe Noah's curse was not on Canaan himself but a prophetic pronouncement on the nation that would come from him.

Disdain of Moses' Cushite wife

In Miriam and Aaron's opposition of Moses in Numbers 12:1-2 we encounter the first incident in the Bible that one might call "racism," but race may be just a pretext for a bigger problem: Numbers 12 tells us that "Miriam and Aaron began to talk against Moses because of his Cushite wife, for he had married a Cushite. 'Has the LORD spoken only through Moses?' they asked. 'Hasn't he also spoken through us?' And the LORD heard this." Moses' wife was a descendant of Cush, the first son of Ham. A Midianite, referred to as an Ethiopian in some translations, she most likely was Zipporah (Exod 2:15-22). The Midianites were Semites, ethnic cousins to the Israelites and worshipers of Baal. Zipporah's priestly father Jethro is called a Kenite. The Kenites travelled with the Israelites to Palestine (Judg 1:16). Zipporah's native country was not Ethiopia below Egypt, but Arabia, which intimates that she may have been dark skinned. As Frank Yamada has noted, "Within the Bible, cultural difference is not identified primarily through physical traits. The more dominant categories were ethnicity and religious difference. Ethnicity is tied to a group's common cultural understanding based primarily in national origin."[16]

Marrying a foreigner was not unlawful; nor was it looked upon unfavorably. Moses had been married to Zipporah for some forty years. Why would her skin color now become an issue? Was her ethnic and cultural distinctness a ruse or smokescreen to hide a larger problem? The issue presented in verse 2 seems to have been the real one: authority. Miriam and Aaron, Moses' siblings, may have wanted prophetic equality with their brother.

Further, God himself had taken the Spirit that was on Moses and placed it on the 70 elders Moses had chosen (Num. 11:24-25). The whole idea of shared governance had, however, been suggested by Moses' father-in-law—but probably inspired by Zipporah who had both taken word to Jethro of her husband's presence in the desert and accompanied him to meet Moses (Exod 18:5). Was Zipporah seen as changing the leadership dynamic by harnessing her father's influence and adding her own to it thus swaying Moses' decision? The selecting of 70 elders may have been seen as a sharing of power which elevated other leaders but diminished the stature and authority of Miriam and Aaron. Did the episode where the Spirit rested on the 70 elders (11:24-25) suggest to Miriam and Aaron that legitimate leaders other than Moses existed? It appears that power-sharing, not race, was the real problem for the opposition of Moses' leadership.

---

[16] Frank M. Yamada, "The Bible and Racism," Session 1: Does the Bible justify or resist racism? Or both?
https://static1.squarespace.com/static/55e9d34be4b0ab8467774bff/t/5d24b3c2c5c86400014f19c7/1562686403217/The+Bible+and+Racism.pdf. Accessed 9/25/2020.

Conquest of Canaan: Ethnic Cleansing?

Regarding racism and ethnic cleansing, no part of the Bible is more troubling than the book of Joshua though the battles between Israelites and the Canaanites were not racial. Biblical scholars, social anthropologists, and archaeologists have determined that there is little to distinguish the Israelites from the Canaanites. They shared a common origin. Yet, God's commission to Joshua to exterminate the inhabitants of Canaan to take possession of the land raises questions of ethics and equity.

The conquest of Canaan and the savagery that attended it can be correctly understood only in the context of the unfolding story of redemption, God reclaiming land from a decadent people long under the aegis of false deities (Deut 7:1-11). The book of Joshua is about the advance of God's kingdom in a world held in the iron grips of pagan gods who demanded worship and claimed hegemony over creation and its peoples. The war for the Promised Land was not Israel's war to conquer territory to which they would lay personal claim; it was the Lord's war executed to prosecute God's program of redemption. Lands and property conquered did not belong to Israel in an absolute sense; they belonged to the Lord.

A dominant Hebrew term in the conquest narratives is *herem*. The verb form (*haram*) means "to devote" or "exterminate" and is commonly used of the destruction of idolatrous nations. The *herem* (Gk. *anathema*) was a person or thing irrevocably devoted to God for destruction (Lev 27:21; 27:28-29; Josh 6:17; 7:1). The word also means dedication of a person or possession to God without the possibility of recall or redemption. Lands conquered by Israel were not their national possession by right of conquest. The spoils of war were not theirs to enrich themselves. Everything—Canaan's people, land, property, wealth—all belonged to God to dispense with as he wished. But the despicable objects tainted by pagan idolatry and immorality had to be cleansed of all vestiges of paganism—hence their decimation. Further, in purging the Canaanites from the land, God could begin anew with his chosen, covenant people who would serve him alone and order their lives according to his will.

Prohibition against Intermarriage with Foreigners

Israel failed to live as God's chosen, covenant people. In disobedience to his law, they adopted the ways and worship of their pagan neighbors, resulting in their deportation to Babylon in 586 BCE. After the exile, having learned from the errors of their evil ways, the returnees were a transformed people imbued with a renewed sense of collective identity, devotion to the law, and nationhood. But the pendulum had swung from one extreme to the other. A consciousness of distinctiveness had emerged among the people that not only led to national and religious particularism, but to an exclusivism epitomized in the Pharisees.

The coming of Ezra and Nehemiah put into high gear Israel's feeling of separateness with a call for a cessation of intermarriage and the divorcing of foreign wives (Ezra 10; Neh 13:23-31). While the prohibition against intermarriage may have a xenophobic tone, Ezra and Nehemiah's appeal was based on religious and spiritual grounds, rather than on race. Foreign wives could lead their husbands and families away from God and into idolatry. Nehemiah explained his action thus:

> I made them take an oath in God's name and said: 'You are not to give your daughters in marriage to their sons, nor are you to take their daughters in marriage for your sons or for yourselves. Was it not because of marriages like these that Solomon king of Israel sinned? Among the many nations there was no king like him. He was loved by his God, and God made him king over all Israel, but even he was led into sin by foreign women.' (13: 25-26).

The book of Ruth provides a more positive picture of Jewish perception of and social interaction with foreigners. Due to famine, a Jewish family resettled in Moab. (The Moabites descended from Lot and were, therefore, relatives of the Israelites. Historically, however, their relationship was one of mutual hostility.) The two brothers of the Jewish family married two sisters of a Moabite family. Naomi, the only surviving member of the Jewish family, returned with her widowed and childless daughter-in-law Ruth to Bethlehem. There Ruth met and married Boaz. From their union came a great-grandson, David as well as Jesus the great "son of David" (Matt 1:1) and Savior of the world. Ruth's placement in the lineage of David characterizes the ethnic diversity and inclusivity of the kingdom of God.

Diversity and Inclusivity in the Ministry of Jesus

As one pivots to the New Testament, it is important to observe the diversity and inclusivity of the genealogy of Jesus, the initiator of the New covenant—a genetic harbinger of the all-embracing Savior he would be. It is no small matter that Matthew, the most Jewish of the Gospels, names five women in the family tree of Jesus, three of which were Gentiles (Tamar, Rahab, and Ruth). This indicates early that parallel with the particularism and Jewishness of that Gospel runs an encompassing universalism. It is Matthew alone that mentions that the Christ Child found refuge in a foreign country (Egypt) and that wise men came from afar to pay tribute to the Baby born king.

Despite Matthew's catholic overtones, his account of the mission of the twelve seems to present Jesus as ethnically insensitive: "Do not go among the Gentiles or enter any town of the Samaritans. Go rather to the lost sheep of Israel," Jesus commands (Matt 10:5-6). Why the prohibition of taking the gospel to the Gentiles and Samaritans? No one can rightfully charge Jesus of ethnic insensitivity. His life and ministry contradict such a claim. Jesus' interdiction may be partially answered theologically. The Jews must be the first recipients of the gospel (Acts 1:8) and the first to take it to the world (Jn 4:22). The priority of the Jews in salvation is acknowledged by Jesus himself: "I was sent only to the lost sheep of Israel" (Matt 15:24) and reiterated by Paul: "For I am not ashamed of the gospel, because it is the power of God that brings salvation to everyone who believes: first to the Jew, then to the Gentile" (Rom 1:16). Paul adopted this order on his missionary journeys, ministering first in the synagogues in the cities he visited and then to the Gentiles in other venues.

In the ancient world a yawning ethnic and cultural chasm separated Jews and Gentiles. The magnitude of the problem was unlike anything the modern world has known. Says New Testament scholar John R. Stott, "It is difficult for us to grasp the impassable gulf which yawned in those days between the Jews on the one hand and the Gentiles (including even the 'God-fearers') on the other hand." He continues, "The tragedy was that Israel twisted the doctrine of election into one of favoritism, became filled with racial pride and hatred, despised Gentiles as 'dogs', and developed traditions which kept them apart. No orthodox Jew would ever enter the home of a Gentile, even a God-fearer, or invite such into his home."[17] J. M. Stifler describes the rift as "worse than the Hindu caste." There was no room for social intercourse. For the Jew, to touch a Gentile "was defiling, his food was an abomination to the devout Israelite, and his religion blasphemy."[18]

William Barclay echoes the sentiments above and the predicament that early Christianity faced:

> Christianity was cradled in Judaism, and, humanly speaking, no message which was meant for all the world could ever have had a more unfortunate cradle. The Jews were involved in a double hatred--the world hated them, and they hated the

---

[17] John R. Stott, *The Spirit, the Church, and the World: the Message of Acts* (Downers Grove, IL: Intervarsity Press, 1990), 185.

[18] J. M. Stifler, *An Introduction to the Study of the Acts of the Apostles* (New York: Fleming & Revell, 1892), 81, 82.

world. No nation was more bitterly hated than the Jews... No nation ever hated other nations as the Jews did.[19]

Jesus' disciples were not ready to undertake a Gentile mission. But God in his inscrutable providence had prepared a man for that mission. That man was Paul. He alone was theologically, socially, ethnically, and spiritually prepared for the task. He alone could bridge the great gulf that distanced the Jews from the Gentiles and the Gentiles from the Jews.

The situation between the Jews and Samaritans was somewhat better. The Samaritans were half-Jews, a hybrid people in race and religion—the offspring of intermarriage between the Jewish remnant left behind after the city's conquest and the foreign people introduced into Samaria by Assyria in 722 BC. Their long history of internecine animosity exemplified in Samaritan opposition to the Jews rebuilding of the Temple (Ezra 4) and wall in Jerusalem (Neh 6), and the Jewish king John Hyrcanus' destruction of the Samaritan temple in 129 BC, had abated little by the time of Jesus and the Church. The words of the Samaritan woman to Jesus at Sychar's well capture the mood and mutual sentiment between these two inveterate enemies: "Jews do not associate with Samaritans" (Jn 4:9). The solution of James and John to the Samaritans' refusal to allow Jesus to spend a night in their town epitomizes how most Jews felt about the Samaritans: "Lord, do you want us to call fire down from heaven to destroy them?" (Lk 9:54).

These hate-filled words amply prove that the disciples were not ready to preach the gospel to the Samaritans. Not till ten years after its birth was the church ready to take the gospel to the Samaritans in fulfillment of the commission of Jesus (Acts 1:8). Yet, it took Philip a Hellenistic Jew with a broader worldview and more accepting disposition to bring it about!

---

[19] William Barclay, *The Mind of St. Paul* (New York: Harper & Row, 1975), 9, 10.

Both Matthew (15:21-28) and Mark (7:25-30) record an episode in the life of Jesus that has historically presented an image of him that is hard to reconcile with that presented elsewhere in the Gospels. In his brief exchange with the Syrophoenician woman, a Gentile (Matthew refers to her as a Canaanite, Mark a Greek) whose daughter was demon possessed, Jesus seemingly compared her to dogs. The demeaning, contemptible epithet is softened only slightly in knowing that these dogs were not the wild, scavenging predators that roamed the streets. The Greek word for dogs (*kunaria*) is diminutive and means "little household pet dogs." Some translations render it "little dogs" (puppies) or simply "dogs." The NIV tries to skirt the ethnic and racial "slur" by translating the Greek "their dogs": "It is not right to take the children's bread and toss it to *their dogs*" (emphasis added, Matt 15:26; Mk 7:27). At first blush the remark seems rude, unkind, and even derogatory. But did Jesus mean to be disrespectful and insensitive to this Gentile woman? Did he carry the same disdain for the Gentiles as the Jews at large?

Matthew situates the event in the mission of Jesus: "I was not sent except to the lost sheep of the house of Israel" (15:24; see also 10:5-6). Mark states it a different way, "First let the children eat all they want" before feeding "their dogs" (7:27). The priority of the Jews as recipients of the gospel is clearly in view. Noted New Testament scholar William Lane has remarked, "By reference to the distinction between the claims of the children of the household and the pet dogs Jesus sharply differentiates between the claims of Israel and those of the Gentiles upon his ministry, which is restricted to Israel."[20] Contra C. E. B. Cranfield,[21] British churchman and New Testament scholar John Nolland has noted that while some rabbis viewed Gentiles as "dogs," the term is not used as a standard Jewish image of Gentiles, as

---

[20] William Lane, "The Gospel of Mark," *NICNT* (Grand Rapids, MI: William B. Eerdmans Publishing Co., 1974), 261.

[21] C. E. B. Cranfield, "St Mark," *The Cambridge Greek Testament Commentary* (London: Cambridge University Press, 1959), 248.

often maintained."[22] Lane says it is "doubtful that Jesus intended a reference to the Gentiles or that the woman understood his statement in this sense."[23] Cranfield agrees.[24]

Allen Black sees the statement not as pejorative, but proverbial. He says, "the basis of the proverb is not an antipathy for Gentiles, but the necessary Jewish focus of Jesus' earthly ministry."[25] Kyle Butt adduces that Jesus was using the term "dog" idiomatically, as we do today, without any disparaging connotation. In this way, his remark to the Gentile woman should not be taken literally. For example, we may say someone shows "bulldog tenacity"; a person is as "cute as a puppy"; someone "works like a dog"; you cannot "teach an old dog new tricks"; he is the "top dog" in the company.[26] It remains to be seen if this interpretation will ever be given a scholarly hearing.

Rather than seeing Jesus' remark as disparaging, it could be seen as Jesus testing the woman in the fashion of the custom of some teachers with their disciples (Jn 6:6) to tease from her the unalloyed genuineness of her faith? Or was Jesus reiterating a commonly known Jewish perception of Gentiles, but with the implication that his view was completely different? Difficult as it may be to satisfactorily determine what Jesus meant, no answer that distorts or contradicts the portrait of him presented throughout the Gospels should be entertained. Our interpretation must be consistent with the Jesus we meet in the Gospels. Unlike other religious men, everywhere in the Gospels, Jesus unconditionally reached out to and accepted the outcast, the prostitute, the foreigner, and the poor—he did not deprecate or rebuff them. Jesus never spurned a seeking or believing Gentile (e.g., a centurion, Matt 8:5-13; Greeks, Jn 12:20-35) and used

---

[22] John Nolland, *The Gospel of Matthew* (Grand Rapids, MI: William B. Eerdmans Publishing Co., 2005), 634.

[23] Lane, "The Gospel of Mark, 262.

[24] Cranfield, "St Mark," 248.

[25] Allen Black, *The Book of Mark* (Joplin, MO: College Press, 1995), 137.

[26] Kyle Butt, "Jesus, the Syrophoenician Woman, and Little Dogs." http://www.apologeticspress.org/ APContent.aspx?category=22&article=317. Accessed 9/28/2020.

them as positive examples in his teaching (Matt 11:20-24; 12:41-42; 21:31, 41, 43). One of his last acts before his crucifixion was the cleansing of the court of the Gentiles in the temple. He did this so that God's house could be a "house of prayer for all the nations" (Mk 11:17).

It was fitting that who Jesus was in life was recognized at his death. Notwithstanding Pilate's malicious intention in doing so, in a strange twist of irony the inscription he hung above the head of Jesus written in Hebrew, Greek, and Latin (Jn 19:20, NKJV) acknowledged and publicized Jesus' universal saviorhood and dominion. Hebrew was the national tongue and the language of religion and divine revelation. Greek constituted the language of culture and universal commerce among the nations and peoples of the world. Latin was the official language that represented law and Roman imperial power.

Pentecost: Unity in Diversity

The occasion of the outpouring of the Holy Spirit on members of fifteen nations gathered in Jerusalem, Pentecost affords us a window into the multilingual, multicultural, multiracial nature and mission of God's new people, the Church. Unlike the confusion of languages at Babel and the attendant dispersal of the people, Pentecost witnessed unity of speech and the joining of many diverse peoples and cultures in united praise to God. Couched in the symbolic language of "each one [of the 15 nations] heard them [the inspired tongues-speakers] speaking in his own language" (2:6, 8) is the Church's mission of world evangelization. All nations must hear the good news of salvation in their own language and acknowledge the goodness and greatness of God.

Noteworthy at this august event and in the flourishing multi-ethnic church that blossomed in Antioch thereafter is the African contingent (13:1). Present at Pentecost were men from Egypt and Libya (North Africa). In the leadership of the Antiochene church were Simeon called Niger and Lucius of Cyrene—capital of Libya (13:1),

90

both of whom were black. In Galatians 3:28 Paul writes, "There is neither Jew nor Gentile, neither slave nor free, nor is there male and female, for you are all one in Christ Jesus,"and Ephesians 2:14-16 echoes a similar note of unity: "For he himself is our peace, who has made the two groups one and has destroyed the barrier, the dividing wall of hostility... His purpose was to create in Himself one new humanity out of the two, thus making peace, and in one body to reconcile both to God through the cross." Did the broadly diverse yet inclusive church in Antioch inspire Paul's vision of the church universal depicted in Galatians and Ephesians?

Hebrews and Hellenists

Overlooking Hellenistic Jewish widows in daily food distribution (Ac 6:1-6) was an early problem in the church that, seemingly, smacked of discrimination. Two kinds of Jews made up the Jerusalem church: Hellenist and Hebrew--both full-blooded Jews, but two separate and distinct groups with cultural barnacles that chafed mutual relationship. Hellenist Jews were born outside of Palestine and spoke Greek. Their attitudes, outlook, culture, and intellectual orientation were strongly Greek. The Hebrews were Jews born in Palestine. They spoke Aramaic or Hebrew and exercised greater traditional rigidity in matters of religion and social interchange. The two groups seemed to have worshiped in their own separate synagogues.

Though complaint by the Hellenists over the neglect of their widows is the problem mentioned in Acts 6, that however was only the lengthened shadow of a much deeper and potentially more explosive issue. Hellenist Christians probably outnumbered their Hebrew counterpart, were generally wealthier, and had the largest amount of money in the benevolence fund. Cultural inertia had led to a monocultural monopoly in the leadership of the church, and Hellenist widows were not receiving their equal share of the community resources. Did the oversight of the Hellenist widows stem from poor organization and micromanagement? Was it the result of nepotism and favoritism which sprang from a deep well of ethnocentrism? Thankfully, the church's leaders saw the rightfulness of the grievance and chose seven deacons—probably all Hellenist—who took care of the problem.

Jews and Gentiles

Acts 10 records the bridging of one of the greatest ethno-cultural divides in human history. To the Jew there were only two kinds of people in the world—Jews and Gentiles. To be Jewish meant to be chosen and divinely favored of God; the opposite was true for being a Gentile. Grounded in an absolute monotheism, Jewish ethnic identity displayed a revulsion for the Gentile idolatrous way of life and fear of contamination any social interaction would invite. On the other hand, Gentiles disdained the Jews' imageless monotheism, magnifying the antipathy. The chasm that separated them was wider than the Grand Canyon.

But bridge it God would. And God would do it with incompatible human timber. Two most unlikely men were the agents of divine reconciliation: Cornelius and Peter. These two men were like repelling poles, as irreconcilable as oil and water. Cornelius was a disciplined and decorated leader of a Roman regiment, Peter the strongly opinionated and orthodox leader of the Church and supernova of Judaism. Two places would be the theaters of divine operation: Caesarea Maritima and Joppa. In both cities and in both men, God began his bridge-building project, softening the hearts of Cornelius and Peter through prayer and lighting their horizons with a new vision.

Peter was not quickly and easily convinced that Gentiles were clean. God had to do some deep cultural excavation in him, projecting the same vision before him three times and enjoining him, "Do not call anything impure that God has made clean" (Acts 10:15). Full and visible manifestation of this truth burst upon Peter's vision when, after traveling nearly 40 miles and preaching to Cornelius and his household, he witnessed their conversion and infilling with the Holy Spirit just as it had happened to the Jews at Pentecost.

This momentous event brought Peter under much suspicion by the Jerusalem church and its leadership. The Christian communities became abuzz with rumor: "the supernova among them has plummeted to earth." Their leading apostle had done the unthinkable: entered the house of Gentiles and engaged in table fellowship with them. Peter had to answer for his action. To verify all that transpired in Cornelius' house he called upon the six Jewish believers that had accompanied him to Caesarea and witnessed what happened in Cornelius' house. They were there when Peter preached his immortal sermon. They were there when the Spirit came. In the face of incontrovertible evidence of God's sovereign work among the Gentiles, Peter's opponents "were silenced" (Acts 11:18 RSV), and "had no further objections" (NIV). God had spoken; the world must remain silent. God had acted; the earth must pause and ponder.

The event in Cornelius' house seared itself into Peter's consciousness, emboldening him to face the Jerusalem Council to defend the legitimacy of Paul's missionary work among the Gentiles (Acts 15). In light of the revelation of God's acceptance of Gentiles (Acts 10), Peter's later withdrawing from table fellowship with Gentile Christians in Antioch at the arrival of messengers from James (Gal 2:12-14) is inconsistent and quite puzzling. As a Jewish Christian leader, Peter's presence at table fellowship was regarded as endorsement of the shared equality of Jews and Gentiles as people of God. Withdrawal from table fellowship, inspired an exodus of like-minded Jews and demonstrated a preference for a common Jewish racial identity over the new reality of the unity of all believers. This behavior influenced even Barnabas and rightly drew the ire and denunciation of Paul as hypocrisy.

The gospel is universal and inclusive in its appeal. This truth laces through the Bible from Genesis to Revelation. Such universality is adumbrated in Acts in the conversion of distant descendants of each of the three sons of Noah before Paul's missionary journeys into Asia and Europe. As all the nations descended from Ham, Shem, and Japheth (Gen 10), so now in Acts a distant progeny of each features in the global outreach of the gospel As Acts records, the Ethiopian (Acts 8) represents the racial family of Ham, Saul of Tarsus (chap. 9), the racial family of Shem, and Cornelius the racial family of Japheth. As the progenitors of the seventy nations that would spread across the earth after the flood and populate it (Gen 10), so now they reappear in Acts as three representatives of the diverse nations and peoples that will blanket the world with the gospel.

All one Family

God's reign in the world is based on justice—a justice God wants for all people. He made all human beings in his image and bestowed on them equal honor and dignity and expects justice from his people toward each other. All humans have sinned and fallen short of God's glory (Rom 3:23), and no one is able to fulfill God's holy requirements without his assistance. God loves all his children equally and sent Jesus to die for all (Jn 3:16). The Holy Spirit is given to all believers without exception as a seal of God's ownership. What is more, in two passages Paul admonishes us that Christ has given believers a new identity which obliterates all religio-ethnic-cultural, socio-economic, sexual, and class distinctions which could serve as a premise for prejudice and discrimination. In Galatians 3:28-29 he writes, "There is neither Jew nor Gentile, neither slave nor free, nor is there male and female, for you are all one in Christ Jesus. If you belong to Christ, then you are Abraham's seed, and heirs according to the promise." Then he adds in Colossian 3:9-11:

> Do not lie to each other, since you have taken off your old self with its practices and have put on the new self, which is being renewed in knowledge in the image of its Creator. Here there is no Gentile or Jew, circumcised or uncircumcised,

94

barbarian, Scythian, slave or free, but Christ is all, and is in all.

Paul is making clear that all barriers are down; distinctions of every kind are eliminated. Racism is gone. Classism is gone. Gender bias is gone. There is nothing that can disqualify a person from God's new family. And there is no basis on which one can build a case for personal superiority or inferiority. In this new family each member has equal access and equal acceptance and shares equally. This is God's vision for his people and God wants to see it become a reality in the here and now.

What Paul says to the church at Ephesus, he says to all the people of God:

Make every effort to keep the unity of the Spirit through the bond of peace. There is one body and one Spirit, just as you were called to one hope when you were called; one Lord, one faith, one baptism; one God and Father of all, who is over all and through all and in all. (4:3-6).

God's promise to Abraham that in him "all the nations of the earth will be blessed" has been fulfilled in Christ. God is the God of all nations. He is the God of all people. He is the God of all races. He has no favorites. It behooves us to translate in word and deed the words of John Oxenham, "In Christ there is no east or west, in him no south or north; but one great fellowship of love throughout the whole wide world." John the revelator telescopes the scene at the end of time when all nations will gather as one undivided family and joyfully parade in unison before the throne of God as trophies of his divine grace and redemption:

After this I looked and there before me was a great multitude that no one could count, from every nation, tribe, people and language, standing before the throne and in front of the Lamb. They were wearing white robes and were holding palm branches in their hands. And they cried out in a loud voice: "Salvation belongs to our God, who sits on the throne, and to the Lamb" (Rev 7:9-10). Amen!

Until then we must daily live out the ethical mandate of the prophet Micah to act justly, love mercy and walk humbly with our God.

A Pentecostal Model for Addressing Racial Discrimination

Patrick L. Kelly

Introduction

As a community under the guidance and power of the Holy Spirit, the contemporary church possesses the potential for answering the challenge of discrimination within a broken humanity. The scriptural narrative of the resolution of such an issue in the New Testament church provides a paradigm regarding how we might resolve our current dilemma amid the racial tension that is an ongoing fixture. By observing how Jesus' redemptive activity is played out in the life of the young church, believers can develop a sense of biblical community that will allow us to live in harmony among ourselves and with others in society.

The church is not a perfect institution. For it, like the rest of humanity, exists within a fallen world. Both biblical and social history reveal that believers are often plagued by the same problems, behaviors, and mindsets that affect the unredeemed. Though reconciliation to God positions us to become, in practice, what Christ has already accomplished through His passion, as imperfect beings, Christian are still subject to the imperfection of a fallen nature.

Still, as the "light of the world" and a "city on a hill," the church is positioned to lead in the righteous conduct that causes men and women to follow and worship God, and to live out their love for their neighbor. Where we fail in that mission, we can adjust through the abiding presence and guidance of the Holy Spirit. Acknowledging Paul's conviction that, "[w]e have this treasure" yet it is contained in "earthen vessels" enables us to admit our frailty in resolving hard challenges and to place our confidence in the continuing power of God to mature and perfect our responses to critical issues.

The book of Acts provides an example of how a Spirit-empowered, yet imperfect, church depended on the Holy Spirit to guide it through a touchy situation that could have derailed the ministry of the infant community and discredited its witness within the broader society. In Acts 1:8, Jesus points to the necessity of the Holy Spirit for accomplishing the church's mission.

> But you shall receive power when the Holy Spirit has come upon you; and you shall be witnesses to Me in Jerusalem, and in all Judea and Samaria, and to the ends of the earth.

The presence and power of the Spirit is integral to the life of the church. Acts 2 confirms this when the promised coming of the Holy Spirit was received on the Day of Pentecost, marking the birth of the church. Luke's narrative describes a community of believers for which the Holy Spirit plays a prominent role in the young church's development and the furtherance of the gospel. As F. F. Bruce opines, within this community, "there is nothing which is unrelated to the Holy Spirit."[1] While most Bible versions entitle Luke's missive "The Acts of the Apostles", it could justifiably have been titled "The Acts of the Holy Spirit."

The Holy Spirit in Acts

Since contemporary issues are not new, revisiting and following the early church's pattern of involvement with and reliance on the Holy Spirit for empowerment might enable us to find clarity for answers to pressing challenges. The church was intended to be a diverse collection of people from various cultures. The Acts 1:8 narrative relates how the sweeping reach of the gospel witness was destined to accomplish began to unfold when "Parthians and Medes and Elamites, those dwelling in Mesopotamia, Judea and Cappadocia, Pontus and Asia, Phrygia and Pamphylia, Egypt and parts of Libya adjoining Cyrene, visitors from Rome, both Jews and proselytes, Cretans and Arabs"

---

[1] F. F. Bruce, *The Acts of the Apostles*. (Chicago: InterVarsity Press, 1952), 30.

(Acts 2:9-11) heard the praises of God in their native languages. That same diversity was reflected when three thousand souls were baptized and united with the disciples on that day.

Hailing from the enumerated regions, these believers were initially drawn to Jerusalem at Pentecost to celebrate their common Jewish faith. Peter's scriptural appeal in claiming the teacher of Nazareth as the promised Savior, produced a collective expression of faith in Jesus Christ. Ethnic and cultural differences became secondary to the desire to learn more about Jesus' teachings as these unified believers continued in fellowship, doctrine, and prayer. The closing verses of the chapter portray a church growing and functioning in harmony, love, and brotherhood. Their experience of koinonia was evidence of the work of the Holy Spirit among them.

The Holy Spirit in Community

The observance of signs and wonders (Acts 2:43) and the continuing conversion of many to faith in Christ (Acts 2:47) were not the only indications that something powerful was taking place. The sharing of resources among the diverse group pointed to a connection undergirded by the Spirit. The fact that each believer was willing to part with his or her resources to contribute to the well-being of another, so that they "had all things in common" reveals a sense of oneness manifested in a desire to eliminate lack for any among them.

In his work on Acts, Willie Jennings refers to this common experience of deep sharing as the "the goal of life together in God. The condition of joined life where the haves and have-nots are bound together in [supportive relationship represents a redefinition] of life where the Spirit invites us to a sharing of space and place, resources and dreams."[2] Though many have interpreted the early church's actions as necessary to address the conditions at the time, we could imagine that this is what heaven will be like. Life with God will position

---

[2] Willie James Jennings, *Acts*. (Louisville: Westminster-John Knox Press, 2017) 9-10.

all of us as needing nothing since God will be the source of all life and existence. In the interim, the Spirit urges us toward the experience of this common oneness here on earth.

The experience of koinonia was so persistent among early believers that Luke reiterates their willingness to sacrifice for the good of the community. Acts 4:34-35 relates,

> Nor was there anyone among them who lacked; for all who were possessors of lands or houses sold them, and brought the proceeds of the things that were sold, and laid them at the apostles' feet; and they distributed to each as anyone had need.

The Holy Spirit in Conflict

The only deterrents to the will of God and the urgings of the Holy Spirit in the church are the schemes of Satan and the frailty of those who hold His treasure in earthen vessels. For, the experience of koinonia is always threatened by the imperfect expressions of a maturing people. The fifth chapter of Acts details the first deliberate assault against the unity of the community. In the account, a husband and wife allowed greed and dishonesty to cloud their actions. Ananias and Sapphira "determined in their hearts" to deceive the Holy Spirit by reporting less than the total proceeds from their sale of land. Thinking that their deed was a secret, they were publicly rebuked by Peter for lying to the Holy Spirit and died in separate, dramatic displays of God's chastisement. The church's response to these events was a greater sense of fear and reverence for the presence of God in their midst as they continued to grow in number and experience of the Spirit's power.

A second assault against the church's fellowship at the beginning of Acts 6, speaks to the argument concerning discrimination within the community.

... when the number of the disciples was multiplying, there arose a complaint against the Hebrews by the Hellenists, because their widows were neglected in the daily distribution.

Among those in the audience at Pentecost and who later comprised the church, two distinct Jewish cultural groups could be found. According to Bruce, one group consisted of "... Hebrews [who] were evidently Jews who habitually spoke Aramaic, whose homeland was Palestine (or any other area where Aramaic-speaking Jews lived). [While the other was made up of] Hellenists ... [who] were Jews who spoke Greek and whose way of life, in the eyes of stricter Palestinians, smacked too much of Greek customs."[3] The Hellenists had been the larger group who witnessed the Pentecost outpouring and responded to Peter's message. However, the distribution of resources to widows was being managed by Hebrews, some of whom were part of the original group of Jesus' disciples and so were entrusted to give guidance to the newer believers. Their oversight favored their own people over the Hellenists. The failure to equally allocate resources to all the widows would not escape the attention of the neglected or of the Holy Spirit. Something needed to be done to answer the complaint and prevent an escalation of conflict in the church.

Discrimination in the distribution to the widows was taking place in the church. In looking out for their own, the Hebrew believers were operating with bias, and the Greek believers were being overlooked. Though some see the appointment of the seven men as the major lesson of the text, this was a serious matter for the new community. The propensity to give preferential treatment still infects some within the contemporary church. But as we consider what was at stake, we don't have to continue making the same choices.

---

[3]F. F. Bruce, *New Testament History*, (New York: Kingsley Books 1980), 217.

Discrimination is sin. It disobeys the Lord's command to love your neighbor as yourself. It fits the charge of James 2:9 in that we are committing sin by showing partiality in the way we interact with others. While God has freely demonstrated love toward all, discrimination devalues some while esteeming others. It rejects the rights of sonship for some and defies the purpose of God through Jesus to make both Jew and Gentile one (Ephesians 2:14-15). It denies the work of the Spirit by whom, according to 1 Corinthians 12:13, "we were all baptized into one body – whether Jews or Greeks, whether slaves or free - and have all been made to drink into one Spirit."

The seriousness of the complaint was not lost on the Apostles who quickly responded to mitigate the issue by convening an assembly to address the concern. After deliberating the seriousness of the breach, the twelve invited the broader community to discuss the matter, for since it was a public breach, it needed to be adjudicated publicly. They knew that all the voices of the community needed to be included. The offenders needed to be confronted, the offended needed to be heard, and the community needed to reach a solution.

Most commentators focus on the selection and appointment of the first deacons in the church. For the issue that gave rise to this response was grave enough to introduce a vital and enduring ministry of the church. The discrimination shown to the women was serious enough that the apostles appointed a group with responsibility to eliminate the problem. The Spirit was at much at work in this incident as in other challenges to the early church. Seven trustworthy men "of good reputation, full of the Holy Spirit and wisdom" were appointed under the Spirit's guidance; they were chosen for character rather than popularity. Daniel Segraves offers this take on their selection.

> … it was necessary to choose men who not only had a good reputation, but who were also full of the Holy Spirit and wisdom. This brings to mind that the Spirit of the Lord that would rest upon the Messiah was first described as the Spirit

of wisdom (Isaiah 11:2). There are other aspects of the Spirit, but this event in the life of the first century church underscores the necessity of wisdom on the part of those involved in any facet of church leadership, and this kind of wisdom comes only from the fullness of the Spirit. Those who are not filled with the Spirit may have good reputations and some level of wisdom, but spiritual leadership requires spiritual direction.[4]

By insisting that those chosen should be Spirit-filled, the Apostles could continue their ministry of preaching and prayer without being concerned that the needs of any group within the community would be overlooked because of bias or prejudice. The guidance of the Holy Spirit in the qualifications of those chosen points to the posture of dependence that the church was determined to maintain. They would not operate absent the Spirit's leading and empowerment in every situation, especially where a possible fracture in the community was concerned. Likewise, racial discrimination is a work of the flesh that fractures contemporary Christian community. Its extermination must involve the presence and power of the Holy Spirit among us.

The church selected seven men of Hellenist origins, but who could maintain koinonia—fellowship—because they were accustomed to interacting within varied cultural contexts. They could be trusted to function with an awareness and sensitivity heightened by their experience and guided by the Spirit. Because of their upbringing, they could operate without bias and prejudice and easily communicate with both Hebrews and Hellenists in the church. And they had the support and confidence of the brethren.

The Apostles' invocation of God's approval of the seven through prayer, again, reveals the need for divine direction. The laying on of

---

[4]Daniel Segraves, *The Holy Spirit in the Book of Acts*. https://danielsegraves.com/2019/07/23/the-holy-spirit-in-the-book-of-acts-study-guide. Accessed July 27, 2020.

hands communicated the significance of the new office and function. The men would need the wisdom and empowerment of the Spirit in the administration of their duties. God's approval was apparent in the elimination of the complaint, the multiplication of the disciples, and the conversion of many in Jerusalem.

A Pentecostal Pattern for Reconciliation

The community's actions exemplify a Pentecostal pattern for addressing discrimination. When the presence and power of the Holy Spirit is given preeminence in the church, believers can anticipate the same experiences as the early church. These believers can more effectively portray the harmony and brotherhood Christ intended, see more dramatic displays of God's power, successfully proclaim the gospel, and more clearly express God's kingdom in society. The directive of Paul in Galatians 5:16 confirms this, "I say then: walk in the Spirit, and you shall not fulfill the lust of the flesh." The failure of the church, and believer, to reflect what God has required is due to a failure to seek the guidance of the Holy Spirit.

Though far too many churches have excused and allowed expressions of racial and cultural bias to infect their operations, discrimination is an affront to the kingdom of God. While most minority groups in America have faced some level of bias, blacks have endured a particularly long and tragic history of slavery, oppression, and discrimination. Unfortunately, the church response has ranged from outright support to silent complicity on the issue. It is only now, as society has begun to revolt against the blatant racism exposed through social that media and news headlines, that some in the church have been examining their own attitudes and actions.

In 2000, Rice University sociologist, Michael Emerson, directed a study of efforts by white Evangelical Christians to address racial inequality. In it, he concluded that, "Evangelicals likely do more to perpetuate the racial divide than to tear it down, largely because they tend to worship in racially segregated congregations and view racial prejudice as an individual, not a societal problem"[5] Two decades later, America is having a vigorous discussion about widespread systemic racism and discrimination. Efforts are being made to address the issue through acknowledgement and action in the church as well as society.

Beyond making apologies, some denominations have appointed African Americans to significant administrative and leadership positions. The Southern Baptist Convention, Church of God of Prophecy, Church of God (Cleveland, TN) and others have taken historic steps in the involvement and recognition of their black constituencies.

Lest those efforts be viewed as token offerings however, the entire American church must confront the issue headlong, with a determination to eliminate discrimination in the body of Christ. To that end, Ed Stetzer sees Anglo-Americans as suffering from the same ethnocentric mindset that characterized the Jews in the new church in Acts. They see themselves and their ways as superior to others. He concludes that "many people will have to forgo their pride and snobbery and be willing to include, follow and even learn from others."[6] The Pentecostal/Charismatic church can draw on its orientation around the active presence and power of the Holy Spirit to lead the way in this endeavor.

The model of the Jerusalem church's resolution of the Hebrew-Hellenist conflict points to significant steps that must be taken. They reveal a three-fold strategy of hearing the complaint, engaging in meaningful discussion, and involving the disaffected in the search for solutions, all under the direction of the Holy Spirit. For just as with the Jerusalem church's response to cultural bias, the contemporary

---

[5] Reported in Tom Gjelten, "Multiracial Congregations May Not Bridge Racial Divide." NPR, July 17, 2020, https:/ / www.npr.org/ 2020/07/17 /891600067/multiracial-congregations-may-not-bridge-racial-divide. His findings were published in, *Divided by Faith*, in 2000, accessed July 27, 2020.
[6] Ed Stetzer, "Truths About Diversity in The Church" *Outreach Magazine,* August 7, 2016, https://out reachmagazine.com/features/18699-diversity-in-the-church.html, accessed July 27, 2020.

church's response to racial discrimination must also involve the guidance of the Holy Spirit.

Rather than dismiss the complaint of the Hellenist widows as mere murmuring among the dissatisfied, the Apostles heeded their outcry. They recognized that any charge of injustice needed to be answered speedily and effectively. The terms of Israel's covenant with God included sensitivity to the plight of the marginalized and called for equity in dealings with each other. The teachings of Jesus reiterated God's expectation of love for one's neighbor and concern for the disenfranchised. Therefore, the presence of the Holy Spirit among the disciples would not allow them to ignore the cry of the widows. Likewise, the contemporary church must heed the persistent charge of under-representation, lack of equal access and opportunity, and condescending attitudes that many minorities suffer from white believers.

The Hellenists' cry was stimulated by the promptings of the Holy Spirit. The record of Israel's history reveals that God consistently fulfilled His purpose through the outcry against injustice. Just as Moses was commissioned to lead God's people out of Egyptian bondage because the people cried out against their oppressors and Judges were raised up in the Promised Land to deliver the Israelites from the hand of their oppressors when they cried out to God, the Holy Spirit's prompting led the widows in the Jerusalem church to complain of neglect. Could that same Holy Spirit be prompting the outcry from marginalized people of color and enabling the cry of discrimination to be uttered within today's church?

The fact that the Apostle's willingness to hear the Hellenist widows' cry resulted in a gathering of the multitude to engage in discussion speaks to the truth that the issue of discrimination cannot be relegated to closed boardrooms and corner offices. Widespread public offenses require widespread public engagement and conversation. In a representative government, public policy reflects the will of the people. In the Church, the will of God is often reflected in the attitudes and actions of a surrendered people. The policies enacted by church leadership must fulfill the expectations of God's word concerning the church's oneness. All voices must be considered valuable in an atmosphere in which the Holy Spirit is authentically celebrated.

The church's diversity demands diversity of participation in discussion regarding its challenges. The Apostles saw the value of collective engagement rather than assuming that their viewpoints and perspectives alone were sufficient. So too, the contemporary church must align the diversity of their leadership to the diversity of their membership to ensure representation of all viewpoints. Esteban Lugo insists that such diversity "encourages critical thinking and helps us learn to communicate with people of varied backgrounds... foster[ing] mutual respect and teamwork. The church's message and witness become credible when the world sees us building relationships regardless of color, ethnicity, or culture. [For only] in the context of diversity [can] the church grow."[7]

The involvement of the multitude of disciples in the search for a solution to the crisis in Acts meant that voices from the disaffected group would be heard. Their opinions were given credence. Their presence gave legitimacy to the Apostle's concern and invested credibility in the consensus that was reached. Had the Hebrews handled the issue alone, it is unlikely that there could have been a satisfactory resolution. Those unaffected by a problem can scarcely be counted on to solve it effectively. Had the Hellenists not voiced their complaint, the Hebrews might have assumed that all was well. The solution demanded the involvement of those who were the object of mistreatment since they held a more accurate perspective of what the actual problem was.

---

[7] Esteban Lugo, "A Theology of Ethnic Diversity: God's Mosaic" *Christian Educators Journal*, April 30, 2013, https://www.cejonline.com/article/a-theology-of-ethnic-diversity-gods-mosaic, accessed July 27, 2020.

The effective dissolution of discrimination in the church must involve those against whom the discrimination is lodged. White believers might be surprised to learn of the negative experiences of their non-white brothers and sisters. Those who deny the reality of racial discrimination might be unaware that their biased, privileged worldview does not allow them to see it though it exists in their communities.

A recent Pew Research Center survey found that most black Christians felt that it was appropriate for pastors to preach about racial relations and nearly 25% deemed it essential. By contrast, the same survey found that the majority of white Christians did not feel it was necessary and 40% insisted that it should not be mentioned.[8] Since many white believers, then, have no understanding of the severity of the issue of racial disparity, they cannot be depended on to resolve the issue on their own. They need the testimony, insight, and wisdom of their minority brothers and sisters.

Some point to the existence of numerous multicultural congregations as evidence that the ideal can be found in an atmosphere where different ethnic groups feel free to fellowship together. Closer inspection reveals that all is not as it seems, however. Emerson recently surveyed several multiracial congregations and found that growth in those congregations has resulted from people of color moving into white churches where they generally feel welcomed "so long as they remain in the minority." When the percentage of white membership drops below 50%, white flight begins. By contrast, few whites seem comfortable joining churches of color and black leaders are not optimistic about the possibility of diversifying their congregations. For, according to Emerson they contend, "it doesn't work. The white brothers and sisters just won't give up their privilege."[9]

---

[8] Daniel Burke, "Why Black Christians are Bracing for a Whitelash." CNN, July 21, 2020, https:// www.cnn.com/ 2020/ 07/10/us/white-black-christians-racism-burke, accessed July 27, 2020.

[9] Gjelten, "Racial Divide."

Conclusion

The Jerusalem church was a multicultural church that faced the challenge of discrimination in their midst. Yet, they were able to address it through the leading of the Holy Spirit. Today's church must return to that same level of dependence upon the Holy Spirit to eliminate the plague of racial discrimination. Our efforts must include hearing the complaint, engaging in discussion, and involving minorities in the search for solutions.

The Acts narrative reveals that, after they solved the problem, the word of God spread, their numbers increased, and a significant number were converted. How much more effective could the ministry of today's church be if it finally eliminated racial discrimination? By adopting the early pattern, the modern Spirit-filled and Spirit-led church is more properly positioned to embark on the journey toward racial reconciliation that is key to more accurately portraying holiness and brotherhood, representing Christ in the world, and accomplishing its evangelistic mandate.

Words Matter: The Structure of Conscious and Unconscious Bias in Everyday Speech

Phyllis Thompson

This essay is framed in the context of the language we use to make sense of ourselves, our world, and our Christian witness. It seeks to illustrate how these words shape our thoughts, feelings, and behavior—how our conscious and unconscious use of language willingly or inadvertently includes or excludes others; how our choice of words can foster prejudices or institutional and systemic racism. In the final analysis, for Pentecostal Christians, *Words Matter*.

In the Beginning was the Word

Words are powerful. The words we use to express ourselves can enrich or deprive, enable, or hinder, heal or destroy. Scripture tells us that, '[t]he tongue has the power of life and death' (Prov. 18:21, NIVUK). Our use of words has specific implications and consequences for private as well as public relationships.

Words express and embody the worldviews, perspectives, memories, aspirations, beliefs, and values of linguistic groups. Words create and communicate a sense of self in relation to others and, as such, provide reference points for social power and hierarchical structures within institutions and society at large.

Words matter. There is an umbilical relationship between the words we use and our experience. They emerge from, as well as impact, our thoughts, feelings, and behavior. They are both instigators and corollaries of our inner being, attitudes, and choice of lifestyles. Words renew and alter us. They express buried secrets and can bring to the surface surprising, controversial, or contentious notions we would rather not own.

We use words to help make sense of our experiences and create meaningful communication with others within our given language groups, and in this respect, language can be understood as a social action. Subscribers to the interactionist approach and sociocultural theory offer a useful way of thinking about the way we learn and use language to communicate and orientate ourselves in the world. Accordingly, our language develops from and is, consciously and unconsciously, reinforced via our social interaction. The extent of control of our language can restrict or liberate us in our social relations. The language we acquire and use can bring about narrow- or broad-mindedness, empowering or disempowering thought processes and outcomes. Guy Deutscher points out that 'Language reflects the qualities of the nation that speaks it'[1] and he goes further in his considered observation to make the sobering statement that 'as the language is, so is the nation.'[2] Thoughts, language, selfhood, and culture are therefore intricately interrelated. Words and language affect our ways of 'knowing,' 'being,' and 'doing,' which in turn interplay with the implicit and explicit values we hold and the worldview they validate. Deutscher raises a pertinent question that provides the Christian community with much to consider: 'Could language have a more than a passive role as a reflection of cultural differences and be an active instrument of coercion through which culture imposes its conventions on our mind?'[3]

Words are repositories of long-ago memories that underlie given thoughts, feelings, or behaviors. Let's take the word 'overseer' for example, which quite a few denominations employ as a title for ecclesial supervisors. What does this term mean for the black and white members of congregations in the light of this discourse? The overt or covert emotions, subtle or blatant intentions, personal or institutional leverage that the word 'overseer' engenders can stem from enormous soul-destroying memories. A good starting point to help us understand

---

[1] Guy Deutscher. *Through the Language Glass: Why the World Looks Different in Other Languages.* (London: Arrow Books, 2010), 1.
[2] Ibid., *5*.
[3] Ibid., *20*.

the sentiment here is to explore answers to the question: 'Soul-destroying memories for whom?' with reference to the following text:

> On large plantations, the person who directed the daily work of the slaves was the overseer, usually a white man but occasionally an enslaved black man—a 'driver'—promoted to the position by his master. Some plantations had both a white overseer and a black driver, especially in the deep South or on plantations where the master was often absent. Of white overseers, former slaves relate harsh memories... Of black drivers their memories are more varied, reflecting the ambiguous state between power and impotence inhabited by the black slave driver.[4]

Words and language convey memories as well as divergent perspectives and worldviews, many of which we are sometimes required to revisit and redress. Since we are commanded (Matt. 22:34–40) and commissioned (Matt. 28:18–20) to bring peace, unity, reconciliation, and hope to our world, we have a moral responsibility to move from 'good to better and better to best' in every sphere of life—whether we call this evangelism, discipleship, integral mission, or social action. In this process, memory is as valued a commodity as is the truth. Truth is not static for, as Paul asserts, 'we see through a glass, darkly [and] know in part' but we will 'know even as also [we are] known' (1 Cor. 13:12, KJV). Our knowledge is partial, and we need to learn from others— 'history' and 'herstory.' We need to hear from the perspective of the 'conqueror' and the 'conquered,' the young and the old, those in the global south and the global north. And, while learning, we must make the necessary adjustments to make wrongs right.

---

[4] The Making of African American Identity: Volume I, 1500-1865. http://nationalhumanitiescenter.org/pds/ maai/enslavement/text4/text4read.htm.

Inclusive or Exclusive Language

Words shape and change people. They include and exclude people. They communicate, validate, and reinforce values, ideas, stereotypes, and prejudices, and negative and positive views. Our conscious or unconscious use of words can include or exclude individuals as well as groups. Words can be offensive, patronizing, enabling, or enriching. Within our faith communities, we need to critically reflect on how we, deliberately or inadvertently, use language to include and exclude people based on skin color, nationality, ethnicity, or race.

To accommodate an authentic multi-racial church, or an international denomination, we must create opportunities for shared learning and praxis in our churches and society. An immense amount of understanding and sensitivity is of paramount importance and ought not to be underestimated or overlooked if we are to take this agenda forward and gain the objectives we desire.

Shared learning and praxis between races rely on good relationships, intentional learning, and focused minds. They also require a major paradigm shift in how we think and interact with each other across racial divides. Yet without such a shift, we are unlikely to see hoped-for changes.

In his classic publication, *Black and British: A Forgotten History*, David Olusoga brings to light occasions when words were intentionally used to include or exclude voices of slaves and how this impacted the slave trade and abolitionist movement. The missionary activities of the 'non-conformist' preachers—Methodists, Moravians and most significantly the Baptists—offered 'the slaves a radical message of redemption and hope.' However, as he discloses, they were:

> instructed by their superiors in Britain that their mission was
> to spread the gospel, not oppose slavery. They were ordered
> to avoid entanglements within the colonial authorities and be
> cautious in their dealings with the slave owners... the planters

regarded the preachers as dangerous intrusion in their world. They feared the impact that the Christian message might have upon the slaves.[5]

In its mission of engaging people in the mission of God, the Church must ensure that its use of language does not gratuitously offend, intimidate, belittle, or exclude anyone, reinforce harmful stereotypes, nor contribute to the unequal status of individuals. Inclusive vocabulary is intrinsic to God's transformative work of including all humanity in the breadth of the Kingdom so that each person is valued and empowered to flourish.

When we consider how words position those within our churches, leaders may have to revise the language, processes, and procedures used to share the gospel in ways that do not include or exclude some ethnic/racial groups and re-imagine their approach to the global missional responsibility.

History, Education and Wisdom

History, education, and wisdom are intricately connected. At its best, education is as much about the quest for truth and wisdom as it is about developing skills to discern and apply that truth to experience. Our experience embodies individual and corporate stories, and a balanced education, whether formal or informal, enables us to examine and learn from our past. Otherwise, we would be teaching and learning, advocating, and celebrating flat earthism! Through history, we learn from the past so we can apply insights to make sense of the present and bring about a better future.

Words communicate truths and lies, accommodate dreams and aspirations, promote wisdom or idiocy, all of which hinder or foster change for our common good. The Christian Church is potentially a force for social change. Many global reforms have come about because

---

[5] David Olusoga. *Black and British: A Forgotten History.* (London: Pan Books, 2017), 225–6.

of Christian intervention. As the recent publication, *Challenges of Pentecostal Theology in the 21st Century*, tells us that,

> [a]ccording to conventional wisdom, questions inspire conversation and conversations enable learning and growth. Learning to ask the 'right' questions, engage in insightful conversations and then identify opportunities to practice what we believe... is clearly a positive way forward... How we facilitate opportunities for meaningful conversations about social injustice... are critical matters and challenges for our time.[6]

Lack of opportunities for genuine and frank conversations in our Christian faith communities inevitably fortify what Brazilian educator, Paulo Freire, calls the 'culture of silence.'[7] Freire used the expression 'critical consciousness' to explain his use of the term 'conscientization,' which refers to 'learning to perceive social, political, and economic contradictions, and to take action against the oppressive elements of reality.'[8] In Freire's thinking, our understanding and use of dialogue in the pursuit of a better world requires an appreciation of words as more than 'instrument[s] which makes dialogue possible.' He presents a convincing argument to support his belief that words serve two active dimensions: reflection and action. If authentic dialogue is to be achieved, he argues, these two constituent elements must be activated, otherwise, the outcome will be 'idle chatter... verbalism... alienated and alienating "blah".'[9]

For Freire, the best education takes place through dialogue in a milieu where both the 'teacher' and 'student' relate as 'learners', with

---

[6] Phyllis Thompson, ed. *Challenges of Pentecostal Theology in the 21st Century*. (London: SPCK, 2020), 11.
[7] Paulo Freire. *Pedagogy of the Oppressed*. (London: Penguin Education, 1972).
[8] Ibid., 15.
[9] Ibid., 60.

respect and sensitivity to each other's dignity and worth and the value of life experience and wisdom each brings to the learning process. He describes this process as a 'dialogical encounter with others.' In this learning environment, he argues, learners who are oblivious to their collusion with the status quo whether by omission or commission can come to:

> perceive [their] personal and social reality as well as the contradictions in it, become conscious of [their]own perception of that reality, and deal critically with it... As this happens, the word takes on new power. It is no longer an abstraction or magic but a means by which [people] discover [themselves] and [their] potential as [they] give names to things around [them]... When [the learner] participates in this sort of educational experience, [they come] to a new awareness of self... a new sense of dignity, and [are] stirred by a new hope.[10]

Black, brown, and white Christians need to ensure authentic personal and corporate conversations about racial justice as we attempt to bring about justice within our local, national, and international church. Yet, in many of our churches, there is not only acquiescence to the 'culture of silence' on the matter of racism; but resistance to efforts to start the conversation and appraise the challenges and opportunities.

Much listening and learning within our global church is required to overcome ignorance and eradicate concord with racist thought processes and practices. This will not happen if the spaces in which decisions are made do not include black, brown, and white leaders who are placed in position because of merit, gifting, or sense of calling rather than as tokens.

---

[10] Ibid., 12.

If we accept that our Christian mission is to lead people by example to God's truth and the hope of our faith we cannot be seen to be in collusion with systemic oppression within our private and public worlds. In their effort to entice customers, the chain of Park Inns owned by Radisson Hotels uses the slogan 'Every meeting is a new story.'[11] Many leaders and members of our churches are becoming disillusioned because they cannot testify to this experience in some of our meetings organized to address issues such as racism within our churches, if, and when, we do have them. Consequently, many of us have little to contribute to society at large on current concerns such as racism.

Every one of us is a work in progress. A dialectical approach to learning involving the cyclical progressive route from thesis to antithesis to synthesis provides a healthy and enriching formative means to mature in our discipleship journey. Our world needs mature Christian disciples, equipped with the clarity, confidence, and skills to facilitate continued growth and transformation in the context of community life. But we must start with ourselves and our own communities of faith: the local church, and our national and international bodies.

The Power of Words

During childhood, many of us were taught that 'sticks and stones may break [our] bones, but words will never hurt [us].' This expression was meant to protect us when we were provoked by cruel words. However, as we have learned, words do hurt and can leave an indelible scar that can only be erased by the grace of God.

The memories of slavery, the slave trade, imperialism, and colonization—whether those of the conquerors or the conquered—are enshrined in many of the words in every sphere, including how we do church. The experience of the church in the African diaspora—the

---

[11] See parkinn.co.uk/meetings.

Caribbean, the United States, Europe, and Canada—bears witness to this. Martin Luther King Jr. is recorded to have said that Sunday morning is the most segregated time in Christian America, but this can be said of our global church. The legacy of slavery still haunts us today and, unless it is redressed, some dreams and hopes will never be fulfilled. As black, brown, and white Pentecostals, we have made a commitment to bear witness to the Great Commandment to 'Love the Lord your God with all your heart and with all your soul and with all your mind and love our neighbor as ourselves' (Matt. 22:34-40). Only then can we successfully commit to the Great Commission to make disciples of all nations (Matt. 28:18–20). Church is not a 'holy huddle' or 'social club.' Instead, we have the responsibility, as Gandhi so effectively puts it, "[t]o be the change we want to see in the world."

The clarion call to the Church by Anglican Archbishop Justin Welby in a recent symposium, '[t]o put its house in order,'[12] highlights the lethargy of the Christian community regarding our responsibilities in this area. In his key input to the symposium, Sir Hilary Beckles, who has worked tirelessly on the matter of reparation for slavery, acknowledged the global conversation energized by rhetoric and action regarding the pain of global black communities who are seeking justice.[13]

A range of models has been instituted by various denominations in attempting to present the fullness of Christ, nullify racial disproportionality, and redress the imbalance in leadership. Galatians 3:28 is a text that is often quoted as the bottom line: 'Faith in Christ Jesus... makes each of you equal with each other, whether you are a Jew or a Greek, a slave or a free person, a man or a woman' (CEV).

---

[12] Church of God of Prophecy, History, Heritage and Identity Symposium November 12, 2020. https://uwitv.org/symp/history-heritage-and-identity-symposium.
[13] Ibid.

Various terminologies and practices are in use to create safe spaces for strategic thinking and action plans to make this a reality, for example in England:

- The Methodist Church in England has an Equality, Diversity and Inclusion Committee including a representative group with responsibilities for the selection of candidates for ordained ministry.[14]

- The Anglican Church has a Committee for Minority Ethnic Anglican Concerns, which is accountable to the Church of England's highest decision-making body, the General Synod.[15]

- The Baptist Union of Great Britain has a Racial Justice Working Group and a National Racial Justice Hub.[16]

- Amongst its set of resolutions for its international constituency, the Church of God (Cleveland, TN) has a Resolution for Multi-Cultural Ministry (2010) in which it states its commitment to build cross-cultural relationships, continue to seek and embrace inter-racial inclusiveness, heighten multi-cultural awareness and unity in concrete policies and behaviors that seek to provide ecclesiastical structures that reflect multi-cultural leadership.[17]

A report in the *Church Times* by Rebecca Paveley on 31 July 2020 is worth quoting at length:

---

[14] https://www.methodist.org.uk/media/1097/counc-mc17-53-equality-diversity -inclusion-april-2017.pdf.

[15] https://www.churchofengland.org/more/policy-and-thinking/ our-views/race-and-ethnicity.

[16] https://www.baptist.org.uk/Articles/529540/National_Racial_Justice. Aspx, and https://baptist.org.uk/ Publisher/File.aspx? ID=215590.

[17] http://www.churchofgod.org/resolutions/multi-cultural-ministry-2010.

Racism is a 'blight' affecting all churches in the UK, the presidents of Churches Together in England (CTE) said this week. "We challenge this unreservedly, recognising the constant experiences of racism, including microaggression, which black people face."

Signed by the Anglican Archbishop of Canterbury, the Roman Catholic Archbishop of Westminster, and leaders of the Free Churches, Coptic Orthodox Church, and Pentecostal churches, the statement was issued after a period of listening to the voices of black people in the UK, after the killing of George Floyd in the United States. This listening was 'deeply moving,' and showed how much action, as well as 'profound change of heart,' was needed, the statement said. It urged all churches to scrutinize themselves and commit to challenging racial injustice and building trust with black communities.

We believe that churches have a significant role to play in combating racial injustice. If we are to be effective in doing so, we must look at ourselves.

We are painfully aware of the racism that blights the life of our churches. We are intent upon a process of identifying racial injustice within our churches—current and historic—repenting of it and taking action to effect real change. This includes the potential for discriminatory behaviour in the way that we make church appointments, which we know can happen at the conscious or unconscious level.

The representatives of these church denominations announced that they would also organize conversations between young black people and the police service to try to improve relationships and urged churches to do the same locally.

We encourage all churches throughout England to do all they can to build trust and improve accountability between black communities, the police, civic bodies and wider community groups. In particular, we call upon groupings of Church Leaders throughout the nation to reach out to their black colleagues in church leadership who are currently absent from their membership, making more inclusive ecumenical leadership.

Our desire is that these groups will create spaces for those in authority to listen, as we have, to the powerful testimony of young black women and men as a step towards greater social cohesion.

The Church of England has announced that it will set up a racism action commission, which will find and dismantle institutional barriers to racial justice, equality, and inclusion. The CTE presidents' statement said that work was also under way in the Methodist, United Reformed, Baptist, and Roman Catholic Churches, and that challenging racism was already a priority for the Orthodox and Pentecostal Churches.[18]

How far these committees, working groups, and resolutions go in changing the way churches present a witness of moral justice and racial equality is worth examining in the light of current global conversations, protests, and appeals. This is indeed a significant moment in history. Slavery and the slave trade may have been abolished, but the legacy is still at large on the global scale. The mentality of slavery and its outworking in the life of the descendants of the perpetrators and the victims is an ongoing impediment. Without rigorous examination,

---

[18]Rebecca Paveley, *Church Times* (31 July 2020), 3. https://publications.hymnsam.co.uk/emags/CT8211/.

some strategies to address this legacy can inadvertently become in themselves shackles of subtle racism.

It behooves us as disciples of Christ to seek insightful answers regarding the underlying assumptions and beliefs that produce our words and deeds aimed at the redemptive mission of establishing God's Kingdom on earth. What informs our understating of the inclusion discourse and what motivates our engagement with the issues? We must be clear on our starting point and our bottom line concerning how we celebrate diversity, our social and cultural perception of the world, how social-relational models will assist our effort, and how we determine our goals. Such clarity will also help to make reasoned decisions and articulate how we work in solidarity with others and evaluate our progress or achievements.

Many Christians have become aggrieved about the dehumanization of black people and the veneration of white people. The prejudicial assumptions that cause many to comply with presentations of Jesus and other biblical characters as 'white Europeans' as opposed to 'Middle Easterners' are still at large. The effort of Thomas C. Oden and others to redress this error is commendable. Their objective to inform us of the contribution made by non-Europeans to Christianity is a welcome repositioning. In *How Africa Shaped the Christian Mind*,[19] Oden challenges the popular view that the formation and development of Christianity is by and large a Western or European accomplishment.

The emotional reaction to the history of slavery is different for those who have inherited vested interests in the institution compared to those who bear its scars. Having come to a degree of awareness of past injustices instigated by slavery, some white people become upset, ashamed, and emotionally paralyzed. On the other hand, some black people resort to riot.

---

[19] Thomas C. Oden. *How Africa Shaped the Christian Mind: Rediscovering the African Seedbed of Western Christianity.* (Downers Grove, IL: InterVarsity Press, 2007).

Before meaningful conversations can take place, much healing is required. Perhaps there is a place for pre-meetings in the awareness-raising process when the history of racism can be examined in a safe place with appropriately trained facilitators.

In his much-acclaimed book, *We Need to Talk about Race*,[20] Ben Lindsay shares insights and advice to enable a measure of understanding about the black experience in white majority churches. In his introduction, he raises a few focal questions: Are ethnic minorities tired of trying to integrate into the multi-ethnic church the Bible describes, when this seemingly appears not to be a reality? Has diversity become just a word on a church website without consideration of how ethnic minority cultures are included within Church life?[21] In his conclusion he cautions, '[w]hite people need to become better listeners to their black brothers and sisters—that is listening without always offering solutions or making swift assumptions. Black people need to be empowered to move from being passive bystanders and towards becoming agents of change.'[22]

Words and language, consciously or unconsciously, define and locate people and at worse marginalize as well as elevate people based on our assumptions, prejudices, bias, and subtle or blatant racism. In response, some white Christians as well as non-Christians have made private and public acknowledgement that they have come from a privileged position and place of power at the expense of black people. Other white people find this admission incomprehensible and are aghast at the thought of owning this perspective. Words can cause trauma, anger, grief, rage, or brokenness, or lead to the sense of disconnection, disrespect, contempt, and pain for black people in racist environments. The result is a distorted sense of self that interferes with congenial interactions between black and white people and deters

---

[20] Ben Lindsay. *We Need to Talk about Race: Understanding the Black Experience in White Majority Churches.* (London: SPCK, 2019).
[21] Ibid., xxvi.
[22] Ibid., 155.

respectable community relations. The global response to George Floyd's murder bears witness to the truth that racism is not a black problem. It is a human problem, a people problem, a societal problem.

Words Divide and Unite

Our choice of words conveys moral feelings and instigates action and reaction. If racial injustice is not considered critically, ill-judged strategies with unhelpful outcomes will further exacerbate the moral deficit. In many parts of the world, we have 'black majority' and 'white majority' churches. These come about by default, spiritual survival in other cases, or because of righteous indignation. In the final analysis, 'black-led' or 'black majority' churches have served as a spiritual, emotional, and mental survival strategy for black people, but do two wrongs make a right?

Church history demonstrates our successes and failures to participate in God's mission to bring redemption and reconciliation into our world. Texts such as '[t]here is one body and one Spirit, just as there is one hope to which God has called you' (Eph. 4:4–9, GNB) have become ideals for the world-to-come rather than goals for the here-and-now. Speaking out against social evil and demonstrating social holiness can be perceived as a threat to the social order, bringing reprisals. Learning the rules of engagement is a must, but courage and faith are requisites to be effective in this arena. In addition, clarity of purpose, clear understanding of the issues, confidence in the Christian message, and the ability to focus on the cause enable us to make wise choices about whom to partner with and which battles to fight. As vested interests come to light, fear of loss of status, defence strategies and resistance will surface. Unexpected alliances and enemies may emerge, but becoming righteously subversive may be the only way forward.

As Christians who aspire to be authentic, we are compelled to engage the sentiment behind the slogan, 'Black Lives Matter.' Alicia Garza, Patrisse Cullors, and Opal Tometi are due thanks for their insight and tenacity in instigating this worthy initiative. Unfortunately, many black, brown, and white Christians, as well as people of other faiths or none apply energy in debating the weakness and strength of this three-word phrase rather than engaging in the opportunities it offers to annihilate the brutal history it encapsulates.

'Black Lives Matter' speaks truth to abusive expressions of power manifested in institutions and issues, such as the penal systems in Western nations, ecclesiastical polity that fortifies systemic discrimination, and global climate change. The phrase challenges moral, political, social, and religious sensitivities. Influential voices are making connections sparked by the current global conversations about the death of George Floyd, and the diverse perspectives on whose lives matter are becoming a unifying or divisive conundrum. Sincere disciples of Christ are compelled to examine the message we communicate through our choice of words.

'Black Lives Matter' incorporates our Christian belief that all life matters. To negate this position in words or action would reflect a grave flaw in our theology. At its heart is our hope for the redemption of human dignity and the world which our Creator considered good. Jesus declares: 'The thief comes only to steal, kill, and destroy. I have come in order that you might have life—in all its fullness' (John 10:10, GNB). The aspirations of the Christian community for well-lived lives must include *black* lives.

Slavery and the slave trade are history, but their legacy is evident in society and the Christian church—including the Church of God. To counter this, it is critically important that laity and leadership within our churches subscribe to explicit anti-racist policies as part of discipleship formation. Engaging members in conversations about addressing the institutional issues that contribute to bias and inequities for black and ethnic minorities could play a significant role in the healing and reconciliation process.

There is much to be gained from peer conversations. The voices of the local, national or global church family add value to dialogues and decision-making processes and heighten commitment to allegiance to biblical precepts. Structural change is a process, not an event. Prejudice does not suddenly disappear; its demolition requires a process of questioning, learning, unlearning, and relearning to equip ourselves with the language to engage the healthy tension of this process.

In the wake of current conversations, now is a good time to examine structures and assess whether they reflect the bias and prejudices of yesteryears and simply protect the status quo. What do we need to change to demonstrate what we believe concerning the biblical premise: 'There is neither Jew nor Gentile, neither slave nor free, nor is there male and female, for you are all one in Christ Jesus' (Gal. 3:28, NIVUK)? Such critical reflection may lead to pleas for honesty, forgiveness and the dismantling of some structures and the establishment of new ones. This will mean liberation for those whose selfhood and sense of calling have been subjugated and stifled, as well as those whose selfhood and sense of calling have been domineering and suppressive. It is an opportunity for all to gain greater self-respect, flourish in their gifting and calling, and engage in new possibilities through their contribution to the denomination.

If 1 Corinthians 12 is taken seriously, and unity in the body of Christ is applied to our thinking and practice of ministry in local, national, and global contexts, we might discover the need for significant changes in the words, images, and structures we use to individually and corporately, project ourselves as Christians. Most churches will say, 'All are welcome.' But how far do we mean this? How do we become a genuinely inclusive Church? How do we authentically celebrate racial diversity? Might terms such as 'black majority,' 'black-led,' 'white majority,' and 'white-led' lose their currency when referring to churches and become relics of the past? Might we discover and replicate visionary multi-ethnic churches that evidence a semblance of the heavenly celebration as referenced in Revelation 7:9 (NIVUK): "there before me was a great multitude that no one could count, from every nation, tribe, people and language, standing before the throne and before the Lamb"?

Learning to Walk the Talk

A reflection on the contemporary crises leads us to conclude the profound realization that, as one student puts it, "[t]he church does not just bring people together for Sunday worship, but prepares people to live their faith in Jesus Christ among their neighbours every day of the week."[23]

Many of us have become preoccupied with questions about what will become the 'new normal' when the current Covid-19 pandemic is behind us. We have all learned new words and phrases and added new meaning to familiar words to make sense of our experiences and engage in conversations whether on social platforms or face-to-face. 'Lockdown, shielding, social bubbles, zoom,' are words that have changed meaning as we think and talk about our lack of and need for interconnectedness and interdependence on a personal and global level. This shift has made us acknowledge that 'the way we do church has got to change.' But this must become more than rhetoric if we are going to rise to the call and maintain credibility.

On the grounds of the Great Commandment (Matt. 22:36–40) and the Great Commission (Matt. 28:16–20), the need to cultivate the ability to communicate effectively with sectors in society beyond our comfort zone is non-negotiable. Sharpening our witness and gleaning from the imagery of 1 Corinthians 12 help us develop a strategy for crafting language and thinking that allows us to become more inclusive in our mission and less exclusive in our ministry. Affirmation of people of color within the body of believers with the requisite skills, gifting, and interest would be a good start. Resourcing and supporting them into opportune zones for ministry could bring about a radical change in our world so that more people could live with dignity, fulfil their

---

[23]Cosmos Mutowa, "Cosmos' Story." *The Link* (Autumn 2020): 12–14. Nazarene Theological College. enquiries@nazarene.ac.uk.

God-given potential, experience the joy of new opportunities, and live life in abundance.

The murder of George Floyd, by police in Minneapolis, Minnesota, USA, has caused a surge of movements of the moment across the globe. The engagement of young people of all ethnic backgrounds and racial groups is remarkable. It is heartening to note their united efforts to be agents of change, to change the narrative and redress the wrongs of the past. Floyd's iconic statement, "I can't breathe," is mind-blowing. It sharpens our reading of Genesis 2:7 that resonates with our Christian conscience: '[a]nd the LORD God formed man of the dust of the ground, and breathed into his nostrils the breath of life; and man became a living soul' (KJV); 'He breathed the breath of life into the man's nostrils, and the man became a living person' (CSB).

The current global outrage compels us to ask about the implications for understanding our Christian mission, ethics, moral leadership, and our pastoral ministry. It has also turned the spotlight on the education and training available for Pentecostal ministry in this twenty-first century. What might be a distinctive Pentecostal response? In the end, we may question the extent of the nurturing, teaching, and preaching in our local churches. We might also question the content of the theological education and training in our institutions, and the work of our Pentecostal scholars to resource us. We might further question how our theology, dogmas, and language are perceived by others. Are they viewed as antiquated stories or valid resources for a better future?

Finally, Christopher Wright challenges us to give wholehearted consideration to our engagement in God's mission and the proclamation of God's word: the good news for the fullness of life in our private and global world.[24] We must critically reflect on the

---

[24]Christopher J. H. Wright. *The Mission of God's People: A Biblical Theology of the Church's Mission.* (Grand Rapids, MI: Zondervan Academic, 2010).

knowledge base, sensitivity, skills, and behavioural outcomes we should facilitate, in our Pentecostal theological and missional teaching and learning events in our pews, pulpits or academic institutions.[25] Are we equipping our adherents for effective Christian service? Are we ensuring that our leadership is 'fit for purpose?'

---

[25]William K. Kay. *Pentecostalism: A Very Short Introduction* (Oxford: Oxford University Press, 2011), 57.

In the Spirit of King and Arnold: A British Pentecostal Reflection

Marcia Clarke

I had missed a call from the eldest surviving patriarch of our family. I returned his call. He was an 'old-time Pentecostal', born and raised in Jamaica before migrating to "farrin."[1] He would periodically call to check on me and the family to ask about everyone's welfare by name. Somewhere in our conversation, I shared a story to which he responded something like, "[the Christian's] job is to save souls not to get involved in politics." As old as I am there is respect for the elders–do I just say yes and ask about his garden or do I probe his statement. I decide to probe.

My relatives' statement is not unique to black Pentecostals, but is a wider Evangelical sticking point. It calls into question the church's relationship to society and social issues. The prophetic voice of African-American, Martin Luther King, Jr. speaks to pneumatological sensibilities on social issues, with a particular emphasis on the issue of race. As a demonstration of a level of respect by a Pentecostal denomination for King's social exegesis his final message was delivered at Mason Temple Church of God in Christ, the headquarters of the Pentecostal body that is the largest African-American denomination in the world. Selwyn Arnold, former General Overseer of the Church of God, England and Wales—a predominantly African-Caribbean church—identified and reflected on the social issues faced by what was then United Kingdom's largest black majority denomination.[2] Against

---

[1] Or farring, meaning aggressive, incomprehensible speech accented by wild gestures and bizarre facial expressions, punctuated with guttural grunts, and lacking clearly defined consonants or vowels.

[2] The NTCG has its inception and doctrinal roots in the Church of God (Cleveland, Tennessee). It began in England 1953, when its founder, Oliver Lyesight (1919–2006) established the first congregation in Wolverhampton. Lyesight, who was invited to preach at various congregations including the Assemblies of God, founded the church due to the newly arrived migrants 'drifting away and backsliding.'

a backdrop of King's Christian spirituality, Arnold and King are brought into conversation in the context of the African-Caribbean Pentecostal experience in Britain.

Skepticism to Hope—The Context and Reason for the Book

In 1981 and 1985, riots erupted in Britain's major cities, due in major part to the institutionally sanctioned harassment of young black men by the police, institutional racism, and rising unemployment. Those same cities are home to at least one New Testament Church of God (NTCG) church. In 1985, a riot took place in Handsworth, Birmingham the home of one of NTCG's larger churches. A fire was set at an old theater, and rioters were looting and burning shops. About 200 yards away, church members were having a church meeting. It was only at the close of the meeting when trying to get home, that they realized roads were blocked due to the riot.[3] This event is analogous with how over the years, despite issues of racism, unemployment, and unjust policing methods, the black church has managed to remain present, yet oblivious and inactive.[4]

The black church has often neglected to participate in the affairs of the 'present world' because of her anticipation of the Parousia, the final judgment, and the restoration of all things. While Arnold held to this theological hope that lay in the literal return of Jesus, he in time also recognized the need for a holistic gospel.[5] Written in 1997, in *From Scepticism to Hope: One Black-Led Church's Response to Social Responsibility*, Arnold presents the migratory backdrop to the presence of the church in the United Kingdom Additionally, Arnold identifies and analyzes factors that led him to see the need for a holistic gospel and the necessity of realizing that this gospel has application in the here and now. The title and task of Arnold's work emerge from this process.

---

[3] Selwyn E. Arnold, From Scepticism to Hope: One Black-Led Church's Response to Social Responsibility (Bramcote, Nottingham: Grove Books Ltd., 1992), 71.

[4] Ibid., 71.

[5] Ibid., 11, 34.

The book begins with a foreword by Prebendary Pat Dearnley and Bishop Wilfred Wood, the Church of England's first black bishop in England. In this foreword, they reference an address by Joel Edwards.[6] In 1991, Joel Edwards, then a NTCG minister—who led the African-Caribbean Evangelical Alliance and would become the Director of the Evangelical Alliance in Great Britain—addressed the *Annual Conference of Evangelical Christians for Racial Justice*.[7] In the address, Edwards outlined four stages in the maturation of urban black churches in Britain. First, "Inception"—the arrival of the first immigrants; second, "Consolidation," the establishment of black-led church headquarters and increasing concern to develop infrastructures within the churches. The third stage was "Initiation" which Edwards places in the 1970s and 80s to witness "a process of escalating community involvement and social action. The final stage, predicted to occur around the time of Arnold's book release, was "Dynamic Transition" a period during which the implication and ramification of the label black church would be explored.[8]

Dearnley and Wood assert that Arnold's book had appeared at a crucial time when Britain, including the police, was institutionally discriminatory and racist and this racism was a major factor in the discontent and disillusionment experienced by Britain's African-Caribbean community.[9] Black men were more likely than their white counterparts to be stopped by the police. Yet the proportion of these stops that lead to an offence was one in twelve.[10] Despite this, black men continued to be disproportionately represented as criminals in the justice system. Concurrently, Britain was experiencing rising unemployment and a failing economy the blame for which was being

---

[6] Ibid., 8.

[7] Ibid.

[8] Ibid., 8.

[9] The term, "African-Caribbean" designates individuals of Caribbean descent who are of African ancestry and live in Britain.

[10] Arnold, 49.

placed squarely on the shoulders of ethnic minorities.[11] In Dearnly and Wood's mind, the black church had a role to play in confronting and combatting such issues of racial inequity.

Perhaps the aforementioned events would not have evoked a response from Arnold, had it not been for the fact that growth in the NTCG had slowed, the pioneers of the church were getting older and would need support, for which the church believed it was duty-bound. Further, younger people were becoming disillusioned with the denomination's response to social issues and, rather than joining the church, many were leaving.[12] Before bringing King's philosophy to bear on the problems of social responsibility found in Arnold's work, a background to Pentecostalism in general and African-Caribbean Pentecostalism is in order, to which I turn to next.

Pentecostalism

Allan Anderson presents William J. Seymour (1879–1922), as a central figure in North American Pentecostalism in particular and its subsequent spread beyond the US in general. Seymour experienced brutal and bitter experiences on account of his race. Yet, despite "innumerable brutalities" Seymour refused to be embittered, but "lov[ed] in the face of hateful racism", striving for ecumenical unity despite the opposing and sometimes hostile social climate.[13] Walter Hollenweger explains that Seymour's resilience in the face of such opposition was due to his Pentecostal spirituality. Seymour himself recognized that the work of the Spirit was not solely in the charisma. This recognition may have contributed to his deviation from the assertion that speaking in tongues (glossolalia) was the initial evidence of Holy Spirit baptism or, any insinuation that every believer who was

---

[11] Ibid., 47.

[12] Ibid., 37.

[13] Walter Hollenweger, 'Pentecostal and Charismatic Movement,' 550; Walter Hollenweger, 'The Black Roots of Pentecostalism,' in *Pentecostals after a Century,* ed. Allan Anderson and Walter Hollenweger (Sheffield: Sheffield Academic Press, 1999), 40.

filled with the Spirit of God had to show evidence of such. Rather, he insisted that "a [surer] sign... was love," and that [speaking in] tongues was not the only true sign of baptism of the Holy Spirit. Seymour attested to the outworking of Holy Spirit baptism over any mechanical formulaic test of its reception."[14]

As a Christian tradition, Pentecostal spiritual practice relates to three principal notions first, it is sourced in Scripture particularly in the Acts of the Apostles and the gospels.[15] Keith Warrington suggests that Peter defended what was experienced by the disciples and spoke of the multi-sensory episode of the feast of Pentecost following Jesus' resurrection as a fulfilment of Joel 2:28–32.[16] Peter does not refer to the languages or the fire, even though these displays went beyond the prophecy found in Joel 2:22. It was perhaps taken for granted that this encounter was outside the norm of how God is known to work, and therefore explanation was not the point. The experience's authenticity was not validated by intellectual rationale but by its effects. In this instance, the effect was to cause those nearby to listen to Peter who presented them with a way of engaging with God.[17]

Second, Pentecostal spirituality does not draw on "abstract theory but attempts to live out gospel values in a positive yet critical manner within specific historic and cultural contexts." Finally, the experience and insights of individuals and groups are not isolated but relate to the wider Christian tradition of beliefs, practices, and community life.[18]

---

[14] Estrelda Y. Alexander, ed., "Seymour, William Joseph 1871-1922," in *The Dictionary of Pan-African Pentecostalism, Volume One: North America.* (La Vergne: Wipf and Stock Publishers, 2018), https://public.ebookcentral.proquest.com/choice/publicfullrecord.aspx?p=5709208.

[15] Phillip Sheldrake, "Preface," in *Encountering the Spirit: The Charismatic Tradition*, Traditions of Christian Spirituality Series (Maryknoll, N.Y: Orbis Books, 2007), 10.

[16] Warrington, *Pentecostal Theology*, 25.

[17] Ibid.

[18] Sheldrake, "Preface," 10; Mark J. Cartledge, *Encountering the Spirit: The Charismatic Tradition*, Traditions of Christian Spirituality Series (Maryknoll, N.Y: Orbis Books, 2007), 20.

Pentecostal spirituality, then, is not just concerned with prayer nor narrowly religious activities but with the whole of human life. This is expressed in terms of a conscious relationship with God in Jesus Christ through the indwelling of the Holy Spirit and within a community of believers.

Britain's African-Caribbean Pentecostals

During the 1950s and 1960s, large numbers of young West Indians of all social classes migrated to Great Britain from the Caribbean.[19] This exodus occurred for a variety of reasons: some had been recruited by British public sector employers, others travelled independently to pursue a career or to study, while others wished to join husbands, wives or fiancés.[20] The vast majority of the émigrés were skilled workers who, like most economic migrants, were in pursuit of better employment opportunities.[21] Jamaican migrants left a

---

[19] Diane Austin-Broos, *Jamaica Genesis: Religion and the Politics of Moral Orders* (Chicago; London: University of Chicago Press, 1997) 22-24. Austin-Broos states Jamaicans had been moving to different countries from the 1800s to the 1920s in search of work. John Catron, 'Evangelical Networks in the Greater Caribbean and the Origins of the Black Church,' *Church History* 79, no. 2 (March 2010): 77 – 114. Catron suggests that Jamaican Christians would travel between the islands and America spreading the message of Evangelical Christianity; Peter Fryer, *Staying Power: The History of Black People in Britain* (London: Pluto Press, 1984), 372, 374; Toulis, *Believing Identity*, 1.

[20] Beverley Bryan, Stella Dadzie and Suzanne Scafe, *The Heart of the Race: Black Women's Lives in Britain* (London: Virago Press, 1986) 25; Toulis, *Believing Identity*, 1. In June 1948 the *SS Empire Windrush* brought 498 West Indians, mainly Jamaicans to England, among them was 1 female stowaway. By 1961 the number of West Indians in Britain had increased to 172,379. Unlike other migratory trends the proportions of women to men were roughly equal. Anthony Reddie, *Black Theology in Transatlantic Dialogue* (New York: Palgrave Macmillan, 2006), 9-10. Doreen Morrison, *Reaching for the Promised Land: The Role of Culture Issues of Leadership and Social Stratification within British Caribbean Christianity*. Unpublished Ph.D. (University of Birmingham), 91. The majority of the men and women that migrated to England were in their twenties.

[21] Peter Fryer, *Staying Power* (London: Pluto Press, 2010), 374, 375. Fryer states that of the West Indians who came to Britain—it is not clear which years he is referring—13 per cent of the men had no skills and 5 per cent of the

country where the cost of living had doubled during the Second World War; where unemployment was high; and where Hurricane Charlie had further added to the islanders' suffering and hardship.[22]

Christianity in general, and Pentecostalism in particular, was Jamaica's national "religious hegemony."[23] Many of the migrants, therefore, were either Christian, from Christian backgrounds or were regular church attendees. These Caribbean Christians would have been unaware of the major role they were to play in the establishment and development of the black Pentecostal church and the black presence in Britain's historic churches, designated collectively as the Black Majority Church.[24]

As with all Pentecostals, the person and work of the Holy Spirit are central to African-Caribbean spirituality. As a classical Pentecostal denomination, the NTCG espouses the baptism of or in the Holy Spirit as a foundational distinctive and considers the work of the Spirit as a continual work in the Christian life. Believers understand themselves as works in progress, moving on to perfection. Pentecostal theologian, Frank Macchia states that not until "the resurrection of the dead and the new heavens and new earth make the entire creation God's dwelling place" will the final word be spoken. We then have to

---

women. One in four men were non-manual workers and over half the women. 46 per cent of men were skilled.

[22] Fryer, *Staying Power*, 373.

[23] Alexander, 'A Mouse in a Jungle,' 90; Foster, 'Women and the Inverted Pyramid,' 46. Austin-Broos, *Jamaica Genesis*, 1. The émigrés were probably expecting the same sort of hegemony in England; Wedenoja states in 1943 census data recorded Pentecostals as accounting for 4% of the Jamaica's population by 1970 this had risen to 20%. Data from a church survey in northern Clarendon, the geographical heart of Pentecostalism in Jamaica record that in 1969 45% of all church goers attended Pentecostal churches while 45% attended denominational churches (see William Wedenoja, "Modernization and the Pentecostal Movement in Jamaica," in Stephen D. Glazier, ed., Perspectives on Pentecostalism: Case Studies from the Caribbean and Latin America. (Washington, D.C.: University Press of America, 1980) 30-31.

[24] Foster, 'Women and the Inverted Pyramid,' 45-68; Alexander, 'A Mouse in a Jungle,' 85-107.

continue to seek until we find and have ears open to hear what the Spirit is saying in our time.[25]

In the African-Caribbean church, it was, mainly, the women who would visit the sick and elderly, and provide economic and physical resources to those experiencing hardship. They supported missionary efforts in Africa and were fundraisers and supplementary school teachers. The idea of having all things common and no one having need (at least not dire need) was part of the lived experience. Hence, while glossolalia signified Spirit baptism and sanctification, it was also about being empowered for service. Yet, there is room for further scope for Spirit-empowered service to include confronting issues of race. Responses to this issue do not, nor should not, emerge only from a political context, but should rather emerge as an integral to Spirit-empowered service. The Spirit in Martin Luther King's Christian theology can help inform the Pentecostal undertaking of racial social justice.

God, Spirituality, and Martin Luther King Jr.[26]

Martin Luther King Jr. is probably most well-known for his "I Have a Dream" speech during the March on Washington, August 28, 1963, when he said,

I have a dream that my four little children will one day live in a nation where they will not be judged by the color of their skin but by the content of their character. I have a dream today.[27]

---

[25] Frank D. Macchia, *Baptized in the Spirit: A Global Pentecostal Theology* (Grand Rapids, MI: Zondervan, 2006), 19.

[26] Many thanks to Dr. Hak Joon Lee, Lewis Smedes Professor of Christian Ethics, Fuller Theological Seminary, for permission to include notes from his class on the Ethics and Theology of Martin Luther King.

[27] Martin Luther King and James Melvin Washington, "I Have a Dream," in *A Testament of Hope: The Essential Writings of Martin Luther King, Jr*, 1st ed (San Francisco: Harper & Row, 1986), 219.

King's fight for civil and economic rights was not principally motivated by politics nor even by his experience of discrimination and oppression. His call for justice was motivated by his Christian faith, shaped by his mother and father under the auspices of the black Baptist church. King would say, "I am… the son of a Baptist preacher, the grandson of a Baptist preacher and the great-grandson of a Baptist preacher."[28] And he would add, "[t]he Church is my life, and I have given my life for the Church." As Pentecostals, we ought to pay attention to this motivation.

In King's theology, God was neither remote nor impersonal; but was able and had true communion with God's people. God could be touched, and as incarnated in Jesus was familiar with temptation (Hebrews 4:15). God had to relate to God's creation because true communion and fellowship can only occur between personal beings. While impersonal beings can interact—I can interact with my car and every time that I drive I interact with other cars and even drivers—this does not equate to fellowship. A personal God brings God's presence to bear in the empowering and encouraging of God's people. It is people, not impersonal objects, who reflect the *imago dei*. As such, humanity has "spiritual and moral capacity to communicate with one another and with God."[29] If God is not both close and personal then God is object and can neither participate in human "spiritual formation" nor "historical transformation."[30]

King was mindful of his spiritual heritage. He drew upon the black Baptist tradition as it incorporated the African spirituality of his foremothers and fathers. Therefore, while King was a civil rights leader, theologian, and movement organizer, he was akin to the prophets and leaders of Scripture that are "called by God for a special

---

[28] Martin Luther King Jr., "The UnChristian Christian," *Ebony*, August 1965, 77.

[29] Hak Joon Lee, *We Will Get to the Promised Land: Martin Luther King, Jr.'s Communal-Political Spirituality.* (Eugene, OR: Wipf & Stock Publishers, 2017), 87.

[30] Lee, 87.

task." The idea of call resonates with Pentecostals particularly as it relates to pulpit ministry. In that black Pentecostal pastors do not make a decision for the ministry, there is a Divine call that is observed in practice and attested to in community. King's call was clear.

King was appointed pastor of the prestigious Dexter Avenue Baptist Church in Atlanta on October 31, 1954.[31] The following year, following the arrest of Rosa Parks, for not giving up her bus seat for a white person, the citizens of Montgomery, Alabama voted to boycott the buses. Mrs. Parks was not the first black person to be arrested. For, over the previous decade, the black citizens of Montgomery had suffered abusive treatment by the transit company and its employees. They were required to enter and pay at the front of the bus, only to get off and enter again, but at the back. Occasionally, the money was taken but the driver would leave before the passenger could re-board. Hence Parks' arrest was just one of many of these occurrences that, sometimes, included loss of life.[32]

The detention of a respected middle-aged black Christian woman was the straw that broke the camel's back and instigated a movement. The Montgomery Bus Boycott was planned for a day but was extended as pastors and citizens continued the action until black citizens received the changes they demanded. On the first night, residents of Montgomery appointed 24-year-old King president of the Montgomery Improvement Association (MIA). In his inaugural speech fifteen minutes after the election, at Holt Street Baptist Church, King declared his faith in Jesus Christ. Further, in advocating for the fair treatment of black citizens he declared that if the MIA was wrong in their cause, not only was the Supreme Court and the US Constitution wrong, but "God, Almighty is wrong and Jesus of

---

[31] Martin Luther King and James Melvin Washington, *A Testament of Hope: The Essential Writings of Martin Luther King, Jr*, 1st ed (San Francisco: Harper & Row, 1986), xviii.

[32] See Jo Ann Gibson Robinson and David J. Garrow, The Montgomery Bus Boycott and the Women Who Started It: The Memoir of Jo Ann Gibson Robinson (Knoxville: University of Tennessee Press, 1987).

Nazareth was merely a utopian dreamer."[33] King, explains theologian James Cone, came from a context in which no reality was more important than God in this life or the next. "God could make 'crooked roads straight' and the 'rough places plain."[34] He was called by this God, who alone bestowed 'somebodiness' on the leader and not white rhetoric nor mistreatment.[35]

For him, the God of Scripture was both personal and relational, powerful, and omnipotent Creator of heaven and earth. God is not malevolent but exercises' God's power through love and justice to restore relationships. Cone explains that Kings' faith cannot be found in the essays and books that bear his name. Rather, King's faith is displayed in his preached word. King's assertion that "God was able" was not a passive statement, God was able through *him*.[36] The promise that God would be with him even to the end of the world was a divine promise. The God that made such promises is not "slack" about keeping them. With every trial, death threat, stabbing and betrayal the promise remained, because the God who promised is moral and cannot lie. "When you know God, you can stand up amid tension and tribulation and yet smile in the process... When you know God, you have some shoes that can help you walk through any muddy place."[37] God, in King's view, was both moral and political "working in history to bring about justice."[38] God vindicates the oppressed and the assurance of God's fellowship meant that the oppressed are never alone as they struggle for justice.[39]

While most scholars agree that King's spirituality was influenced by his black Baptist upbringing and African American religious

---

[33] *Martin Luther King Speech, Holt Street Baptist Church (Text + Audio)*, 2012. https://www.youtube.com/ watch?v=GGtp7kCi_LA&feature =youtu.be.

[34] James H. Cone, *Martin & Malcolm and America*, (Maryknoll, NY: Orbis, 2002), 25.

[35] Ibid.

[36] Cone, 126.

[37] King, "Discerning the Signs of History," sermon given November 15, 1964 at Ebenezer Baptist Church.

[38] Lee, *We Will Get to the Promised Land*, 87.

[39] Ibid.

tradition, Hak Joon Lee asserts that Kings' spirituality was also communal-political in its nature and emphasis. In this sense, Lee understands communal-political as,

> a spiritual and moral thrust that seeks enduring mutuality, fellowship and shared understanding among persons. This term has special meaning in African American contexts, since "racism" means noncommunity. African Americans struggles have been those of searching for community.[40]

Hence community, in this sense is existential.

Politics, in Lee's understanding, is situated in the context of racism and economic uplift and as such endows King's politics with a particular meaning. In this sense politics signifies the struggle to be *recognized* as an American with all the human and citizens' rights that the designation carries. Such a designation includes participating freely and equally in the process of decision making and sharing power. The thrust is engagement in or concern for the affairs of the nation. As such, preachers should be involved in politics, for,

> Who… is supposed to articulate the longings and aspirations of the people more than the preacher? Somehow the preacher must be an Amos, and say 'let justice roll down like waters and righteousness like a mighty stream' somehow the preacher must say with Jesus the spirit of the Lord is upon me because he hath anointed me to deal with the problems of the poor.[41]

However, King acknowledged that not all preachers embraced this aspect of the ministry. While commending some who had been

---

[40] Ibid., 10.

[41] Martin Luther King and James Melvin Washington, "I See the Promised Land," in *A Testament of Hope: The Essential Writings of Martin Luther King, Jr*, 1st ed (San Francisco: Harper & Row, 1986), 284.

jailed and beaten for their "political" stance he was clear that "often preachers are not concerned with anything but themselves…I am always happy to see a relevant ministry."[42]

Bishop Selwyn Arnold Meets King

Selwyn Arnold was an experienced preacher and administrator but what bearing did this have on the wider society? Was his, in the words of King, "a relevant ministry?" In what follows, I provide a biographical outline after which I discuss some of the convergences and divergences in the thought of King and Arnold.

Selwyn Arnold Sr, born on May 29, 1934 in Scarborough, Tobago, as the youngest of 11 children. He was raised in what he describes as the "strict traditions of the early Methodists."[43] In 1953, following baptism by immersion, Arnold joined a group of young believers called the "Christian General Assembly." While a member of this group, Arnold received the "Baptism of the Holy Spirit and was called to preach."[44] He and the group joined the Church of God in 1955. In England, he served as the Dean of Students at Ebenezer Bible Institute (circa 1963) the first theological institution started by a black church in England.[45] He served as a pioneer missionary Overseer to Ghana, West Africa from 1966-1976.[46] From 1976-1984 he served as missionary Overseer to Nigeria, assuming the leadership of the United Kingdom church in August 1984.[47] In 1993, the NTCG England and Wales, for the first time, chose its leader who was ratified by, instead of being appointed by, the International Office in Cleveland, TN.[48] Presumably,

---

[42] Ibid., 282.

[43] Arnold, *From Scepticism to Hope*, 30.

[44] Ibid.

[45] Ibid., 30; "Selwyn Arnold Obituary (2013)" *The [Trenton] Times*, https://obits.nj.com/amp/ obituaries/trenton/167941744. Accessed January 11, 2021.

[46] Arnold, *From Scepticism to Hope*, 30.

[47] Arnold, 30.

[48] "Dr Selwyn E Arnold | New Testament Church of God," https://ntcg.org.uk/about/history/dr-selwyn-arnold/, accessed January 11, 2021

his only publication, *From Skepticism to Hope: One Black-Led Church's response to Social Responsibility,* was published in 1992. According to Arnold, it was written for the Church of God and for the attention of black-led Churches in the United Kingdom.[49] It is a self-reflection and response to concerns from "younger members who recognize a need for progress and self-achievement in the struggle for survival."[50] There was perceived divergence between NTCG's theology, doctrinal principles and traditions and the changing values of the society on the one hand; and its silence on issues of racism and social responsibility on the other.[51]

Convergence: African Undergirding

An overarching characteristic of Pentecostalism is its contextual adaptability. Once in the Caribbean, American influenced Pentecostalism was "modified and inserted into a pre-existing order of socio-religious status assertion. Here it acquired cultural significance in the solution of the problem of an individual's social identity."[52] Although different in expression, the African roots of spirituality are common to both black Baptists and African-Caribbean Pentecostals. Slavery, despite its force and terror, served only to repress African spirituality. It did not decay but, as Wilmore asserts, was strengthened and enhanced in those "subterranean vaults."[53] Cornel West identifies three principal African resources. "Kinetic orality" is displayed in black preaching, song, prayers, and hymns. "Passionate physicality" that is

---

[49] Arnold, *From Scepticism to Hope,* Preface.

[50] Ibid., 11.

[51] Ibid.

[52] Nicole Rodriguez Toulis, *Believing Identity: Pentecostalism and the Mediation of Jamaican Ethnicity and Gender in England,* Explorations in Anthropology (Oxford ; New York: Berg, 1997), 82.

[53] Gayraud S. Wilmore, *Black Religion and Black Radicalism: An Interpretation of the Religious History of African Americans,* 3rd ed. (Maryknoll, N.Y: Orbis Books, 1998), 27.

144

the exercise of agency over the body that sense of "somebodiness."[54] And, "combative spirituality" embodied in the preacher, deacon and choir, whose responsibility it was to encourage the discouraged and engender hope in the hopeless.[55]

Central to African-Caribbean spirituality is the presence of the Holy Spirit and an emphasis on dynamic worship as a transformative experience. This is neither symbolic nor merely cerebral but encompasses both the physical body and emotion. Walter Hollenweger attributes the expansion of Pentecostalism to its "black root." This can be described in terms of the "orality of liturgy," "narrativity of theology and witness," "maximum participation," "inclusion of dreams and visions in personal and public forms of worship," and, "an understanding of the body/mind relationship that is informed by experiences of correspondence between body and mind."[56] Both King and Arnold understood their visions as communal.

Divergence: Engagement with Entities beyond of the Church

Jesus, the Apostles and King engaged with people from different walks of life, perspectives and philosophies. King was middle class, educated at renowned universities where he studied the philosophies of Reinhold Niebuhr and Paul Tillich. As Baptist ministers, King's father and grandfather's experience contributed to King being comfortable and conversant with the church and the sensibilities of her people. He engaged with the teachings Mahatma Gandhi, from whom he developed a nonviolent approach to civil rights activism. He met world leaders, spoke with US Presidents. Yet he was also beaten, stabbed and eventually killed because of his Christian theology. Racism wrong in the eyes of the God of Scripture, whom King espoused as such he called out racism and its concomitant structures as immoral.

---

[54] Cornel West, *The Cornel West Reader* (New York: Basic Books, 1999), 428.

[55] Ibid.

[56] Walter J. Hollenweger, *Pentecostalism: Origins and Developments Worldwide* (Peabody, Mass: Hendrickson Publishers, 1997), 18.

Such a hermeneutic was at theological odds with prevailing white Evangelical Christian belief and practice. For King, this was not an intellectual assent but one which emerged from the existential experience of African-Americans. His idea of "Beloved Community" required "mutual dependence and cooperation" individual human life is only actualized in community.[57] It was necessary for the "government to support and ensure that the talents and potentials of persons are actualized to the full extent."[58]

Wilfred Wood in *Scepticism*'s preface critiques the African-Caribbean church's absence from the chambers of national and local government stating that "[d]oubtless the legacy of the 'holiness movement' with its suspicion of politics as heavily tainted by 'the world' is largely to blame for the reluctance of Christians from black-led churches…" to address matters of secular politics.[59] Conversely, Toulis argues that while there may not be overt resistance, the "politics of representation is achieved through relative passivity."[60] African-Caribbean Pentecostalism enables members to deal with racism by controlling their own thoughts regarding themselves."[61] Arnold recognized that this was not always enough. Young people were attracted to "secular community-based organizations" because they offered a fitting response. The response of the church however was deemed narrow and apolitical. For such young people, the only way to be involved in social responsibility was to leave the auspices of the church.

Convergence: The Power of the Gospel

Christian theological hope necessitates that the gospel message is preached. For King, the gospel was key because only the gospel had the power to liberate from personal sin *and* social evils. Arnold was

---

[57] Lee, *We Will Get to the Promised Land*, 91.
[58] Ibid., 92.
[59] Arnold, *From Scepticism to Hope*, 9.
[60] Toulis, *Believing Identity*, 206.
[61] Ibid., 207.

aware of the "social imperatives enshrined in the gospel of Christ", imperatives that could be contextualized in lived experience.[62] Arnold refers to King stating,

> ...it might be that Martin Luther King Jr. and the black Church in America found some means of incorporating the hope of liberation from the humiliation of slavery and economic oppression, with the hope and themes of liberation from sin, and the hope of a better life.[63]

Yet Arnold was aware that although equipped to live out their faith and prepare through practices and rituals for the life to come, "members need to be equipped to influence the social development of their own society in the here and now."[64]

It was from the same Christian faith that King garnered the strength to love.[65] Such a love included tough-mindedness "characterized by incisive thinking, realistic appraisal and decisive judgment."[66] Such a mind King believed was able to break through the legends and myths to discern truth from falsity. However, a tough mind without love only values people in terms of their usefulness to the cause and not in terms of their humanity.[67]

"The NTCG must accept the challenge to respond to racism in the society not only for its own survival, but because racism is alien to the principles of the gospel of Christ."[68] King takes this further

---

[62] Arnold, *From Scepticism to Hope*, 34.

[63] Ibid., 62.

[64] Ibid., 11.

[65] Martin Luther King, *Strength to Love*, 1st Fortress Press ed (Philadelphia: Fortress Press, 1981) The book is dedicated to his mother and father "whose deep commitment to the Christian faith and unswerving devotion to its timeless principles have given me an inspiring example of the Strength to Love."

[66] Ibid., 16.

[67] Ibid.

[68] Arnold, *From Scepticism to Hope*, 51.

perceiving the church as the "chief moral guardian of the community." It is to the church that society should look for moral guidance. This may require the church to disconnect from the status quo to address issues of inequity; to be neither master nor servant, but rather to be conscience.[69]

Arnold established a task force that had as one of its tasks to search the Bible for references that support God's concern for the poor and the oppressed, since he felt that such a focus had been lost due to the church's overemphasis on the Parousia.[70] Yet, he was aware that for "modern youth" social issues required sources other than the Bible. In the eyes of the younger generations, the black Pentecostal church which upheld Scripture as central to life and practice but which, over the previous ten years, had been declining numerically and not growing spiritually, was outmoded, The team realized this decrease was, in part, due to a neglect of the whole person. Their heavy emphasis on preparing people for heaven left people ill-prepared for living and participating in society and bringing about needed change.[71]

King understood neoliberal capitalism to be driven by competition and self-interest that was antithetical to community and denies human interdependence.[72] He understood that failure to treat people as reflections of the *imago dei,* but as consumers with endless desires, is anti-spiritual. In so doing, he felt, the culture becomes "thing-orientated" discouraging self-discipline and civic responsibility.[73] Further, all human beings should have access to everything necessary to attain their full potential. King did not advocate welfare, but favored full employment and income and reckoned that a guaranteed annual income could be achieved for

---

[69] Mervyn A. Warren, *King Came Preaching: The Pulpit Power of Dr. Martin Luther King, Jr* (Downers Grove, IL: InterVarsity Press, 2001), 127.

[70] Arnold, *From Scepticism to Hope,* 35.

[71] Arnold, 35.

[72] Hak Joon Lee, *The Great World House: Martin Luther King, Jr., and Global Ethics* (Cleveland, Ohio: Pilgrim Press, 2011), 157.

[73] Lee, 157.

twenty-billion dollars, while the Vietnam conflict was costing thirty-five billion dollars and the expedition to the moon twenty billion dollars.

Arnold's Task Force set two major goals by which the denomination, through its churches, could increase involvement in social and economic issues. First, it called for development and launch of the Department of Social Responsibility to increase local churches' awareness and understanding of the social issues that confronted the black community. The second was to sensitize African-Caribbean people to the benefits of a cooperative endeavor.[74]

Arnold was aware that some of the members were reflecting solely on the Church of God and its relationship to black experience. While he wanted to draw more broadly on black theology, liberation theology, and King, his work does not critically engage these perspectives or offer a systematic framework for the church's reflection. Presumably, he wanted the team, based on their findings, to devise a contextualized framework.

Arnold was fortunate to have been raised in a majority context. He migrated to Britain as an adult with aspirations of being a medical doctor and could not identify an instance where his color was a barrier. Having spent 18 years in ministry leadership positions in Ghana and Nigeria, he had not been exposed to the harsh treatment of growing, up nor ministering, in the inner city. Unlike some team members, he had not been exposed to social rejection so, at first, he struggled to understand the fuss about black theology and white theology. As a boy, he did not consider himself as black nor white. This is not unique, many people from majority contexts as the Caribbean, learned they were black when they arrived in Britain.

Prior to initiating the Task Force project, Arnold insisted that color did not matter in the Kingdom of God. And, not seeing himself as a target of blatant discrimination he was oblivious to the racism church members experienced and could not fully empathize with

---

[74] Arnold, *From Scepticism to Hope*, 36.

them. The project awakened him to who he was. He saw the project as serving as a point of spiritual renewal in the denomination and felt that there had been advancement that enabled him to "conceptualize hope in the here and now."

The experience of Arnold is tangential to that of King. One was raised in a majority community under colonial rule, the other came from a middle-class family upbringing in racially segregated Georgia. King had grown up seeing police brutality, lynching and the intimidating rides of the Ku Klux Klan and these experiences informed his responses.[75] His time at Morehouse College helped him deal intellectually with the injustice of the US.[76] He held that Christian pastors were called to speak on issues of justice without being selective.

King engaged in four basic steps. *Fact gathering; negotiation*—talking with both political and business leaders. *Self-purification*—inner reflection and workshops on non-violence and *finally non-violent direct action*. King understood that freedom is never voluntarily given up by the oppressor it must be demanded by the oppressed.[77]

Conclusion: The Pentecostal Call to Social Justice in Acts 6:1

These two black leaders represent different geographical contexts but were subject to the same existential reality of racism and discrimination and recognized the gospel as a central response to their reality. The foregrounding of the Parousia fueled a fervor to spread the gospel and informed the priorities of migrant British black Pentecostals. Yet Britain had experienced a cry from young black Christians for whom navigating through racial injustice had become impossible. Unlike King, who left leadership of a church to concentrate solely on civil rights, Arnold led what was then the largest

---

[75] Lee, *We Will Get to the Promised Land*, 62–63.

[76] Ibid., 64.

[77] Hak Joon Lee, "Church and State in Kings Ethics" (Lecture 6, The Theology and Ethics of Martin Luther King Jr., Fuller Theological Seminary, Summer 2020).

black denomination in the United Kingdom within the confines of a white-controlled American denomination.

Pentecostal biblical scholar Trevor Grizzle states the situation with the widows in Acts 6 occurred because the "church had developed a cultural stress fracture along hidden fault lines of ethnic exclusiveness."[78] The passage conveys the plight of the Greek widows who were being overlooked in the daily distribution of food. A year or so had passed since the multi-sensory occurrence in the upstairs room; the church had grown to somewhere in the region of 20 to 25,000 people.[79] Grizzle asks how this burgeoning "megachurch on multiple campuses" would deal with this social justice issue, I suggest that the black British church was in a similar position. Grizzle, also a pastor, explains that "authentic church growth is a visible fruit of divine favor... Individual human needs... can become a blur of indistinguishable sights and sound. This is never intentional it just happens."[80]

The frequent references to widows in the Old Testament often relate to their impoverished state. Perdue explains that widows without families to support them were destitute despite having protection under charity laws (e.g., Deut 10:18; 24:17-21; 26:12-13). Those who subverted the justice against widows were, according to Deuteronomy 27:19, cursed. While, clearly, the Acts passage indicates that difference in treatment was based on ethnicity (and probably gender); was it also due to the Jewish Christians not feeling obligated to care for *non-Jewish* Greek widows because they were not like them?[81] The Apostles attended to the matter quickly making the "spiritual" their priority. For "both the distribution of rations" (Acts 6:1) and preaching (Acts 6:4)

---

[78] Ibid., 100.

[79] Trevor Grizzle, *Church Aflame: An Exposition of Acts 1-12* (Cleveland, TN: Pathway Press, 2000), 100.

[80] Ibid., 102.

[81] Leo G. Perdue, ed., *Families in Ancient Israel*, 1st ed, The Family, Religion, and Culture (Louisville, KY: Westminster John Knox Press, 1997), 194–95.

are *diakonia* or ministry.[82] Could this be a viable leadership model? Only leaders who are confident in their calling and abilities can recognize that they were not called to do everything. That sense of purpose and confidence frees them from personal intimidation thereby permitting others to take the lead.

God's design for Pentecostal clergy is to equip and release the laity (see Ephesians 4:12). As Grizzle states, "[e]ach church] has all the resources necessary for effective ministry locked in its membership."[83] African-Caribbean Pentecostals believe in and practice the theology of the priesthood of all believers. Laity function in a variety of ecclesial roles; they play instruments, sing, preach and pray. But, are our young people becoming more frustrated and our churches becoming stagnating because these are the only roles afforded recognition? Do we exclude development and application of strategies to confront the social issues that face the African-Caribbean community?

As the church, we cannot remain silent. Clearly, black people are being overlooked in economic, civil, and educational opportunity. In speaking out against the US presence in Vietnam, King exclaimed, "a time comes when silence is betrayal."[84] Jeremiah wanted to stay silent, yet it was like fire in his bones. To douse the fire and remain silent would be a betrayal of the call on his life.[85] In examining the actions and inactions of European citizens during the holocaust, David Gushee concludes that the lack of response by those who professed to be Christians is "moral failure" and indifference to the suffering of others is in conflict with the teachings of Jesus.[86] The black Pentecostal church cannot remain indifferent to social justice. As people who experience the hard reality of racism, poverty, and oppression, like the

---

[82] Grizzle, *Church Aflame*, 103.

[83] Ibid., 103.

[84] King and Washington, *A Testament of Hope*, 231.

[85] David Gushee, *(David Gushee, The Righteous Gentiles of the Holocaust: A Christian Interpretation (Minneapolis: Fortress Press, 1994)*, (Minneapolis: Fortress Press, 1994), 84.

[86] Ibid.

non-Jewish widows, it needs to speak up. The Christocentric nature of King's approach to social justice is clear, Arnold (as a Pentecostal) recognized that the Spirit-empowered gospel had a wider application, that includes the individual and the society. Both are necessary."

Race and Gender Equality in a Classical Pentecostal Denomination: How Godly Love Flourished and Foundered

Kimberly Ervin Alexander and James Philemon Bowers

In the lore of early Pentecostalism, perhaps no line is more often quoted than that penned by Frank Bartleman, "The color line was washed away by the blood."[1] Indeed, what was perhaps most startling to those who visited the revival at 312 Azusa Street in Los Angeles, California, in the spring and summer of 1906 was the multi-racial and multi-cultural nature of the revival meeting. Azusa St. historian, Cecil M. Robeck, contends that the Apostolic Faith Mission was primarily an African American congregation, with an African-American, William J. Seymour, clearly acknowledged as pastor. It is notable, however, that he was assisted by a group of leaders, who were black and white, male and female. Robeck has documented membership not only including blacks and whites but also Latinos, Asians, and Native Americans.[2]

Revival attendee Gaston Barnabas Cashwell's story is illustrative. A Holiness preacher from Eastern North Carolina, Cashwell traveled to Azusa in 1906 after hearing of the revival. When he arrived and saw the interracial congregation, he realized he would have to be prayed for by African Americans. Unable to move beyond this at that first service, he returned to his hotel and prayed about his prejudice. He returned to the mission after days of soul-searching and prayer, asking Seymour and others to lay hands on him and pray that he might be baptized in the Holy Spirit. By his account, he immediately received the experience. In an age of Jim Crow segregation and the influence of British-Israel theory in populist politics and religion, in both the academy and society, the Pentecostal outpouring *on all flesh* was

---

[1] Frank Bartleman, *How Pentecost Came to Los Angeles.* (Los Angeles: Frank Bartleman, 1925), 54.

[2] Cecil M. Robeck, *The Azusa Street Revival and Mission: The Birth of the Global Pentecostal Movement* (Nashville: Nelson Reference and Electronic, 2006), 24-25.

scandalous to the outsider, but a sign of authenticity to those on the inside.

The experience of Cashwell and scores of others who attended the Azusa St. revival or one of its many replications around the United States in the early twentieth century included conversions and healings but also experiences of sanctification and an experience identified as a baptism in the Holy Spirit understood as parallel to that of the disciples in Acts 2. Those seeking a way to articulate that experience, in the form of a testimony, may have utilized the biblical language but also described dispositional changes. The following example is especially noteworthy:

> A Nazarene brother who received the baptism with the Holy Ghost in his own home in family worship, in trying to tell about it said, 'It was a baptism of love. Such abounding love! Such compassion seemed to almost kill me with its sweetness! People do not know what they are doing when they stand against it. The devil never gave me a sweet thing, he was always trying to get me to censuring people. This baptism fills us with divine love.'[3]

A similar testimony, found in the same issue, narrates the experience of a minister who was baptized in the Spirit at the revival: "He is filled with divine love. His family were first afraid to see him speaking in tongues, thinking he had lost his mind, but when his wife and children felt the sympathy and divine love which the Holy Ghost puts in people's hearts, they said, 'Papa was never as sane in his life.'"[4] There is a noted *affective* change in the person and the language used to articulate this experience is "divine love" or "baptism of love."

Though emerging creedal statements and explanations of the Pentecostal distinctive of Spirit Baptism identified the purpose of the

---

[3] *The Apostolic Faith.* 1:1 (September 1906), 1.
[4] *The Apostolic Faith,* 1:1 (September 1906), 1.

experience as "power for witness," testimonies reveal that participants understood the experience as bringing about an ontological and dispositional change. As a result of these collective experiences, Pentecostal communities were transformed into activists for the cause of Christian unity. Robeck argues that Seymour had a "vision of shared experience and communal cooperation between various Christian groups."[5] Seymour exclaimed, "We are not fighting men or churches, but seeking to displace dead forms and creeds and wild fanaticisms with living, practical Christianity. 'Love, Faith, Unity' is our watchword."[6]

In this ethos, Godly love flourished. As defined by their own testimonies, divine love, infused through an infilling of the Spirit, expressed itself in compassion for others, in a desire for unity in the church, and, most notably, in the crossing of culturally imposed or regulated lines of demarcation regarding gender and race. Racial lines were seemingly erased to the horror of those who observed the revival.[7] White ministers, male and female, submitted to the leadership of African American ones. In addition, there was real, if restricted, elevation of the status of women within the movement. Estrelda Y. Alexander describes this effect:

> Within the revival, white women from various walks of life ministered alongside black washerwomen and household servants with no formal Bible or theological training. Both were given free rein to exercise their ministry gifts of speaking in tongues, interpreting glossalalic messages, prophesy, and intercession…In fact, one element of the revival that drew public attention---and a degree of derision of the secular

---

[5] Robeck, 8.

[6] "The Apostolic Faith Movement," *The Apostolic Faith.* 1:1 (September 1906), 2.

[7] Robeck, 87-128; 129-186.

press---was the regular sight of white men, many of them somewhat prominent members of the clergy or community, kneeling before black women who prayed with them to receive prayer for Holy Spirit baptism.[8]

Beyond the confines of Azusa Street, women took on positions of some power and influence such as pastor, evangelist, missionary, and teacher. In some cases, women carried out so-called "priestly duties" such as the administration of sacraments. Alexander does conclude that this egalitarianism was never fully realized.[9]

An examination of this earliest period of the Pentecostal movement reveals that the experience of Spirit Baptism was understood by revival participants as resulting in a change in the status of persons of color and of women. Utilizing the typology developed by Lee and Poloma, it can be stated that within the early revival there were exemplars of Godly love who could be classified as "Changers" (those who work for structural changes in society). Though it may not be argued that these exemplars had a complete reform of society in view, nevertheless, a change in social status such as was experienced was, in reality, a social change. Beyond this, it is clear that Seymour, or others, did have an explicit agenda of renewal of the church in view, that would place him in the category of "Renewer."[10]

Disturbingly, this flourishing of Godly love began to wane relatively quickly. As early as 1907, insiders began to react to the interracial nature of the movement, perhaps, at first, unaware of the racist overtones of their reaction but nevertheless playing into the eventual accommodation to segregated culture. Two examples will

---

[8] Estrelda Y. Alexander, *The Women of Azusa Street* (Cleveland, OH: Pilgrim Press, 2005), 11-12.

[9] Estrelda Y. Alexander, *Limited Liberty: The Legacy of Four Pentecostal Women* (Cleveland, OH: Pilgrim Press, 2008), viii.

[10] Matthew T. Lee and Margaret M. Poloma. *A Sociological Study of the Great Commandment in Pentecostalism: The Practice of Godly Love as Benevolent Service.* (Lewiston, NY: Edwin Mellen Press, 2009), 62.

illustrate this foundering. First, in the January 1907 issue of *Triumphs of Faith* an editorial appeared in which editor Carrie Judd Montgomery commented on the lack of unity among Christians in the work in Los Angeles. She reported: "Some of the white people who first received the special blessing among the colored people in the Azusa Street meetings, have organized little gatherings in different parts of the city, and continue to receive gracious manifestations of God's presence." She continued, "Much that seemed excitable and abnormal about the work has died down, but a real work of grace and power remains in many hearts."[11]

The second example comes from William H. Durham, who had his initial Pentecostal experience at Azusa St. in 1907. When Durham moved his headquarters from Chicago to Los Angeles in 1911, with the intent of re-defining the soteriology of the entire movement, he attempted to redirect the revival at Azusa St. In an article in his periodical *The Pentecostal Testimony* titled "The Great Revival At Azusa street Mission---How It Began and How It Ended," Durham describes the "sad condition" of the "work in Los Angeles" as a consequence of "incompetent leadership." Durham clearly sees the subsequent rejection of his message by the leadership of Azusa St. as falling along color lines when he writes, "When we came to the Mission Tuesday we found that Seymour had influenced a few of the officers of the Mission, men of his own color, to stand with him, and they had locked and bolted the door." He describes a power-play for control of the revival at Azusa Street in terms of Seymour's "scheming" and trying to gain "a place" or position.[12] He goes on to say that he had "always found an excuse for his failures and blunders," finally pronouncing that "the power of God had entirely left him."[13]

---

[11] Carrie Judd Montgomery, "The Work in Los Angeles." *Triumphs of Faith* 27.1 (January 1907), 14.

[12] It should be noted that Seymour was still pastor of the mission.

[13] William H. Durham, "The Great Revival at Azusa St.--How It Began and How It Ended," *Pentecostal Testimony* 1:8 (1911), 3.

Given this larger history of the movement, it seems appropriate to utilize cases of race and gender to assess the presence and productivity of Godly love within the Pentecostal community. Particularly notable is Sorokin's description of the five dimensions of love: *intensity, extensity, duration, purity, and adequacy.*[14] By examining the development of a Pentecostal group's responses to the issues of race and gender equality it is possible to test these dimensions; of most interest are the *intensity, extensity,* and *duration* of the experience.

In this investigation, the issues of race and gender equality as expressions of Godly love will be examined within a classical Pentecostal denomination, the Church of God (Cleveland, TN). The Church of God (COG) was one of many small Holiness groups coming into the Pentecostal movement after contact with the Azusa St. revival. The formation of the church took place in a very different context: The Southeastern United States, in predominantly rural settings. By examining the period of its infancy and adolescence (approximately 1906 – 1923) one sees a similar pattern of the flourishing and then foundering of Godly love but within a more self-contained structure. By the teens, the COG was nearing a decade of Pentecostal identity and was in the throes of contemplating the meaning of "church," the form that the organization should take, and attempting to find the biblical model of church government. The reflections, discussions, and decisions made during this period of maturation are revealing and there is no better evidence of the ambiguity that marked the church's hermeneutic and worldview (and, perhaps, that of the larger Pentecostal movement) than that seen in the response to issues of race and gender. The denomination was shaped by a curious mix of the acknowledgement of the important role of spiritual experience and a fundamentalist hermeneutic all poured through the filter of the dominant culture of white male paternalism. In the final analysis, the transformative potential of Pentecostal

---

[14] Pitirim A. Sorokin. *The Ways and Power of Love: Types, Factors, and Techniques of Moral Transformation.* Philadelphia, PA: Templeton Foundation Press, 2002 [1954]), 15-16.

spiritual experience in the interest of racial and gender equality is largely negated by the adopted hermeneutic and conformity to cultural norms.

The "Law of Love": Church of God Visions

The impulse to "displace dead forms and creeds," as seen at Azusa, was one shared in common with other restorationist movements of the day, including an emerging movement in the Southeastern United States, one that produced this poetic expression:

The law of love by Christ was given,
To guide the church from earth to heaven;
It almost makes my heart to bleed
To see a change for human creed.[15]

This stanza from *The Lost Link*, a book by early Pentecostal preacher and COG founding influence, R. G. Spurling, is but one of several poems in the text depicting his version of the church history. Spurling's restorationist view was that the church fell from Christ's intention; that is, the church was to be guided by the "law of love" (designated as "the Lost Link") but had fallen in 325 CE by allowing doctrine and particularly an imposed "human creed" to divide the church. For Spurling, "Godly love" was impeded by humanly-devised ("men-made") creedal statements and their attending interpretations of orthodoxy.

In 1886, Spurling, his father, and seven others covenanted together to form the Christian Union with the understanding that they desired to,

be free from all men made [sic] creeds and traditions, and to take the New Testament, or law of Christ, for your only rule

---

[15] R. G. Spurling, *The Lost Link* (Turtletown, TN: R. G. Spurling, 1920), 34.

of faith and practice; giving each other equal rights and privilege to read and interpret for yourselves as your conscience may dictate, and are willing to set [sic] together as the Church of God to transact business [as] the same.[16]

Explicit in this covenant was a restorationist vision of New Testament Christianity and an egalitarian understanding of the Body of Christ. Ten years later, the Holiness revival would serve to transform the lives of even more believers in the Unicoi Mountains of Tennessee and North Carolina. William F. Bryant, a Baptist lay leader who experienced sanctification during this revival, described his reaction to the severe persecution he and his fellow Holiness adherents faced:

> We lay on our faces and cried to God to keep us sweet and let us do nothing to grieve the Holy Ghost. There [were] a number who would hazard their lives for this wonderful Spirit we had, so we asked for the signs to follow us more and more.[17]

When members and leaders of the community were to be prosecuted for severe persecution, Bryant appealed for judicial leniency. Spurling joined Bryant's group to form the Holiness Church at Camp Creek in 1902. The related visions of Christian Unity and Holiness joined together to establish what shortly became the COG under the leadership of A. J. Tomlinson.

Tomlinson, a native of Indiana with Quaker roots, had been influenced by various strands of the radical wing of the Holiness

---

[16]David G. Roebuck, "Restorationism and a Vision for a World Harvest: A Brief History of the Church of God." (https://fliphtml5.com/jjnr/qodq/basic, 1999), 1.

[17] David G. Roebuck, "Faithful Pilgrims: Establishing the Church of God," *Servants of the Spirit: Portraits of Pentecostal/Charismatic Pioneers*, ed. Andrea Johnson (Des Moines, IA: OBC Publishing, 2010), 43.

movement and by Frank Sandford's vision of restorationism[18] As a missionary to the region, he believed the group he encountered in the mountains to be the Church of God of the Bible, united with them, and later became the dominant leader. In January 1908, Tomlinson, as a result of the preaching of Cashwell, experienced a Pentecostal baptism in the Holy Spirit. Tomlinson's account of the experience described both the physical manifestations and the *affective* change:

> As I lay there great joy flooded on my soul. The happiest moments I had ever known up to that time. I never knew what real joy was before. My hands clasped together with no effort on my part. Oh, such floods and billows of glory ran through my whole being for several minutes! There were times that I suffered the most excruciating pain and agony, but my spirit always said "yes" to God.[19]

Beyond this, he described in great detail a kind of visionary travel to remote parts of the world:

> In a vision I was carried to Central America, and was shown the awful condition of the people there. A paroxysm of suffering came over me as I seemed to be in soul travail for their salvation. Then I spoke in tongues as the Spirit gave utterance, and in the vision I seemed to be speaking the very same language of the Indian tribes with whom I was surrounded.[20]

He continued to view South America, Africa, and then Jerusalem where he "... endured the most intense suffering, as if I might have

---

[18] R. G. Robins, *A. J. Tomlinson: Plainfolk Modernist* (New York: Oxford University Press, 2004), 120-121.

[19] A. J. Tomlinson, A. J. *The Last Great Conflict* (Cleveland, TN: Walter E. Rodgers, 1913), 234.

[20] Ibid., 235.

been suffering similar to that of my Savior on Mount Calvary. I never can describe the awful agony that I felt in my body."[21] From there he traveled across Europe and back to his home where he saw his wife and children. His interpretation of the vision is significant; for Tomlinson, he and his family would be on a mission to carry the gospel light throughout the world. It was that vision, along with the influence of Spurling's restorationism, which shaped his future and that of the COG.

Tomlinson led the fledgling movement into a vision for world evangelization and to engage in a campaign he described in his book *The Last Great Conflict*. He dedicated his *magnum opus* to the denomination "…whose duty it is to preach the gospel of the kingdom in all the world for a witness, and then be presented to Jesus Christ '[a] glorious church, not having spot, or wrinkle, or any such thing."[22] In the second chapter, titled "Abounding Love," he explains how Godly love is expressed to and may be expressed by humanity:

> The display of love that was in Jesus was so extreme that the human mind has not been, and never will be able to grasp it in its fullest sense; yet as this great treasure has been displayed in full measure in Jesus Christ, by His divine power and unreasonable methods it has been, and is placed by Him, within the reach of him who is willing to go through all the changes and departments of suffering that is required to gain such possession.[23]

He continued to describe Jesus' act of *kenosis*, his works of mercy, healing, and redemption. He writes,

---

[21] Ibid.

[22] Tomlinson, 4.

[23] Ibid., 22.

Such a display of love on the part of our Savior is beyond the comprehension of our finite minds; but we are to go beyond our understanding and comprehension, if we go into the mystery of godliness and pass into "the love of Christ which passeth knowledge." It evidently takes this extreme experience in the realm of divine love to place us in the experience for which our hearts are crying out and our prayers are ascending; that state of being filled with all the fullness of God." Not until our lives are saturated with divine love are we even approaching anyways near the desired haven.[24]

He continues to instruct that while he is "in favor of" manifestations of the Spirit and signs and wonders, there is yet "a silent but all powerful force...Divine Love."[25] He contends that a "revival of love" would have needed effects: "Such a deep sense of love, such a saturation of love that would silence the tongue in times of the deepest distress and trial; that would forever put an end to fault finding, mote hunting, backbiting, chafing, ungodly conversation, hypocracy [sic] and false teaching."[26] He argues that Bible teaching and preaching as well as manifestations of the Spirit have "failed to bring unity, power and the fulness [sic] of Pentecost"[27] With this foundation, Divine Love, Tomlinson contends the church can move toward her vocation to win the lost.

Racial Diversity

Recent scholarship has shown that the COG originated in an essentially tri-racial society, though white culture undoubtedly

---

[24] Ibid., 24.
[25] Ibid., 24.
[26] Tomlinson, 24.
[27] Ibid., 25.

dominated the region of east Tennessee and western North Carolina.[28] Harold Hunter has shown that from late 1908 (within the same year of his Spirit Baptism experience) Tomlinson was involved in interracial Pentecostal worship experiences. Hunter cites accounts in Tomlinson's diary in which he documents a visit to a 'Pentecostal convention' led by Charles H. Mason" (Nov. 12, 1908) and multiple visits to the Pleasant Grove (Florida) camp.[29] Receiving evangelists' credentials from him (May 1909) after a Pentecostal experience at the camp meeting, were Rebecca and Edmond S. Barr.[30] Rebecca was a native Floridian who had met and married the Bahamian immigrant, Edmond.[31] In November 1909, shortly after their Pentecostal experience, the Barrs carried the Pentecostal message to the Bahamas. In 1911, Tomlinson himself visited the Bahamas, preaching throughout the islands. Hunter quotes his diary: "Blacks and whites all come to meeting together."[32] He goes on to cite examples of

---

[28] Hudson reconstructs the probable Cherokee and African-American influences on the history and spirituality of the Church of God. See Andrew S. Hudson, "An African Reading of an Appalachian Church: An Intentional Reconstructive Ethnohistory of the Church of God." M.Div. Thesis. Princeton Theological Seminary, 2011.

[29] A. J. Tomlinson, diary, vol. 2, Nov. 26, 1908 (Manuscripts Division, Library of Congress, Washington, D. C.) in Harold D. Hunter, "A Journey Toward Racial Reconciliation: Race Mixing in the Church of God of Prophecy," *The Azusa Street Revival and Its Legacy*, eds. Cecil M. Robeck Jr. and Harold D. Hunter, (Cleveland, TN: Pathway Press, 2006), 277-296. Charles H. Mason was co-founder and presiding bishop of the Church of God in Christ, a predominantly African-American Pentecostal denomination headquartered in Memphis, Tennessee. COG historian David G. Roebuck, however, questions whether or not the 1908 Memphis meeting was led by Mason, as he can find no evidence of this claim by Hunter. [Email correspondence with Roebuck, June 3, 2021.]

[30] Interestingly, David Michel does not mention that Rebecca Barr was licensed as an evangelist though he briefly discusses Edmond Barr's licensure and subsequent appointment as State Overseer of Florida. See David Michel, *Telling the Story of Black Pentecostals in the Church of God.* (Cleveland, TN: Pathway Press, 2000).

[31] David G. Roebuck, "Unraveling the Cords that Divide: Cultural Challenges and Race Relations in the Church of God," *Skin Deep*, p. 188, n. 6.

[32] Tomlinson, diary, February 15-16, 1911, in Hunter, 285.

Tomlinson attending a convention in a Spanish-language congregation in New Mexico (1912) and of three congregations in New Mexico that are designated in the 1913 minutes of the Annual Assembly as "Spanish-speaking." The pastor of one of these congregations, Juan B. Padilla, eventually served on the Council of Seventy (1921-1922).[33] In addition, a Native American addressed the Annual Assembly in 1917 and, according to Assemblies of God archivist, Darrin Rodgers, what was probably the first Native American Pentecostal church in North Dakota was a COG congregation.[34]

Clearly, Tomlinson's Spirit-given vision was inclusive of other races. It is also apparent that he, and the COG, struggled over this counter-cultural expression of inclusivity, especially where African Americans were concerned. In 1912, he ordained Edmond Barr and discussed the decision about whether to do so in his diary: "Held a conference meeting yesterday to consider the question of ordaining Edmond Barr (colored) and setting the colored people off to work among themselves on account of the race prejudice in the South."[35] Significantly, ordination offered Barr the right to grant ministerial credentials and to organize churches.[36] The minutes of the 1915 Annual Assembly note that on Saturday, November 6, a similar discussion over the appointment of a "colored man as state overseer over the colored work in Florida" took place.[37]

The assembly record later indicates that Edmond Barr was appointed overseer of the "colored work" in Florida.[38]After an

---

[33] Hunter, 285.

[34] Hunter, 286; Darrin J. Rodgers, *Northern Harvest: Pentecostalism in North Dakota* (Bismarck, ND: North Dakota District Council of the Assemblies of God, 2003), 38-39, 241-242.

[35] Tomlinson, diary, June 2, 1912, cited in Hunter, 285.

[36] Roebuck observes that there was growth in Florida over the next two years with an expansion from seven black churches to thirteen and from 111 to 200 black members. See Roebuck, "Unraveling."

[37] *Minutes of the Eleventh Annual Assembly of the Churches of God.* (Cleveland, TN: 1915), 21.

[38] The "colored work" consisted of seven churches, four with pastors, and 111 members. Four men are listed as deacons; seven evangelists are listed, three

investigation of Barr's capabilities as an administrator over the churches, however, Florida state overseer Sam C. Perry wrote to Tomlinson, "…from all accounts it appears that it would only work an injury to the work to place Bro. Barr over it."[39] According to Roebuck, Perry's investigation involved talking to persons in three of the eleven congregations. The minutes of the Annual Assembly of 1916 report Barr as overseer of the "colored work," but by 1917 Barr had resigned his Miami pastorate and both the black and white congregations in the state were supervised by Perry.[40] C. F. Bright, another African-American minister in Florida, addressed the assembly in 1919 on the subject "The Colored People and the Church."[41] Bright is also listed as having been appointed as overseer over the colored work in Pennsylvania.[42] However, Roebuck contends that he left the COG to join the Church of God in Christ in 1919 lamenting, "the colored will never be recognized with the whites."[43]

What is very revealing, beyond statistics and records of activities, are the letters and descriptions of these interracial episodes. The incipient racism, though perhaps mediated by a degree of Christian charity, is evident. From the 1919 minutes, a letter from Thomas B. Smith, a black minister, to the COG in Miami reads:

> Dear saints, the COG with headquarters at Cleveland, Tenn. is right. We know it is right. Don't let anyone turn you around. They are already making provisions for a party of the

---

of which are women, including Rebecca Barr. Edmond Barr is the only Bishop delineated. *Minutes,* 26.

[39] Roebuck cites Edmond S. Barr's Ministerial File in the Office of Business and Records, Church of God, Cleveland, Tennessee. The file contains the Perry correspondence to Tomlinson. (Roebuck, "Unraveling", 9.)

[40] *Minutes of the Thirteenth Annual Assembly of the Churches of God* (Cleveland, TN: 1917), 51-53.

[41] *Minutes of the Fourteenth Annual Assembly of the Church of God* (Cleveland, TN: 1919), 33.

[42] Ibid., 31.

[43] Roebuck, "Unraveling", 9.

saints of Nassau and the saints of America (colored) to come to the next Assembly. They are giving us a wonderful good time. The white saints love us. God bless them, but *we want to have wisdom and not cause them any trouble.*[44] (italics mine).

A report/letter from C. Sowell of Jennings, Florida describes the service designated for the black members and ministers:

The music and testimonies of the colored brothers and sisters are worthy of mention. The whole Assembly was delighted with their singing and instrumental music. They have the baptism with the Holy Ghost and the fellowship was easily felt. *They proved to be intelligent, loyal saints. One stated that he did not expect the white saints to treat him as they treated each other for him to know they loved him. He knew this without such demonstration.*[45] (italics mine).

What is clear from the accounts by Smith (black) and Sowell (white) is that there was a socialized racism in operation. Smith expresses a kind of gratitude for the inclusion of black ministers and members in the predominantly white meeting. He goes on to *warn* black constituents to use "wisdom" and not cause "trouble" for the gracious white leaders. Sowell expresses the characteristic "delight" at the musical abilities of the black participants and goes on to claim that they have "proven" themselves to be intelligent and loyal; the implication is that there was a question about their intelligence level before this assembly as well as about their loyalty. These statements, on the part of both the black and white writers, reveal that racism and paternalism were the prevalent dispositions: blacks were understood to be less intelligent and were troublemakers; black people should be grateful for the opportunities given to them by the white majority.

---

[44] *Minutes of the Fourteenth Annual Assembly*, 47.
[45] Ibid., 48.

Several other accounts from the assembly minutes are notable. Each reveals the ambiguous position of the white leadership toward the "place" of persons of color within the organizational structure. In 1920, Tomlinson's annual address to the Assembly included a plan for missionary activity among the "Spanish speaking people who are constantly flowing into the United States." The plan was to find a way to have evangelistic materials printed in Spanish, distribute these among those living in the US, "get them saved and into the Church of God" with the goal of some of them returning with the message to their native Mexico. This plan ("to get among these people, get them filled with the Holy Ghost and settled in the COG and let them go back to their native land as missionaries to their own people") could also be applied, according to Tomlinson, to the Chinese in New York City as well as the "Japanese in the west, and almost all other nationalities in the north and north-west [sic]." He cites the advice of missionaries who made the claim "that a native convert does much more good than the missionaries themselves." He concludes, "God is sending foreigners to this country for a purpose. They are coming from every nation under heaven. This reads like Pentecost when it was said, at Jerusalem there were men out of every nation under heaven." He then recommends that the assembly should approve his "plan." [46]

What is noteworthy is Tomlinson's apparent belief in the ability of the "natives" to do the work of evangelism. This position, however, is contradicted by the appointment of Carl M. Padgett, a white minister, over the Bahamas. Padgett's address to the Assembly reveals that he was unable to go to the Bahamas to oversee the work and that William R. Franks, a "native[,] has had oversight of the work under my management." [47] As had been the situation in Florida, earlier, a white minister had jurisdiction over the black churches and ministers. In the case of the Bahamas, the implication is that a white overseer who is geographically distant, is superior to the oversight of a black minister

---

[46] *Minutes of the Fifteenth Annual Assembly*, 26-27.
[47] Ibid., 46.

present in the region. Though Tomlinson had earlier stated his contention that "natives" were better equipped to evangelize their own, *oversight*, and therefore, authority, was designated to a white leader. This was a pattern that would continue in missionary activity in the COG for the majority of the next century.

The 1922 Annual Address is significant in that Tomlinson specifically spoke to the topic of the place of African Americans in the COG in a section of his address entitled, "Our Colored People." The point of the address was to deal with the apparent departure of some of the black ministers to a predominantly African American Pentecostal denomination (most likely the Church of God in Christ). Because of Jim Crow laws in effect "South of the Mason and Dixon line," Tomlinson states, "it is difficult to show them all the courtesy that we would like to." He maintains that the "purpose" of the COG was to "make them feel at home with us." Nevertheless, some black left the denomination because they were not able to "be perfectly free in every respect." This freedom included the opportunity to serve as overseers and "the privilege" of holding their state and local Assemblies. And, perhaps "General" Tomlinson's paternalistic language, "make them feel at home with us," is significant in that this statement, and his further rhetoric, implied that the white leaders owned the home, and the black constituents are "guests."[48] It is, in fact, the language of the benevolent dictator, making room for those who "act right."

Tomlinson reports that appeals have been made, and that he has written letters, "trying to encourage and console them." He maintains that despite the "courtesy" and "love" he showed to them, they were still leaving. Characteristically, Tomlinson cites Acts 15:9, "And he put no difference between purifying our hearts by faith," as scriptural warrant for having no "separations between nationalities and races." But he insists that "it is not always convenient, *neither is it best*, for

---

[48] A. J. Tomlinson, "Overseer's Annual Address," *Minutes of the Seventeenth Annual Assembly of the Church of God* (Cleveland, TN: 1922), 25.

different races to meet together regularly for worship." (italics mine). While Tomlinson maintained the rhetoric of equality based on Scripture, the prevailing cultural norm wins the day: "neither is it best, for races to meet together regularly for worship." He goes on to propose that a committee be formed and given the task of consulting with the ministers who have left the COG and authorized to "do any business required for the best interest of the church and the colored people" up to and including a separate organization with an African-American overseer "selected by them in their Assembly subject to the approval of the General Overseer." This overseer would be given the power of appointment of state overseers "in a territory where required." Tomlinson concludes such a" basis of union and fellowship" would "save to the Church of God all who are now members and bring back all who have gone away."[49]

Several days later, Thomas J. Richardson, an African American minister, was appointed over the "colored work." The notation in the *Minutes* reads: "It was decided to appoint a colored man to superintend the colored work, giving him the same authority of a state overseer."[50]

The following year, J. H. Curry of Florida addressed the Assembly on behalf of the "work with the colored people": "We have had our conflicts along with the other brethren, but have come out more than conquerors and are sticking to the Church. We feel good to be here. *When we get a little place in the building, we stick good."*[51] (italics mine). This was followed by commentary on "others" (presumably black ministers) who intended to remain loyal and the summary, "Then the colored folks sang, 'I Will Not Be Removed,' with great inspiration."[52] Again, one sees that the understanding that the African-American

---

[49] Tomlinson, 26.

[50] *Minutes of the Fifteenth Annual Assembly*, 57. Richardson was succeeded by David LaFleur in 1923. *Minutes of the Eighteenth Annual Assembly*, 45.

[51] "Call of States and Their Responses," *Minutes of the Eighteenth Annual Assembly*, 7.

[52] Ibid., 7.

ministers are less deserving has been socialized within the black community; they simply need "a little place in the building."

That same year, M. S. Lemons suggested that consideration be given to establishing an orphanage for "colored children, and that it be left with them for their consideration and to report later to the Assembly."[53] Consequently, it was reported that "the colored brethren" had given it consideration and thought they would be better served with the establishment of a Bible school for ministry training, with the orphanage to be considered at another time. The minutes read, "After viewing the subject from all angles, it was decided that the colored brethren select the place and building for their Bible School, and the Church would furnish them with a white teacher for present."[54] Again, there is a lack of parity. The black ministers were given the freedom to make a decision regarding the orphanage, deciding upon a school instead, but there is disregard for their autonomy and abilities or their particular cultural needs; a "white teacher" will be needed to prepare them for ministry.

What is apparent is that Tomlinson's Spirit-given vision, one infused with Godly love, was to be made a reality but the implementation of what was necessary for world-wide evangelism was, at this juncture, to be administered by the white male leadership. The *mission* and its implementation were all-important; it must be handled in the most expedient way. That way mirrored that of the dominant culture: "separate but equal."

Women and Ministry in the Church of God

In the earliest meetings of the COG General Assembly or "Annual Assembly" as it was called, women were full participants. Accounts of the first assemblies beginning in 1906 verify the presence

---

[53] Ibid., 43-44.
[54] Ibid., 53-54.

of women in an informally structured meeting with male leadership but no strict separation of persons based on clerical status, gender, age, or race. As the church began to formalize its meetings and organizational structure under the leadership of Tomlinson, a shift in practice with far-reaching consequences for the role of women took place. After initial affirmations of the call and gifting of women placing them in equal eldership in the COG, Tomlinson, M. S. Lemons, and other key ministers articulated biblical and pragmatic arguments for circumscribing the access of women to the decision-making process of the fledgling denomination and to local church leadership and ordained ministry.

Evidently, it appeared to early COG leaders that God was doing something special among women. Five of the eight persons who founded the COG as the "Christian Union" were women.[55] Further, the Golden Text of the Pentecostal movement —Joel 2:28—affirmed the outpouring of the Spirit on men and women. The growing presence of women who functioned as "women preachers," church leaders, and charismatically gifted tongue speakers further substantiated the need for a new view of the role of women.

Whatever factors contributed to their outlook, COG leaders expressed affirmation of women and gave visibility to their presence. Numerous references to "men and women" can be found in the Church of God Minutes and in the writings of Tomlinson.[56] Tomlinson wrote in *The Last Great Conflict*, "It is our purpose to encourage both men and women, young and old; to undertake great things for God and expect great things from God."[57] There were discussions about credentialing women as evangelists and deaconesses as early as 1908.[58]

---

[55] Tomlinson, *The Last Great Conflict*, 186.

[56] *Echoes from the General Assembly Held at Cleveland, Tennessee January 9-14, 1912* (Cleveland, TN: 1912), 14; Tomlinson, 32.

[57] Tomlinson, vii.

[58] *Original Handwritten Minutes 3rd General Assembly January 8-12, 1908 Cleveland, TN* (Cleveland, TN: 1908), 33.

Of special note is the role one woman played in affirming Tomlinson's leadership and helping him get the result he wanted in a COG Annual Assembly. Tomlinson was moderating a contentious discussion of divorce and remarriage and met resistance when he attempted to delay resolution of the issue for a later assembly. Although women were experiencing diminishment of their voice in the Annual Assembly, a "message in tongues" from a female attendee guided the resolution of the controversial matter in 1915. As the minutes of that Assembly recalls,

> Reference was made to the divorce and remarriage question and the general overseer said as the people were so equally divided, a decision could not yet be reached and the matter will be continued. He was about to read from the last year's minutes the plan under which the church had been previously working as the only method to pursue another year, when some spoke out abruptly and said they were unwilling for the question to pass this assembly without a settlement. These abrupt expressions brought a pause and a spirit was manifested to force the general overseer to a conclusion, but he insisted that he could step down and out if they wished to put someone else in the position, but as the division was so marked and equally divided he did not feel that he could take any further steps toward a decision at present. About this time the power of the Lord began to fall and a sister was lifted from her place in the congregation and on the platform behind the general overseer and threw a vail [sic] or shroud over his head and face and said, "What will you do when he is gone?" This was done by the power of the Spirit and brought a thrill of fear and fright over the entire congregation. The overseer stood trembling before the Lord awaiting results, while the congregation fell upon their faces in weeping and prayer. A few brief messages and interpretations followed.[59]

---

[59] *Minutes of the Eleventh Annual Assembly*, 20-21.

Following this demonstration, others spoke words of support for Tomlinson and his leadership was reaffirmed and the controversial "question" was left unaddressed, as he had desired. Ironically, then, two practices later deemed inappropriate in "business meetings" — a woman speaking, and a message given in tongues—helped preserve Tomlinson's power while simultaneously legitimizing his preference to defer discussion of divorce and remarriage until a later assembly.

As early as the assembly of 1908, the COG affirmed the ministry call of women to serve as men did in the diaconate. They apparently believed women served as deacons in the New Testament and affirmed them functioning according to their gifts in local churches:

Deaconesses and their duties: Discussed at some length and decided that women who are qualified and feel the call to the work as outlined in Rom. 16:2 in connection with Acts 6:3 which indicates that she is a female Deacon, therefore her work is similar to that of a Deacon, should be appointed by the Church to exercise such qualities as she is gifted with. We further recommend her as the woman mentioned in Titus 2:3-5 which duty she should exercise as directed by the Spirit. Also, she may along with the elder men, take her part of 1 Peter 5:1-4.[60]

Several important affirmations appear in this summary of the assembly discussion. First, the basis for recognition of women as deacons was for them to "feel the call to the work." While discussion of calling is correlated with scriptural texts, what is ultimately determinative is "the call." There is also affirmation of the Church appointing women to "exercise such qualities as she is gifted with." This affirms giftedness as the primary basis for appointment to ministry rather than a particular interpretation of scriptural texts. The

---

[60] *Original Handwritten Minutes,* 33.

176

sovereignty of the Spirit to lead women into and for ministry is also noted. Finally, women are authorized "with the elder men, take her part of 1 Peter 5:1-4." Interestingly, this text speaks of exercising oversight of the church and uses the primary word from which the term "bishop" is derived.

Increasing ambivalence about the differences between how the Spirit was working among women and how key leaders understood Scripture eventually led to contorted interpretations of the role of women. The tensions present were manifested in assembly discussion in 1909:

> Female ministers—Deaconesses and Evangelists. This subject was discussed, and decided that female ministers had their place in the Lord's vineyard in the days of the Apostles and must be recognized in these days, but for lack of precept or example in the New Testament for ordination the assembly advises for the present, that the wives of the deacons be considered and appointed deaconesses by virtue of the position and ordination of their husbands. The assembly advises further that the women who engage in the ministry of the Word be acknowledged by the church and supplied with a certificate or license showing date of appointment and by what church. Also, that above certificate or license be conferred to un–ordained male ministers.[61]

Clearly, the statements in 1909 represent a significant shift in perspective on the basis for the diaconate ministry of women.[62] Rather

---

[61] *Original Handwritten Minutes 4th General Assembly January 6-9, 1909 Cleveland, Tennessee*, 40.

[62] Baptists in the region had long proposed a subordinate role for women in diaconate ministry. Adoption of "Deaconess" language implied women were authorized to serve based on their husband's call and office and were

than being grounded in call, giftedness, and the leadership of the Spirit, women are now portrayed as ministering based on "the position and ordination of their husbands." Women without husbands have no affirmation for serving as deacons. What emerged, as determinative in this assembly, was a particular reading of Scripture that concluded there was a "lack of precept or example in the New Testament for ordination."

In the Annual Assembly of 1911, Tomlinson presented a list of subjects for discussion. The questions concerned basic organizational matters that were deemed to need attention as the COG struggled to define herself. The last question on Tomlinson's list concerned the role, behavior, and discipline of women: "If women are not allowed to speak in the church (1 Cor. 14) how are they to be dealt with in case of offence."[63] Women had, in Tomlinson's question, moved from being equal contributors to Pentecostal mission, ministry, and worship to being a problem calling for disciplinary action.

M. S. Lemons gave expression to the negative momentum driving a growing restriction of the role of women in the assembly the following year. He associated the leadership of women with corruptive influence in the church.

One thought here might be helpful. The government of Israel had no women judges until it began to be corrupt, and then because God

---

subordinate to male "Deacons." Charles W. Dewesse concluded: "Probably the most influential book written about Baptist deacons and deaconesses in the 1800s was R. B. C. Howell's 1846 work, *The Deaconship: Its Nature, Qualifications, Relations, Duties*. Howell, would gain even more influence through his eight-year presidency of the Southern Baptist Convention in the 1850s. He designated deacons the executive board of the church and deaconesses as their non-ordained assistants. Howell's views of deacons and deaconesses, coupled with those of the Landmark movement, helped guarantee that, for decades, churches would treat deaconesses as subordinate to deacons" (Charles W. Deweese, "Baptist Women Deacons and Deaconesses: Key Developments and Trends, 1609-2005." *Baptist History and Heritage*. Summer (2005), 3.

[63] *Original Handwritten Minutes 6th General Assembly January 3-8, 1911 Cleveland, Tennessee, 58.*

could not find a man, He had to take a woman. So, in the Church of God. The law of God forbids the women to speak, but in the meeting house she may preach, pray, and do all she can to lead souls to Christ. Not all gatherings are the church. But when they have met with the elders and business is being transacted the women must be quiet, and under no circumstance hold any important office. But if it were not for the women this old world would have gone to pieces long ago. The women need to stay humble and keep in their place and they will move the world. She doesn't need to have a big voice, but just the quiet voice of Jesus.[64]

Women are now mere substitutes for absentee men leaders and are *not* portrayed as equal participants in "business" with elders. Distinctions are drawn between gatherings for business purposes and those focusing on worship with women excluded from the former while they are allowed to "preach, pray, and do all she can to lead souls to Christ." Paternalistic statements lauding the importance of women for the world coupled with admonitions for them "to stay humble and keep in their place" evidence a growing resistance to the involvement of women in decision-making and church leadership.

Following on the heels of Lemons' presentation circumscribing the role of women in business meetings in 1912, Tomlinson articulated a fuller polemic against women being active in decision-making at any level in *The Last Great Conflict*:

Church then means government—Christ's government: His Church. Here then is where women are to keep silence: that is, they are to have no active part in the governmental affairs. (1Cor. 14:34)… There were no women speaking in the council at Jerusalem: no-one talking in tongues. They were a judicial body, searching for and applying the laws to a particular case.[65]

---

[64] *Echoes from the General Assembly Held at Cleveland, Tennessee January 9-14*, 12-13.

[65] Tomlinson, 59.

Tomlinson expressed the strange idea that the Church exists in government. He used a rather wooden way of reading Pauline texts to propose a bizarre ecclesiology that dichotomizes worship and polity or spirituality and structure. When the church meets to transact business, it is truly the church and, then, women are to be silent. Tongue speech—judged to be the *sine qua non* of Pentecostal spirituality—was deemed inappropriate for contexts where decision-making and leadership were being expressed. This line of reasoning was a convoluted way of barring women—since they could not legitimately be excluded from Pentecostal worship and experiences of the charismata. Others will follow Tomlinson's lead and began to express arguments against the participation of women in leadership and decision-making.[66]

Consequently, beginning in the assemblies as early as 1917, there is mention of the local church "Business Meeting" with admonition for members to attend. Interestingly, men and women are admonished: "Every member, both men and women, should take an interest in and make it a point to attend every business session if possible." But women are "to take no open active part in discussing or deciding questions but should always be there and silently pray to God to give wisdom and direct the men and show forth God's glory in being the glory of the men."[67]

Women are affirmed as evangelists, preachers, and recruited to serve as teachers in the COG. Illustrating the inconsistent scriptural interpretation and paternalistic approach, Tomlinson appointed Nora Chambers as "primary teacher" of the Bible Training School but named himself Superintendent.[68] Their presence is valued but they are

---

[66] M. S. Lemons, *Questions Answered*. Cleveland, TN: n.d.), 19; Homer A. Tomlinson, *Book of Doctrines: Issued in the Interest of the Church of God* (Cleveland, TN: Church of God Publishing House: 1922), 111.

[67] *Minutes of the Fifteenth Annual Assembly*, 72.

[68] Kimberly Ervin Alexander and R. Hollis Gause. *Women in Leadership: A Pentecostal Perspective* (Cleveland, TN: Center for Pentecostal Leadership and Care, 2006), 16.

restricted no later than 1920 from active involvement in leadership and decision-making. Thus, a rhetoric of affirmation is maintained in the face of the reality of negation.

Conclusions and Implications

In the COG, as in the larger Pentecostal movement, Godly love—as expressed in racial and gender equality—flourished in both intensity and extensity for only a limited time and under certain conditions. It is also apparent that the extensity of this Godly love began to founder very quickly, at least regarding race and gender.

Godly love can be said to flourish when spiritual experience transcends or transforms cultural norms in benevolent ways (such as increasing racial and gender equality) and is given precedence over limiting factors—in the cases considered, certain theological presuppositions and literalistic biblical interpretation. If interpreted through the lens of Pentecostal spiritual experience, racial and gender equality flourished. A. J. Tomlinson attended and led interracial worship services in Tennessee, Florida, and the Bahamas in the years immediately following his experience of Spirit Baptism (1908). Women spoke freely in assemblies and apparently held roles equivalent to those of men in the diaconate (1908). Clearly, the closer the Pentecostal movement was to its original spiritual impetus and core, the more Godly love found fertile ground and flourished in both intensity and extensity.

However, Godly love is impeded—at least in extensity—whenever Pentecostal spiritual experience was negated or subjugated to fundamentalist/literalist interpretations of Scripture. More importantly, the further the movement distanced itself from its original spiritual impetus and core, the more likely it was to filter spiritual experience and biblical interpretation through the sieve of dominant cultural norms. Jim Crow laws and Southern social mores held precedence over early experiences of Godly love that fostered inclusivity. Biblical interpretation, too, was shaped by these cultural norms. Further, fundamentalist and literalistic hermeneutics, normative in the region's Baptist churches that had excommunicated the early Holiness-Pentecostal constituents, were now embraced above a more dynamic hermeneutic congruent with Pentecostal experience. In effect, the dominant cultural norms became the authority.

The shift toward cultural conformity also reinforced legitimation of hierarchical structures that left power and control remained in the hands of the few. In a society where one gender and one race were understood to be in a position of superiority, polity, structure, and hermeneutics that protect that power became essential. The result was that the decision-making process and outcomes had to be controlled. In the case of gender and race, this paternalistic control comes at the expense of equality and voice. Contributing to this concentration of power at the top was the curious distinctive ecclesiology of the early COG that bifurcated worship/spirituality and business/structure. With such a bifurcation, women and persons of color could be kept in their place; they were given liberty to preach, prophesy, sing, give messages in tongues, and interpret them in worship settings. The arena of worship, however, was separate from the arena of "business," the sphere of influence and power in the COG. Extensivity, as measured by racial and gender equality, characterized Godly love in close temporal proximity to the founding spiritual experiences of the COG and Pentecostalism more generally. But it was quickly relegated to a second-tier of importance. In Sorokin's understanding, its *duration* was short-lived. This bifurcation had ongoing effects on the development of leadership, structure, and organization in the denomination and has sustained the exclusion of women and persons of color in places of power and authority.

In the final analysis, conformity to cultural norms incongruent with the spiritual experience of Pentecostals meant that this denomination abrogated its prophetic witness and identity as a counter-cultural movement. Although leaders wrestled with the tensions between the transformative cultural potential of their spirituality, a rather conventional cultural status quo shaped polity and practice. In the language of Tomlinson, the church became a place where Divine Love no longer abounded. Godly love, having originally flourished even in a larger culture of racism and misogyny, had now foundered.

Unraveling Cords that Divide: Cultural Challenges and Race Relations in the Church of God

David G. Roebuck

While conducting interviews with black ministers and members, I occasionally heard accounts of an event that occurred at a Church of God General Assembly. Although I have not located any contemporaneous document describing the episode, which likely occurred in the 1930s, the oral tradition among our black constituency continues to shape their understanding of race relations in the movement.

Mother Evelyn Gooden reported that her father witnessed the episode. According to Gooden, Bishop John Henry Curry was dancing in the Spirit during a General Assembly worship service. A Bahamian immigrant, Curry was a significant leader who served as pastor of the prominent Fifth Avenue Church of God in Fort Lauderdale, was national overseer of the "Church of God Colored Work" from 1928 to 1939, and served on the Supreme Council of the denomination from 1932 to 1938.[1] While segregated seating was common for public events in the southern United States, the incident involving Curry was unusual. "Overshadowed" by the power of the Holy Spirit, Curry was dancing and shouting when his extended arm caught the rope dividing black and white seats and pulled it down. Black worshippers recognized the event as a work of the Spirit bringing down that tangible cord of division. However, white leadership chastised Curry for violating the laws of the land. This event, the different reactions to it, and its continued telling in oral tradition illustrate some of the challenges regarding race relations in the Church of God.[2]

---

[1] Louis F. Morgan, "Bishop J.H. Curry: An Eminent Church Leader," *Church of God History and Heritage*, Winter/Spring 2003, 3-4.

[2] Evelyn Gooden and James Gooden, interview by author, Ft. Lauderdale, 25 August 2009; George Wilson and Dewey Wilson, interview by author, Kathleen, Florida, 29 August 2009; and Kimberly Marcelle Egbulonu, interview by author, West Palm Beach, 24 August 2009. Mother Gooden commented,

Although the Church of God outside the United States is racially and ethnically diverse, membership within the United States is far less so. One of the most visible examples of racial and ethnic separation is in Florida where proximity to the Caribbean Islands as well as to Central and South America facilitates arrival of people of various races, ethnicities, nationalities, and languages. In response to this diversity, the Church of God presently operates three jurisdictional offices: an office in Tampa primarily serves Caucasian congregations, another office in Tampa primarily serves Spanish-speaking congregations, and an office in Cocoa primarily serves African descent congregations. This structure illustrates the continuing challenges of race relations in the Church of God. This chapter will survey how this situation came to exist and hear black voices reflect on the history and continuation of this governmental structure.

The Florida Harvest

The ministry of the Church of God in Florida began with General Overseer A. J. Tomlinson whose 1908 Spirit-baptism experience revolutionized his evangelistic ministry. On April 29, 1909, Tomlinson boarded a train with T. L. McLain bound for Tampa. Florida became his greatest harvest field,[3] and ministry there changed the face of the Church of God from a Caucasian to a multicultural denomination and from an American network of congregations to an international movement.

After establishing a congregation in Tampa, Tomlinson visited the Pleasant Grove Camp Meeting in nearby Durant, where he preached

---

"My dad said the Holy Ghost was using him at that time. And I believe it because it is possible." Bishop Gooden reported on the reaction of the white leadership, "He was scourged very heavy about it."

[3] Tomlinson's message of restoration of the Church of God brought many independent congregations into the denomination. By January 1912, there were twenty-four congregations in Florida, ten more than the next largest number in Tennessee. See Church of God, *Echoes from the General Assembly*, (Cleveland, Tenn.: n.p., 1912), 7.

the Pentecostal message and the importance of restoring the Church of God. Ecclesiology has been foundational in the development of the Church of God, and as we have strived to restore a biblical government some have taught that we were the supreme representation of God's church. This was a primary theological emphasis of Tomlinson, and although it proved controversial, it provided a theological glue that held together black and white members during the period of segregation. Before leaving for home, Tomlinson had received 174 members and credentialed nineteen ministers including Edmond and Rebecca Barr, who were likely the first black members and ministers in the Church of God.[4] On May 31, 1909, Tomlinson licensed Edmond and Rebecca as evangelists.[5]

Edmond Bar provided the first international connection for the Church of God. Edmond had emigrated from the Bahamas to Florida

---

[4] David Michel observed that the holiness movement in general, and the Pleasant Grove Camp Meeting in particular, was more open to integration than most areas of American society. See David Michel, "The Importance of Florida for the Early Pentecostal Movement" (Selected Annual Proceedings of the Florida Conference of Historians, Vol. 12, February 2005), 102, http://fch.fiu.edu/ FCH-2005/Michel-The Importance of Florida for the Early Pentecostal Movement.htm accessed 3 January 2011. Quan Miller suggested that the Barrs were not the only black attendees at Pleasant Grove Camp. He reported Peter C. Hickson's affirmation that the Solomon family, who were instrumental in establishing the Church of God in Webster, Florida, attended. Eddie Solomon reported that his grandfather John Henry Solomon Sr. was a charter member of the church and family tradition believed it was the second or third black Church of God congregation in Florida. Quan Miller, interview by author, Clermont, Florida, 27 August 2009. Eddie Solomon, interview by author, Ft. Lauderdale, 25 August 2009.

[5] See "Church of God Record of Bishops, Evangelists, and Deacons" ledger. Dixon Pentecostal Research Center, Cleveland, Tennessee. Tomlinson's life experiences made him more open to inclusion of persons of color than many but with limitations. See Harold D. Hunter, "A Journey Toward Racial Reconciliation: Race Mixing in the Church of God of Prophecy," in *The Azusa Street Revival and Its Legacy*, ed. Harold D. Hunter and Cecil M. Robeck Jr. (Cleveland, TN: Pathway Press, 2006), 277-96; and H. Paul Thompson, Jr., "'On Account of Conditions that Seem Unalterable': A Proposal about Race Relations in the Church of God (Cleveland, TN) 1909-1929," *Pneuma: The Journal of the Society for Pentecostal Studies*, 25: 2 (Fall 2003), 240-64.

in 1893 where he met and married Rebecca. Desiring to take the Pentecostal message to his homeland, the couple travelled to Nassau in November 1909.[6] Following the accepted definition of a missionary as one who takes the gospel to another culture, Rebecca Barr became the first Church of God missionary. Robert and Ida Evans, along with Carl M. Padgett, joined them in January 1910. Their partnership represented the growing breadth of the Church of God—multinational with members from the United States and the Bahamas, multiracial with persons of European and African heritage, multigenerational with mature and young participants, and gender-inclusive with male and female ministers.[7]

The Barrs returned to Florida in 1911 and settled in Miami where they established a black congregation among Bahamians, and soon there were additional black congregations in Jacksonville, Coconut Grove, and Webster.[8] On June 4, 1912, Tomlinson wrote in

---

[6] Although many Church of God accounts consider Rebecca to have been Bahamian, she was born in Georgia. See Michael S. Swann, *The Holy Jumpers: A Concise History of the Church of God of Prophecy in the Bahamas (190-1974)* (Maitland, FL: Xulon Press, 2018).

[7] See James E. Cossey, *R. M. Evans: "The First of His Kind"* (Cleveland, TN: Pathway Press, n.d.); and Charles W. Conn, *Like A Mighty Army: A History of the Church of God, 1886-1996* [Tribute Edition] (Cleveland, TN: Pathway Press, 2008), 129-32.

[8] There was a large Bahamian population in Miami. A co-worker of the Barrs, Sampson Ellis Everett, returned to his home in Jacksonville and ministered to his family there. The Coconut Grove church was likely a Bahamian congregation as well. E. L. Simmons published the earliest history of these events in 1938. Although Simmons did not cite sources, he was a contemporary Georgian and may have been acquainted with the people involved. His tentative recollection and the lack of citations suggests a need for additional verification. See E.L Simmons, *History of the Church of God* (Cleveland, TN: Church of God Publishing House, 1938), 85. In 1954, Peter C. Hickson included a historical survey of the "Church of God Colored Work" in the minutes of the black General Assembly. For the earliest decades, he quoted from Simmons. See Peter C. Hickson, "History of the Church of God Colored Work" in *Minutes of the 30th Annual Assembly of the Church of God Colored Work* (Jacksonville: Church of God Colored Work, 1954), 10-131, especially 10-11; and Michel, "The Importance of Florida." Miller reported information on

his journal: "Held a conference meeting yesterday to consider the question of ordaining Edmond Barr (colored) and setting the colored people off to work among themselves on account of the race prejudice in the South."[9] Ordination allowed Barr to establish churches and grant ministerial credentials. In 1915, Tomlinson appointed Barr as overseer of black churches, while W. S. Caruthers served as overseer of white churches in Florida.[10] During the next two years, the numbers increased from seven to thirteen black churches and from 111 to 200 members.[11]

A Culture of Segregation

Tomlinson's 1912 journal entry regarding Barr's ordination acknowledged the deep racial divide in the early twentieth century. The evils of segregation led to separate and very unequal opportunities. Jim Crow laws excluded people of color and created difficulties for them to function in society. In the south, black Christians could not drink from the same water fountains, eat in the same restaurants, or stay in the same hotels as their white brothers and sisters—if water fountains, restaurants, and hotels were available at all. This made evangelism

---

the Coconut Grove congregation in our interview. Miller, interview. See also Swann, *Holy Jumpers*, 23-27.

[9] A. J. Tomlinson, *Diary of A. J. Tomlinson, 1901-1924* (Cleveland, TN: White Wing Publishing House, 2012), 190.

[10] The 1915 General Assembly minutes state: "Question was raised as to whether it would be best to appoint a state overseer for the colored people. After a few remarks it was decided best for the general overseer to appoint a colored man as state overseer over the colored people in Florida." Barr had previously addressed the Assembly, and the minutes report, "His few minutes talk was interesting and all enjoyed it." The minutes list Barr as state overseer of "Florida Col[ored]" comprised of seven congregations, one bishop, four deacons, seven evangelists, 111 members, and 100 persons attending five Sunday schools. See Church of God, *Minutes of the Eleventh Annual Assembly* [1915] (n.p.: n.p., n.d.), 21, 18, and 26.

[11] Church of God, *Minutes of the Thirteenth Annual Assembly* (Cleveland, Tenn.: n.p., 1917), 53.

difficult, especially when bi-vocational pastors drove long distances to the churches they served.[12]

Church of God members were not exempt from these harsh laws and customs, which remained in effect until the 1960s. Although it is tempting to discuss these conditions abstractly, they affected real people in real situations, and interviewees reported vivid memories of the harsh realities. Dewey Wilson remembered there were no school buses for children attending his all- black school.[13] Although there was a closer white school, Viola Albritton walked two and one-half miles to attend a black school. She recalled the difficulty of going shopping in downtown Jacksonville, where the J. C. Penny store had the only "decent" restrooms for black people. The trip by bus from her neighborhood to Penny's, as well visits to other downtown stores, had to be planned so that one was not too far from a needed restroom.[14] Out-of-town trips required greater care. James Gooden noted that the absence of restaurants and motels available to black travelers meant packing meals, eating by the side of the road, sleeping in cars, and discreetly relieving oneself in roadside bushes. Summarizing these restrictions Gooden lamented, "That is what we had to do in those days. We did not have any other choice. We had to live with that."[15]

While black members were welcome at Church of God General Assemblies, Jim Crow laws demanded seating designated for "colored" attendees. Conversely, when white visitors attended the black Assemblies in Florida, they sat in designated seats as well. When asked if the Church of God's acquiesce to Jim Crow laws was simple

---

[12] State overseers frequently changed pastoral appointments forcing bi-vocational pastors with good jobs such as Gooden and George Wilson to live in one city and drive long distances to their appointments. Some such as Percell Sanders Sr., who was a barber, could more easily take their job with them and relocate with a new appointment. Gooden, interview; George Wilson, interview; and Percell Sanders Sr., interview by author, Jacksonville, 31 August 2009.

[13] Dewey Wilson, interview.

[14] Viola Albritton, interview by author, Jacksonville, 31 August 2009.

[15] James Gooden, interview.

obedience to the law or prejudice in their hearts Mother Gooden responded, "They could not help it. It was both."[16]

Such laws and customs made it practical and desirable for many black persons to be part of predominantly black denominations and most denominations accommodated this reality. The Fire Baptized Holiness Church divided along racial lines in 1908, and Assemblies of God encouraged people of African descent to join the Church of God in Christ.[17] Michel noted that by 1916, 95% of black Christians belonged to black denominations.[18] Among these were the Barrs who left the Church of God and joined the Church Of God In Christ.[19]

The ecclesiology of the Church of God captured the convictions of many, however; and the influence of the Anglican Church on black Caribbean immigrants may have enabled adherence to the Church of God's commitment to restore one church. Despite racial inequalities, many black members stayed because they were loyal to "Church of God" ecclesiology[20] Evelyn Gooden reported of her father's generation, "He loved the Church. He loved the Church of God really. Then everybody did. That's the way it was. When I grew up the Church

---

[16] Segregation at the General Assembly existed at least as early as 1920 when Minutes of the Fifteenth Annual Assembly reveal a separate section for prayer. Albritton reported being turned away from seating for white attendees at the 1960 General Assembly in Memphis where ropes still divided the races, and she said the Colored Assembly in Jacksonville set aside two rows for whites. Lois Heastie reported that the "eastern side" of the Jacksonville auditorium was for whites. The discrepancy in descriptions may reflect different occasions they attended the meetings. Albritton, interview. Lois Bright Heastie, interview by author, Jacksonville, 31 August 2009; Church of God, *Minutes of the Fifteenth General Assembly* (Cleveland, Tenn.: Church of God Publishing House, 1920), 54; Evelyn Gooden, interview; and George Wilson and Dewey Wilson, interview.

[17] Estrelda Y. Alexander, *Black Fire: One Hundred Years of African American Pentecostalism* (Downers Grove: InterVarsity Press, 2011), 20-21.

[18] Michel, "Importance of Florida."

[19] Swann, *Holy Jumpers*, 27.

[20] George Wilson noted that he liked the teachings of the Church of God and that it was his life. George Wilson, interview.

of God was number one in everybody's life."[21] C. F. Bright, who later served as general secretary-treasurer for the "Church of God Colored Work" left in 1919 claiming "the colored would never be recognized with the whites." Yet, after a brief time in the Church Of God In Christ, Bright returned to the Church of God fully convinced it was God's church. Like many who stayed, his love for the Church of God along with the theological belief that they were restoring God's church fostered allegiance to the movement.[22]

Establishing the "Church of God Colored Work"

From 1917 to 1922, black churches and members served under the same state jurisdictions as white churches. Although not many black members attended the General Assembly, they were welcomed and recognized. In 1919, Tomlinson introduced the practice of black delegates having responsibility for one service at each Assembly by announcing, "We have deviated from our former practice by giving a place on the program for our colored brethren. We have recognized them and loved and fellowshipped them as brothers and sisters and members, and given them opportunity for extemporaneous utterances, but this is the first time we have given them representation on the program." Maintaining, "God is no respecter of persons," Tomlinson continued, "in some states in the United States, it is more expedient for them to have their own churches and schools separate, but when it comes to religion there is no difference, and we feel that it is right for them to be recognized in the Assembly."[23] Despite Tomlinson's assertion that there was "no boundary in the church," General Assembly services remained witnesses of deep seated segregation as

---

[21] Evelyn Gooden, interview by Roebuck.

[22] Interviewees repeated this theme. See also Trudy A. Pratt, "Building the Kingdom: Memories of Bishop Crawford F. Bright," *Church of God History and Heritage*, (Winter/Spring 2003), 2; and C. F. Bright, "Stick to the Church of God," *Church of God Evangel*, (29 March 1924), 2.

[23] Church of God, *Minutes of the Fourteenth Annual Assembly* (Cleveland, TN: Church of God Publishing House, 1919), 13.

black and white delegates sat and prayed in the segregated meeting house.

Ostensibly, because joint meetings continued to prove difficult throughout the south, black members requested their own overseer and structure. Tomlinson acknowledged the request in his 1922 General Assembly address.

> ... The time has come that some mention should be made about our colored people. There is a problem confronting us that is yet to be solved. South of the Mason and Dixon line it is difficult to show them all the courtesy that we would like to. It is our purpose to make them feel at home with us and they do in a sense, but on account of conditions that seem to be unalterable a number of them are going away from us each year. They are joining with an organization of colored people. They say they love the Church of God and would love to remain, but under the circumstances they feel better to be in a church to themselves where they can be perfectly free in every respect.[24]

In attempting to accommodate black members, the General Assembly agreed to appoint a black overseer over black churches, and the Executive Committee appointed Thomas J. Richardson over black congregations in Georgia, Kentucky, North Carolina, Virginia, West Virginia, and Florida.[25]

Challenges remained for black advancement, however; and in 1926, black ministers requested that the General Assembly find a way to "better take care of our affairs among the colored work." Not willing to acknowledge the possibility of a separate denomination, the

---

[24] A. J. Tomlinson, "Overseer's Annual Address," in Church of God, *Minutes of the Seventeenth Annual Assembly* (Cleveland, TN: Church of God Publishing House, 1922), 25.

[25] Church of God, *Minutes of the Seventeenth Annual Assembly*, 49 and 57.

Assembly agreed, "that the colored people be allowed to have a colored Assembly and they still are and shall be recognized as the Church of God, and that we all belong to the body of Jesus (the Church of God). Neither shall it be construed that they are a body separate and apart from the General Annual Assembly of the Churches of God, therefore the General Secretary and Treasurer shall have charge of their tithes to be used exclusively for them." The Assembly also agreed that black churches should be able to promote their orphanage in the *Church of God Evangel*, should be able to select their own general overseer, and "attend to their own business."[26] Over the next four decades, black churches developed a structure referred to as the "Church of God Colored Work." Congregations created a national office and built an Assembly Auditorium in Jacksonville, selected national leaders, appointed state overseers, and constructed an orphanage and industrial school in Eustis, Florida.

Ethnic and National Tensions

Beginning in 1958, the Church of God appointed white overseers to supervise the "Church of God Colored Work." J. T. Roberts served as national overseer from 1958 to 1965, and David Lemons served from 1965 to 1966. Roberts was a fiery preacher who had been a national evangelist and state overseer in Florida and Alabama. Lemons was the son of pioneer M. S. Lemons and considered a kind and gentle man. Those who knew them testify that they did good work. Roberts' construction experience facilitated several new church buildings.[27]

---

[26] Church of God, *Minutes of the Twenty-First Annual Assembly* (Cleveland, TN: Church of God Publishing House, 1926), 38-39. The next year a committee presented the recommendation that, "We, the bishops of the Colored Work present at the Assembly have agreed that our work shall continue as it was before the action of the 21st Annual Assembly, with a colored overseer to supervise the colored work." This allowed northern black congregations to choose to remain under white state overseers rather than the "Church of God Colored Work." See Church of God, *Minutes of the Twenty-Second Annual Assembly* (Cleveland, TN: Church of God Publishing House, 1927), 39.

[27] James Gooden, interview; and Sanders, interview.

Yet, the question must be asked, why did the Church of God appoint white overseers to lead the "Church of God Colored Work," especially as the Civil Rights Movement was gaining momentum? Some suggested denominational leadership selected a white national overseer because black leadership could not agree on an overseer.[28] Others believed white leadership would improve growth. James Gooden reported that, "[b]lack ministers were not advancing like we thought we should have. I don't know if it was due to a lack of vision or what. I think headquarters thought the same. Headquarters decided to give us a different leader... We did not know why. But we said we would wait and see how it works out."[29]

Charles Conn assessed race relations during the period of the "Church of God Colored Work" with the observation that there was little contact between white and black congregations other than the General Assembly. He wrote, "The Executive Committee and Supreme Council gave occasional consideration to ways of increasing black growth and involvement in general church outreach. Ironically, that concern led to miscalculations and tension that were painful to both blacks and whites. In the setting of that period, answers were difficult to find, or they were typically superficial. In many ways the Church of God reflected the national frustration and inertia of the times." Conn continued, "… it was felt by some that a more vigorous evangelistic leadership would be helpful to the black work. However benign that consideration may have been, its consequence was painful."[30]

David Michel noted the significance of ethnic and national tensions among people of African descent in American society and in the Church of God, and several interviewees suggested that the Executive Committee appointed white overseers in part to mitigate

---

[28] George Wilson and Dewey Wilson.
[29] James Gooden, interview.
[30] Conn, *Like a Mighty Army*, 377.

Bahamian dominance in the "Church of God Colored Work."[31] Most early growth in the Church of God was among Bahamian immigrants, especially in the lower half of Florida,[32] and many national overseers were Bahamian.[33] Mother Gooden, the daughter of Bahamian immigrants, reported fights in public schools during her childhood between immigrant and US-born children over who was or was not American. She believed that with their chronological primacy in the Church of God, Bahamians expected privilege in leadership and teaching roles. Not being from Florida, Bishop Gooden described the culture in south Florida as very different from that of South Carolina and Ohio where American-born black persons were the majority. He reported, "The Bahamian culture dominated everything [in Florida]. So, I either had to accept it or pull away. And I certainly was not going to pull away because I gave my life to the Lord, and I chose this church as my church. So, I made up my mind to adapt to whatever I came into contact with."[34] A connected issue was how the Church of God's white constituency might have related differently to immigrants and non-immigrants. Miller, whose family was Bahamian, acknowledged that black Americans believe they experience more prejudice in the Church of God than do Caribbean or Africa immigrants.[35]

---

[31] Michel, "Importance of Florida."

[32] The Goodens reported that due to the proximity between the Bahamas and south Florida, Bahamians tended to settle on the east coast and south of Daytona. Black persons living in Florida north of Daytona tended to be American born from southern states such as Georgia, Alabama, and Mississippi. Goodens, interview.

[33] The Goodens included David LaFleur, J. H. Curry, N. S. Marcelle, and George Wallace, but not W. L. Ford. They were uncertain about Richardson. James and Evelyn Gooden, interview. The Bahamian influence did not end with the dissolution of the "Church of God Colored Work." For example, the family of Bishop Quan Miller, who served as Florida state overseer from 1990 to 2002 was from the Bahamas. Quan Miller, interview. State Overseer C. C. Pratt was born in the Bahamas, and Sanders reported that other state overseers with Bahamian roots included Walter Jackson, and W. C. Menendez. Sanders, interview; and Pratt, interview.

[34] Goodens, interview.

[35] Miller, interview.

Viola Albritton, who served as J. T. Roberts' secretary, stated that Bahamians had a monopoly on the bishopric and Roberts intentionally ordained other qualified men to dissipate that monopoly.[36] Percell Sanders Sr. affirmed that few black men were ordained before Roberts.[37]

From "Colored Work" to "Cocoa Office"

Despite Roberts and Lemons being good leaders, many considered their appointments regressive, and black ministers eventually called for change. Conn, who served on the Executive Committee at that time, wrote, "It was considered an affront to African-American ability that they must be directly supervised by white leadership. There was no question of their loyalty to the Church of God, for many of them had been a part of the church longer than most white members. They simply wanted African-American leadership of their endeavors, an understandable desire."[38]

Growing dissatisfaction with white leadership and changes in American culture pushed the Church of God toward integration. The General Assembly passed a "Resolution on Human Rights" in 1964 and dissolved the "Church of God Colored Work" in 1966. Yet, changes some viewed as a victory for equality others regarded as a loss. With the dissolution of the "Colored Work," most black ministers who were serving as state overseers, youth directors, evangelism directors, and state council members lost their positions. They became a minority in a white jurisdiction shaped by historical prejudices. Fewer opportunities and a perceived lack of white consultation with black leaders led many to question their place in the Church of God.[39]

---

[36] Albritton, interview.

[37] Sanders' father was among those Roberts ordained. Sanders also stated that many of those who left the Church of God when integration occurred in 1966 were Bahamians. If this is correct, some of the defections may have been about losing power among black communities. Sanders, interview.

[38] Conn, *Like a Mighty Army*, 378.

[39] James Gooden, interview. For a more complete discussion of factors leading to integration, see Mickey Crews, *The Church of God: A Social History* (Knoxville: The University of Tennessee Press, 1990), 163-72.

The largest number of black congregations were in Florida, and black ministers there implored the Executive Committee to appoint a black overseer for black churches in Florida—in effect returning to the days of Edmond Barr with white and black overseers.[40] The Executive Committee acquiesced and appointed Walter Jackson as state overseer. This action was too little for some who left the Church of God to establish a separate denomination using the name "National Church of God" with offices in Ft. Lauderdale.[41] For those remaining, the former national office in Jacksonville served as the state office until they purchased property in Cocoa in 1978.[42] Today, the office in Cocoa serves most of the black congregations in Florida. Black congregations in other regions throughout the United States work under their regional jurisdictions.[43]

Following integration, the Executive Committee appointed H. G. Poitier as a black liaison officer in Cleveland. A well-respected leader, Poitier increased communication, worked to resolved problems, influenced some ministers not to defect, and represented the denomination in property disputes. Civil Rights legislation and Church of God integration did not immediately change hearts, however. Poitier's appointment did not come with an office in the headquarters building. Nor did it negate the fact racism limited the neighborhoods in which his family could reside and motivated multiple death threats in the town many Church of God people euphemistically call the "Holy City."[44]

---

[40] George Wilson and Dewey Wilson, interview; and James Gooden, interview.

[41] James Gooden, interview; and Beatrice Davis Marcelle, interview by author, West Palm Beach, 24 August 2009. Gooden was on the black National Council that made the request.

[42] C. C. Pratt, interview by author, Cocoa, Florida, 8 October 2008.

[43] Joseph E. Jackson, *Reclaiming Our Heritage: The Search for Black History in the Church of God* (Cleveland, TN: Church of God Black Ministries, 1993), 14-15. C. C. Daniels continued to serve as black overseer of black churches in Mississippi for a brief period.

[44] Xenobia Anderson and Treva Culpepper, interview by author, Virginia Beach, Virginia, 30 July 2005; and Clinton Culpepper and Treva Culpepper,

Outside of Florida, there continued to be few black leaders. In 1978, the Church of God created the position of Southeastern Regional Evangelism Director and appointed Wallace J. Sibley Sr. His responsibilities emphasized evangelism among black populations of Mississippi, Alabama, North Carolina, North Georgia, South Georgia, and Tennessee. This position expanded to Evangelism Director with national responsibilities in 1983, and C. C. Pratt served until 1992. With the appointment of Joseph Jackson, the position became Director of Black Ministries. In 2010, Church of God International Offices made numerous personnel reductions and added other responsibilities to the Director of Black Ministries. With growing discontent with a "Black Ministries" office on the national level, the office was renamed Intercultural Advancement Ministries in 2018.[45]

Symbol and Opportunities

Although black ministers in Florida requested separate state offices as a solution to perceived diminishing opportunities in 1966, the support for this structure has not been uniform nor remained static. Some continue to see the separate jurisdiction as a necessary antidote to complete subjugation,[46] but many no longer see a need for jurisdictions based on race. Clinton and Treva Culpepper lamented that separate jurisdictions in Florida keep black and white members and ministers from fellowshipping with one another.[47] Eddie Solomon conveyed that while older ministers may prefer the Cocoa office for opportunities and support, younger ministers are weary of explaining

---

interview by author, Ft. Lauderdale, 24 August 2009. Anderson and Treva Culpepper are daughters of Poitier and reported the difficulties of not being able to live near other Church of God officials along with death threats made to their family.

[45] Jackson, *Reclaiming Our Heritage*, 44. For a survey of the development of Church of God Black Ministries see David Michel, *Telling the Story: Black Pentecostals in the Church of God* (Cleveland: TN: Pathway Press, 2000.

[46] Egbulonu, interview.

[47] Clinton Culpepper and Treva Culpepper, interview.

segregated ministry.[48] Quan Miller added that young ministers view segregation in Florida as an attempt by white leadership to maintain control, and many black youths see membership in the Church of God as a stigma. As a result, the Church of God continues to lose young black ministers—especially to the Church of God in Christ. Despite concern about the negative symbolism of a separate black jurisdiction, Miller reported ongoing fear by some that if the Cocoa jurisdiction is dissolved, black ministers may lose leadership opportunities. According to Miller, black members of the Church of God continue to ask, "Where are black leaders?"[49]

Of course, the Cocoa jurisdiction is not the only symbol that matters. Many perceive the 2008 elections of Wallace Sibley as secretary general of the Church of God[50] and Barack Obama as president of the United States as positive and hopeful signs in church and society. Pastor Kimberly Egbulonu regarded the election of an African American president as opening possibilities. With increasing comfort as a black, female pastor she affirmed, "Today the sky is the limit." While issues of segregation once caused feelings of exclusion and reduced participation in the Church of God, she no longer viewed the Cocoa office nor the history of American slavery and segregation as obstacles to her ministry. Yet, she supported integration of the Church of God in Florida as both a necessary change to move forward and a symbolic recognition that blacks can lead. She hoped the Church of God would move beyond the fear of talking about racial issues so we might resolve them. Yet, for Egbulonu, moving beyond does not mean forgetting the past. She expressed a desire to see acknowledgement of the "labor, blood, sweat and tears" of black pioneers and recommended a museum, video, named buildings, and scholarships as fitting honors for black forebears. Finally, she proposed that a voting system designed to enfranchise those unable to

---

[48] Solomon, interview.

[49] Miller, interview.

[50] Miller, interview; Egbulonu, interview.

travel to the United States to attend General Assemblies would change the landscape and color of Church of God leadership.

Conclusion

What conclusions can we draw from a brief historical survey of the development of segregated ministries in the Church of God? It can no longer depend on allegiance to theologies of church, government, and authority as a significant bond of unity, and a predominantly white-led denomination must articulate other reasons for unity of the body. Differences of language, nationality, ethnicity, regionalism, and culture influence human relations of all races, and any hope of healing our continuing divisions demands hearing a variety of voices from diverse backgrounds.

Opinions vary regarding continuing a separate jurisdiction for black congregations in Florida. Yet, behind the symbolism of the Cocoa office is the hope of black members that leadership opportunities will be available. With or without the Cocoa office, the Church of God must find ways to signal that such opportunities are and will be forthcoming.

A review of the history of race relations in the Church of God should provoke questions about our faithfulness to the Bible and to the leading of the Holy Spirit. Too often, we read the Bible on issues of race through the lens of southern culture rather than with Spirit-led discernment, and our blind loyalty to unjust laws precluded prophetic voices against the injustices of racism.[51]

The temptation with all human endeavors is to ask for both forgiveness and forgetfulness in an effort to move beyond the ugly realities of the past. Yet, as William Faulkner's character, Gavin Stevens, understood in *Requiem for a Nun*, "[t]he past is never dead. It

---

[51] Some Church of God leaders attributed the growing unrest generated by the Civil Rights Movement to be the result of Devil-inspired Communism seeking to provoke civil war. Others argued that segregation was God ordained to prevent mixing of the races, and attempts to dismantle segregation defied God's law. Crews, *The Church of God*, 163-65.

is not even past." Our past continues to shape our self-understanding, our decision-making, and our relationships. Regarding race, the Church of God should acknowledge our past and honor those black women and men who have labored in our vineyard.

The story of J. H. Curry pulling down the dividing cord of segregation at a Church of General Assembly remains a powerful symbol in the heritage of black members, while it is virtually unknown among our white majority. Perhaps hearing this story and discussing our differing interpretations may enable us to move forward in meeting the ongoing challenges of race relations in the Church of God and American culture.

Bridging the Divide: The Racial Ecclesiology of the Church of God

Bradley D. Ramsey

Introduction

Discussion of the racial separation in one of the largest Pentecostal organizations in the world must begin with an understanding of a racialized ecclesiology and polity that gave way to such separation. The division of the Church of God in Florida along racial lines occurred in the early twentieth century as the denomination began expanding throughout the American South. As we examine the ecclesiology and polity of this classical Pentecostal denomination, we can discover and dissect how the issue of race continues to divide the denomination in the "Sunshine State." This work aims to give a clearer picture of the history, context, and social/ecclesiastical paradigms of this continuing racial separation.

Florida has and always will be at the heart of the racial struggle in the Church of God. From its beginning, with the appointment of Edmond Barr, it has been the beacon of black leadership within the denomination. Most of its black leaders have either come from, or have moved to, Florida during their ministerial career. Therefore, any attempt to deal with racial separation must directly engage the black church in Florida, as the last iron curtain of segregation in the church. What is surprising is that the two groups still exist as separate operational units while other states have integrated since the civil rights era.

This essay explores the rise in social nuances driving such division and why it is still occurring in the 21st century. Finally, it offers suggestions for a way forward for addressing the issue in Florida and a path toward unity and renewed fellowship.

Social Context

Segregated churches were a part of a broader sphere of racism known as "Jim Crow"—a set of strictly enforced policies that severely discriminated against American blacks in virtually all aspects of their lives. Church traditions were as much a part of that system as sharecropping, job discrimination, restricted voting rights, mandatory segregation on public transportation, racial divisions in dining establishments and lynching. However, it was not so much discriminatory 'separateness' that vexed black members of the Church of God as the principle of legal segregation and the denial of ministry promotion and funds that accompanied it. The primary concern of voluntary segregation was to advance the black work and its voice within the Church, not to separate blacks from whites. Blacks approved of and favored the potential for maintaining the cultural identity of their community that segregation fostered. However, they disliked being treated as second-rate members and having no representation at higher levels of the church.

Since the advent of "praise houses" on plantations in which slaves worshipped and held services, the black preacher has exhorted, instructed, and guided the community.[1] Segregation—whether voluntary or imposed—fostered solidarity and black leadership. Since Reconstruction, black preachers served as community leaders, organizers, diplomats, surrogates, and the voice of blacks.

The Church had always functioned as the institutional, emotional, spiritual, and social anchor of black American life. Further, the black Church functioned as a training ground for black leadership that provided a launching pad for leaders such as Martin Luther King Jr., Rev. Jesse Jackson, and Ralph David Abernathy. This was just as true before, during, and after segregation.

When the late 1960s brought about the integration of schools and public spaces, black ministers and church members in Florida were

---

[1] "Praise House," The New Georgia Encyclopedia.
http://www.georgiaencyclopedia.org/nge/Multimedia. jsp?id=m-8797# (retrieved April 2009).

ambivalent.[2] On the one hand, they welcomed the removal of Jim Crow laws, but on the other, they were reluctant to relinquish the freedom and control they had experienced with ownership of their own work. Imagine the diminishing of power for the black preacher and church within their own community. The psychological ramifications would be great. The discontinuation of the black-led and black-operated Church would drastically alter the position of the preacher in the community.

Integration would undermine those functions and diminish the relative status of black preachers. The greatest obstacle to integration is the fear of the loss of identity. Far greater than their white counterparts, black preachers had identified with their communities. Since black ministers were seldom if ever considered for promotion to higher levels of the church hierarchy, they remained in leadership positions at their local churches for much longer than the average white minister. This long tenure and the social function performed by such black preachers gave them deeper ties to their congregation and community. Although segregation provided them fewer resources, black preachers compensated for poor buildings, inadequate equipment, and lack of funds with hard work. In the eyes of the community, black churches owed their existence and progress to the vision and sacrifice of black preachers.

Black Congregations Within The Church Of God: Florida

In Florida, The Church of God is comprised of two separate communities under one denominational framework. While Conn's authoritative history, *Like a Mighty Army*, references the story, in-depth investigations of the separation of the white and black constituencies are found in *Reclaiming our Heritage: The Search for Black History in the Church of God* by Joseph E. Jackson and David Michel's *Telling the Story:*

---

[2] The reversal of practices of segregation resulted from the historic Brown vs. the Board of Education Supreme Court decision which found racial segregation illegal.

Black Pentecostals in the Church of God.[3] While Michel's work is largely biographical, it recounts the circumstances of the separation, Jackson's work looks closely at the neglected history of black people in the Church of God and examines racial separation.

An examination of the Church of God in Florida is indispensable for understanding how whites and blacks interacted and coexisted during the nineteenth and twentieth centuries. Unless the narrative is told in full, including the origins of the separation and the emergence of the black church in the early twentieth century, the reason for black ambivalence over integration may seem unclear. This narrative includes how the black church in Florida came into being and coped with the challenges of racism and prejudice. It also speaks to the Church of God's history of race relations and the untold story of the 1966 racial split in Florida. Though Bahamians would figure prominently in the denomination's early history in the state, the black church there also includes African Americans, Jamaicans, and Haitians.

Separation was not wholly the creation of white racism, and was, at least partially, black-initiated because many blacks preferred to be led by members of their own community, even on the district and state levels of the church. Church government is deeply political, and in the American South, ever-present and sometimes-violence politics was linked with church governance so that black ministers were always on the front lines in battles over leadership.

The obvious difference between white and black ministers is that the latter had fewer resources and were treated as second class in both

---

[3] See Joseph E. Jackson, *Reclaiming our Heritage: The Search for Black History in the Church of God* (Cleveland, TN: Church of God Black Ministries, 1993). David Michel's *Telling the Story: Black Pentecostals in the Church of God.* (Cleveland, TN: Pathway Press, 2000) Other substantial works that deal with the Church of God include Charles W. Conn, *Like A Mighty Army: A History of the Church of God 1886-1976.* Cleveland, TN: Pathway Press, 1977; Mickey Crews, *The Church of God: A Social History* (Knoxville: The University of Tennessee Press, 1993); and R. David Muir, *Black Theology, Pentecostalism, and Racial Struggles in the Church of God.* PhD. Dissertation University of London: King's College, 2003.)

society and church. Conn asserted that whatever difficulty white preachers faced, black preachers had it doubled. However, a history concerned solely with the material disparities between the white and black Church of God congregations in Florida would fail to reveal how black ministers in the denomination played a role as leaders in their communities.

The Beginning of Racial Separation

The black work began almost simultaneously with the white work in Florida with Barr at the forefront. This work was the first ground broken for the Church of God in the black community. Its earliest members and ministers were Bahamians and African Americans.

Barr, along with R.M. Evans, was part of the first missionary venture of the Church of God.[4] In 1909-1910, the team went to Barr's native home, the Bahamas, preaching salvation and the Pentecostal message.[5] The first meetings of the missionaries were held in Nassau. In 1910, as overseer, Evans worked with Barr to set forth two congregations on the island of New Providence.[6] In 1911, A.J. Tomlinson arrived in the Bahamas and joined the group visiting Exuma, Long Island and Ragged Island.

By 1912, there were three black congregations in Florida: Jacksonville, Miami, and Coconut Grove.[7] However, according to his diary, Tomlinson questioned himself about ordaining Barr as the first black minister and segregating the young work. He wrote:

Held a conference meeting yesterday to consider the question of ordaining Edmond Barr (colored) and setting the colored people off to work among themselves on account of the race prejudice in the South.[8]

---

[4] Conn, Like A Mighty Army, 132-133
[5] Ibid., 132.
[6] Michael Swann, The Holy Jumpers (s.l.: Xulon Press, 2018), 28.
[7] Ibid., 133.
[8] Harold Hunter, A Journey Toward Racial Reconciliation, 285.

This was the first mention of segregation between the black and white churches and the racial problem seemed to begin with the birth of the Church of God in Florida. In the American South, the birth and growth of American Pentecostalism coincided with the intensely difficult racial climate of American culture. Therefore, when blacks and whites entered Pentecostalism, they bought with them social attitudes of the day. Barr's 1912 ordination as Bishop and 1915 appointment as Overseer of the black work in Florida was the first act of racial separation in the Church of God.[9]

There are two types of separation that have historically taken place in both Church and society—voluntary and involuntary. Examples of voluntary separation include the African Methodist Episcopal Church, which in 1816, was born in protest to racism and oppression of black people.[10] This break occurred over sociological differences rather than theological ones. A second example would be historically black colleges that developed around the 1850s, the first being Lincoln University (Pennsylvania), whose purpose was to serve and educate black Americans. These educational institutions resulted from the exclusion of black students from predominately white higher educational systems.

Most voluntary separation of the black communities, whether educational, corporate, or ecclesiastical, has been in response to the existing social climate that excluded blacks from participation in many realms of American life. Therefore, blacks developed living spaces for the progress and maintenance of their own communities. The church was no different. Historically, involuntary separation of American society has often been affirmed by laws created to justify and uphold such injustice. Examples of involuntary separation include segregated public and private schools, restaurants, theatres, and transit. Such was

---

[9] Ibid.

[10] James H. Cone, "God Our Father, Christ Our Redeemer, Man Our Brother: A Theological Interpretation of the AME Church." *AME Church Review*, CVI:341 (1991), 25.

the psychology of inferiority that when blacks entered churches, they were directed to a separate section. Further, participation in the liturgy was limited or non-existent.

Tomlinson's 1915 appointment of Barr created an involuntary form of segregation. Hunter reveals that according to Tomlinson's diary, because of the racial climate in Florida, he wanted to appoint a leader for the black work before the separation occurred and even before Barr's ordination, he was the most likely candidate for the assignment. Nothing in Tomlinson's diary suggests that the blacks in Florida either asked or wanted separation.[11]

It might have been inevitable for such separation to take place due to the sociology and psychology of the time. However, there is no evidence to suggest anyone involved in the black work of 1915 approached the leadership about being separate, as they did at the 1926 General Assembly.[12] Clearly, the initial racial separation was involuntary, and imposed by the church's leadership. Twenty-nine years after its initial formation as the Christian Union, racial separation was already playing a role in the Church's practice and polity.

After only two years in office, Barr was removed as Overseer and the black churches came under a white minister, Sam C. Perry, as overseer of the entire state.[13] While little information exists to adequately explain Barr's removal, Hunter sheds light on it by noting, that "[m]inisterial records... dispel the notion that racial prejudice removed Barr from office."[14] Those same records, kept private until now, indicated that Barr was removed based on charges of sexual infidelity and moral misconduct. Barr insisted, however, that he was innocent and no formal charges were ever brought against him, nor

---

[11] Hunter, 285 (As recorded in Tomlinson's diary, "A. J. Tomlinson, diary, vol. 2, June 4, 1912, Manuscripts Division, Library of Congress, Washington, DC).

[12] Conn refers to a group of black ministers approaching the General Assembly asking for their own assembly; see *Like A Mighty Army*, 199-200.

[13] Peter C. Hickson, *History of the Church of God Coloured Work*, (Cleveland, TN: Church of God Black Ministries, 1968).

[14] Hunter, *A Journey Toward Racial Reconciliation*, 285.

did church leadership take action regarding these charges. In any case, a once-prominent figure in the Florida Church of God suddenly vanished from the scene and there is no mention of Barr's activity with the Church of God after that time.

Though again, Barr was the only likely candidate for the position and Tomlinson had him in mind as Overseer before his ordination. On his departure, he was not replaced by another black minister, but instead, the work was now under the leadership of a white minister. Three years later, in 1919, however C. F, Bright, a black minister was placed as Overseer of Pennsylvania in and subsequently as Overseer in New Jersey in 1920.[15]

Because the black work in the Church of God grew, in 1922, T. J. Richardson, a favorite of Tomlinson, was appointed as the first National Overseer of the black work.[16] He held this position for one year, but left the Church in the infamous split when Tomlinson was ousted and subsequently, established the Church of God of Prophecy.[17] Following their departure, David La Fleur a credentialed black minister was appointed overseer.[18]

The first Florida convention seems to be in 1925 with the decision by the General Assembly to sanction separate meetings following in 1926. Notably, Iain MacRobert, contends that, organizing a separate black assembly extended the apartheid which already existed in that state to the whole organization.[19] This step moved the line of racial separation from Florida to the rest of the Church of God.

Florida would play a prominent role in the black work and broader affairs of the denomination in the United States. The black work began there, all the denomination's black congregations were there for several years, and from its inception, the Office of the National Overseer of

---

[15] Ibid., 285.

[16] Ibid., 287.

[17] Ibid.

[18] Hickson, *History of the Church of God Coloured Work.*

[19] Iain MacRobert, *The Black Roots and White Racism of Early Pentecostalism in the USA*, (Eugene, OR: Wipf and Stock, 2003). 67.

the black work was there and the early overseers of the work came from the state. The only exception was W. L. Ford, from Evergreen, Alabama who moved to Jacksonville upon his appointment.[20] The duty of the National Overseer of the Colored Work was to appoint State Overseers in states where there was a strong African American presence. Florida would receive the bulk of his attention since his office was there; and again, the majority of the black membership was there. [21]

An Attempt at Racial Integration

Perhaps the biggest moment of reckoning for the Church of God regarding racial separation occurred in 1966, 40 years after the General Assembly officially divided the church. While the divide occurred much earlier with Barr's 1915 appointment, the 1926 development of the National Black Assembly formalized the separation.

It cannot be ignored that the Church of God is a product of its southern heritage, with its inception taking place in the mountains of Monroe County, Tennessee. The unrest of the Civil Rights Era, beginning about 1955, set the stage for conscientious change within a Holiness Pentecostal church that was still deeply anchored in the American South. With most of its membership in Georgia, Tennessee, Florida, Alabama, and North Carolina, and its general headquarters in Cleveland, TN, the Church of God knew all too well the social injustices and deprivation that plagued its black constituency.

With the advent of the civil rights movement in an atmosphere of societal reform, institutions, including schools and churches, could not help but be influenced by the fight for equality by black Americans. The movement provided the necessary boldness for blacks in

---

[20] Please see Hickson's "*History of the Church of God Coloured Work,*" which chronicles the Black National Overseers of the Black National work.

[21] E.L. Simmons, *History of the Church of God* (Cleveland, TN: Church of God Publishing House, 1938), 85-88.

organizations like the Church of God to speak out against the degradation they had experienced.

One must wonder what would have happened if the national movement had not provoked thought and action against segregation and inequality. Would the Church of God still have instituted a civil rights measure? Interestingly, the Church inaugurated the measure in 1964 at the zenith of the civil rights era. Their action coincided with the 1964 Civil Rights Acts created by John F. Kennedy since the church could not ignore the steps taken by society to correct its wrongs.

The consciousness of human rights had been sparked and the church issued its "Resolution on Human Rights," that recognized the dignity and worth of every individual.[22] and asserted that,

> no American should, because of his race or religion, be deprived of his right to worship, vote, rest, eat, sleep, be educated, live and work on the same basis as other citizens."[23]

The rhetoric of the measure was noble, but no concrete action was taken until two years later with the disseverment of the Black National Assembly.

The leadership moved from rhetoric to action at the 1966 Assembly when it eliminated the separation of ethnic or racial groups in the Church of God and banned references to race or color from Church of God records, and as Conn writes "all racial barriers broken down."[24] While these actions integrated most of the black churches back into the general body, the notable exception was the black churches in Florida, which constituted the overwhelming majority of the black constituency in the denomination.

---

[22] Conn, *Like A Mighty Army,* 352-353.
[23] Ibid.
[24] Ibid.

The human rights measure was a noble endeavor, but fell short of addressing the problem of separation. With the further measure of dissolving the Black National Assembly and the position of Black National Overseer the black churches in Florida remained separated under their own overseer. Moreover, these black churches still consist of most of the denomination's black constituency. With this, failure to resolve racial separation in Florida remains a failure to resolve the issue of separation in the Church of God.

Separation Remains

Florida has and always will be at the heart of the racial struggle in the Church of God in the United States. From its beginning, it has been the trailblazer and beacon of black leadership within the denomination. Since the appointment of Barr, every major black leader on the general level in the Church of God has either come from Florida or been assigned there at some point. Therefore, any measure to deal with racial separation must directly engage the black church in Florida, as it stands as the last bastion of segregation in the church.

Since 1966, nothing has been done to materially improve the church's racial trajectory. Blacks continued to sit in the balcony sections at General Assemblies with little or no participation in the leadership structures and whites continue to maintain power and control of the church.

From 1966, the office of the National Black Overseer and the National Black Assembly ceased to function as the denomination attempted to re-integrate the black churches back into the community of faith on terms acceptable to its white constituents. However, this paradigm left the black churches in Florida under their own leadership and out of the process.

One must question, however why Florida-Cocoa did not re-integrate with the rest of the church following the 1964 human rights measure? This is still a pressing issue for the Church of God, which, after 90 years, is still experiencing the effects of separation between the white and black churches.

A Racial Split

While there has been talk about "race and race relations" in the Church of God and the separation of racial groups, namely, blacks and whites, nothing has been said about an ecclesiastical and social split behind the "middle wall of partition" as named by A. J. Tomlinson in a previous address to the General Assembly.[25] Yet the split, a result of the ideological and social "middle wall of partition" seems to be radical, defying the prevailing thought that even in the climate of heightened racial indifference, blacks remained loyal to the Church of God.

H. Paul Thompson questions whether "segregation and discrimination were both so intrinsic to and explicit in the southern religious-cultural ethos, [that] if every other Pentecostal group completely divided, why not the Church of God too?"[26] He further asks, "[i]f racism and discrimination were an issue, why did blacks not completely leave the denomination and form their own?"[27] The framing of such questions demonstrate the view that the Church of God managed to escape the "unalterable conditions" of social norms that caused other Pentecostal denominations to split along race lines.

While the Church of God did not experience a large withdrawal of black churches on a national level, the withdrawal of churches in

---

[25] Roger G. Robins, "A.J. Tomlinson: "Plainfolk Modernist"," in James R. Goff Jr. and Grant Wacker, eds. *Portraits of a Generation: Early Pentecostal Leaders*. (Fayetteville: University of Arkansas Press, 2002), 227. Also see Harold D. Hunter, A Journey toward Racial Reconciliation: Race Mixing in the Church of God of Prophecy in Cecil M. Robeck and Harold Hunter, eds. *The Azusa Street Revival and Its Legacy* (Eugene, OR: Wipf and Stock Publishers, 2009). 294-296.

[26] H. Paul Thompson, "On Account of Conditions that Seem Unalterable: A Proposal about Race Relations in the Church of God (Cleveland, TN) 1909-1929" *Pneuma: The Journal of the Society for Pentecostal Studies*, 25:2 (Fall 2003), 240–264.

[27] Ibid.

Florida was significant enough that a court battle ensued over church property and the issue has since been deemed sealed and classified by the General Offices in Cleveland, TN.[28] The revealing of the split in Florida also respectfully challenges the notions of Mickey Crews as stated by Randall J. Stephens that blacks were given opportunities to serve in leadership positions they would not have had within traditional denominations.[29] Thompson seems to contradict this view, by asserting that:

> The minutes document the absence of blacks from the Council of Twelve [Elders]... quickly became the most powerful governing body in the Church—and it was all white. This probably sent the message that although they were good enough to pastor black churches, blacks were not good enough to exercise significant authority over whites.[30]

The split in many ways reflects the discontentment among blacks in Florida over being excluded from the governing process of the Church, yet, while contributing financial support to the well-being of the organization. This discontentment rests at the heart of the 1926 racial split. Moreover, when the governing body decided to dissolve the offices and department of the "National Colored Work," tensions rose and the inevitable occurred.

---

[28] The court case that resulted from the split took place at the Circuit Court of the 17th Judicial Circuit in Broward County, Florida; it was the case, Reverend Walter Jackson (State Overseer for the Church of God General Assembly and State of Florida) vs. Reverend John B. Ferguson, Reverend J. Z. Smith and Church of God Coloured Work, Inc., 1968.

[29] Randall J. Stephens', *Assessing the Roots of Pentecostalism: A Historiographic Essay.* http://are.as.wvu.edu/pentroot.htm, *retrieved* August 14, 2009.

[30] Thompson, *On Account of Conditions that Seem Unalterable, 248*

Dissolution of the National Colored Work

In 1966, Bi-annual General Assembly ruled to integrate the National Church of God Colored Work and desired all groups white, black, and Latino/a to be governed under the General offices.[31] Upon this ruling, offices of the Colored Work were abandoned and the department dissolved; the Annual Assembly of the "Colored Work" was discontinued as well.

The Church of God Colored Work consisted of every black church in the United States, as well as congregations that were part of the New Testament Church of God in England and the Caribbean.[32] Black leaders came together every year for a 'National Convention' in Jacksonville, Florida. Interestingly, the black churches reported directly to the Colored Work, not to the General Headquarters. The funds had gone directly to the black work and not the general offices.

This level of self-control may have provided some relief in a racially tense denomination and may have kept many of the blacks in the Church of God although they were unhappy with the social ethos of the organization. However, when this ceased to be the case, blacks felt slighted that they lacked support and representation at the highest levels of leadership, although their finances now went to support the very ones who retained most of the power.

Church leaders sought to change the structure of the denomination so that the entire Church of God organization have one General overseer and each state have a representative/State Overseer, (which was later named State administrative Bishop) whom all reported directly to the headquarters in Cleveland.

---

[31] Church of God General Assembly Minutes of the Fifty-first General Assembly, 1966.

[32] Special thanks to Bishop Otis Williams and Bishop James Gooden who allow me to interview them by phone about the history of the split of the National Church of God and the Church of God (Cleveland, TN). Special thanks is also owed to Veronica Cooper the first secretary of the newly organized National Church of God. She was provided information and documents including a copy of its Charter book.

This change signaled a major problem for black who felt that the action was not full integration and that white bishops still wanted to rule over the black pastors. Therefore, black members protested, desiring to remain separate. However, after the 1966 decision, these positions were cancelled immediately, and the office of National Church of God Colored Work was dissolved.

Immediately following, General Headquarters appointed Walter Jackson as the first State Overseer over Florida. The building in Jacksonville was considered the Florida State Office. Jackson, a black ordained Bishop, held this position for five years. The time in office was four years but since he was not elected but appointed by General Headquarters, the first year was not considered part of the standard four-year tenure.

In 1966 after Jackson was appointed as the first Overseer of the once again separated state, many blacks withdrew from the Church of God, each going in their own direction, (though some contend these sparse withdrawals had little effect on the denomination). One group formed their own organization, the National Church of God. Inc. Others stayed only because they could not take their church buildings with them.[33]

A Breakaway: Forming The National Church of God, Inc.

As State overseer, Jackson was responsible for retrieving all of the Churches of God properties from pastors who left the organization. A major property, 5th Avenue Church of God in Ft. Lauderdale, was at the center of the court battle between the two denominations.[34]

---

[33] The Church of God has a history of dealing with defected ministers who attempt to take church property with them. The most famous case is A.J. Tomlinson who battled the Church regarding the name "Church of God." A long court battle in Hamilton County Judicial Court resulted in a ruling in favor of the Church of God.

[34] See, for example, Reverend Walter Jackson (State Overseer for the Church of God General Assembly and State of Florida) vs. Reverend John B. Ferguson. Reverend J. Z. Smith and Church of God Color Work, Inc.

Bishop Causeway (the pastor of 5th Avenue Church of God at the time) was not in agreement with the split and wanted to stay with the Church of God (Cleveland, TN). However, the majority of the members of the local congregation wanted to leave the denomination and fired Causeway. In his stead, Bishop J.B. Ferguson became their pastor and joined the other pastors to form the new body. Because Ferguson had the bigger building at the time, the church was named the National Church of God, Inc. and the first National Convention was held there in 1967. Thereafter, several more conventions were held while the battle over the church building continued. The court battle began a year earlier and legal proceedings continued for approximately four years before the court ruled that the building should be returned to the Church of God (Cleveland, TN).[35]

Racial Organization And Development

David Muir's dissertation, *Black Theology, Pentecostalism, and Racial Struggles in the Church of God*, engages both critical race theory and black theology in examining the racial struggles that have long beleaguered the Church of God.[36] It also investigates the racial discourse he sees running through American Pentecostalism. Primarily because the bulk of Muir's contribution is in history and politics, its racial/religious dimension has received little consideration and been often overlooked by church leaders.

Muir asserts that racialization of organizational development set the scene for the politics of race and its cultural assumptions becoming the norm in Pentecostal polity and practice. Leonard Lovett takes it a step further and boldly calls this "institutional racism" which he defines as "*the conscious manipulation of institutions to achieve racist objectives.*

---

[35] The final ruling resulted in the warranty deeds of the 5th Avenue Church of God being signed over to the Church of God through Bishop Walter Jackson, the Florida State Overseer.

[36] David Muir, Black theology, Pentecostalism, and racial struggles in the Church of God, Ph.D. dissertation, King's College, London, 2003.

To this end, racist institutions are but extensions of individual racial thought."[37] Lovett's seemingly harsh critique merits consideration as we assess the possibility that the ecclesiology of some Pentecostal groups may be inherently racist?

The separation in Florida has been due to the institutional structure and polity of the Church of God in which black members have felt excluded from enjoying full equality. As stated as early as 1926, when a group of black ministers shared at the General Assembly:

> We feel… somewhat embarrassed and handicapped to the extent we cannot make much progress that we really desire, and we are asking you brethren, with the consent of all our brethren present at this Assembly, if there can be a way formulated by which we can arrange better to take care of our affairs among the colored work.[38]

Interestingly, the Church of God in Florida has always been separated, but now its black ministers sought to have their own General Assembly within the framework of the National General Assembly. They wanted to set up their own means of developing and propagating polity and institutional structure. A look into the function and purpose of the General Assembly gives further insight into the reasons and advantages of blacks hosting their own assembly.[39]

Bridging The Divide: Ecclesiastical Restorative Justice

---

[37] Leonard Lovett, "The Present: The Problem of Racism in the Contemporary Pentecostal Movement." *Cyber journal for Pentecostal-Charismatic Research* http://www.pctii.org/cyberj/cyberj14/lovett1.html, accessed May 7, 2009.

[38] Conn, *Like a Mighty Army*, 199.

[39] In 1926, "a group of Negro ministers" approached the General Assembly with the request of hosting their own assembly. This request was not well received with the initial thought that the move could lead to their further separation from the general church. See *Minutes of the Twenty-first Annual Assembly*, 1926, 27-29.

When focusing on the racial struggles in the Church of God, Muir presents several of issues which merit serious reflection by those desiring to abolish any prejudice that continues to stain the history of the Church of God movement. Muir accurately observes that meaningful effort at overcoming the legacy of racial tension and division must shift the linguistic paradigm from theologizing to practice. This calls for the Church to act on its discourse and dialogue. We must cease simply talking about racial reconciliation or equality and put policies and action that implements racial reconciliation in place. We must now undergird sermons and songs about love and unity, by putting practical, concrete feet to the theology which the Church espouses.

Secondly, Muir addresses the Church's institutional racism and the phenomenology of denial. Many leaders have aborted the true character of early Pentecostalism that saw whites and blacks worshipping together as equals. As racial reconciliation proponents point out, the oppressor must admit before the oppressed, all the instances and grievances of past oppression, or else both risk remaining in their current state.

Vinson Synan addressed this point as a future strategy for racial reconciliation, saying, "let us... acknowledge our successes and failures as Pentecostal believers." However, we must go beyond the act of 'acknowledgement' to employ the word 'admit,' because it linguistically places a stronger emphasis on verbal confession rather than simply recognizing past faults.

Thirdly, Muir notes that there is a need for resolving historic organizational inequality and arguments for succession. Though Muir does not frame it in this way, this moves racial reconciliation from words to actions and can involve an ecclesiastical form of reparations to resolve past organizational inequality?

Applying restorative practices and principles could maximize justice for minority peoples by, first, refocusing reconciliatory efforts on the restoration of human respect and dignity rather than on the restoration of property rights or monetary payments, and second, acknowledging the wider social relationships in which such conflicts arise. Using restorative justice in situations of historical inequality (i.e., ecclesiastical instances) may impact the practice of restorative justice itself. First, the roles and relationships of those involved will change as we reconsider the role of the superior to the subordinate. Second, applying restorative justice in situations of historical grievances highlights the collective nature of such conflicts and the collective, contextual nature of evolving notions of justice. To make all of this work, ecclesiastical restorative justice entails:

1. Advancement and placement of people of color in key ministry positions proportionate to that of either whites or the percentage population of non-whites groups to that of whites.
2. Funding ministry resources for people of color proportionate to that of whites.
3. Equal involvement and participation of people of color in the General liturgy and services of the organization, i.e., General Assembly.
4. Proportionate coverage and visibility of blacks and Hispanics issues and concerns in Church publications and media resources to that of whites.

While Muir insists that racial discourse must take place among Pentecostals, six elements be in place for intentional dialogue to be meaningful:

1) It must be affirming of the setting and dialogue taking place. Value should be place on the need for and importance of such discussion.

2) It must be honest. Openness must be welcomed and encouraged for participants to feel comfortable in opening up about internalized racial feelings.

3) It must exhibit racial sensitivity. There must be an understanding of the sociological concept of race and how it is experienced in Society at present.

4) It must not neglect responsibility. There must be an assessment of what sense of responsibility has not entered the conversation and acceptance that we have all hurt one another.

5) It must extend a hand. We must move forward together and recognize the healing value of apologies.

6) It must move from dialogue to practice. Participants are called to practical action to solidify insights and extend the benefits of the conversation.

Fourth, In addition to this foundational work of dialogue at the General Church level, jurisdiction dialogues must take place within districts with a gathering of two or three churches.

Fifth, to move toward meaningful reconciliation, the sociology of power in the Church of God oligarchy must substantially change. The church must allocate the distribution of higher-level positions for people of color in proportion to their representation in the denomination.

Sixth, transformations in polity and organizational culture remain impervious to the dignified arguments of black ministers in the US and NTCG leaders in the United Kingdom for a move towards an inclusive ecclesiology and away from structures which perpetuate 'an ethos of parent-child role.'

Finally, classical Pentecostal denominations must realize that racism is a sin—a barrier to realizing God's vision for human relationship. Racism hurts all by violating the reflection of the image of God in us.

While racism is present throughout our society, including in our church and congregations, all areas of society suffer from its debilitating effects, and many do not understand the effects of racism, or how to undo them.

Restorative justice is a necessary component if true and lasting reconciliation within the Church of God is to occur. This involves a process by which those who have caused harm take responsibility for their actions, and those who have been harmed being allowed a central role in the reconciliation.

For racial reconciliation and race relations in Pentecostal organizations to advance, adherents must recognize, address, and work to rectify the racialized ecclesiology within their practice and polity that has lent itself to these divisions. Until then, we'll still be two separate bodies exiting within one Church of God: one comprised of predominantly white churches represented by the Tampa Office; the other of predominantly black churches represented by the Cocoa Office.

What Black Christians Want the White Church to Know

Estrelda Y. Alexander

As we acknowledge, wrestle with, and faithfully attempt to answer hard questions as Christian brothers and sisters, who hold the truth of Scripture in high regard, we desire to live in obedience to God's desire that we walk in authentic Christian unity. From the beginning, humankind was created to live in divine relationality such that we collectively reflect the full image of God. Racism, as a disruption of that relationality, is sin. Though for over four hundred years, black Christians, along with the entire African American community, have continued to share in the common experience of racist oppression, we now find ourselves constrained to address what for us is an urgent issue.[1]

Most white Christians do not consider themselves racists. What they think of as simply personal prejudice, however, is part of a complex system of hierarchies and inequities. While racism begins at this individual level, its broader outworking includes institutional and structural forms that bring social or material benefit to an individual or group, or, in which they participate at others' expense.[2]

The simplest form of racism ascribes certain (positive or negative) attributes to persons or groups as predictable ways of behaving in specified situations based solely–or primarily–on their racial identity.

---

[1] This essay solely deals with racism in the American church and society, for a more complete discussion of the issue of racism globally see, Martin Bulmer and John Solomos, Racism. New York: Oxford University Press, 1999, or Charles W. Wills, "Global White Supremacy" in Paula S. Rothenberg, ed., *White Privilege: Essential Readings on the Other Side of Racism.* New York: Worth Publishers, Inc., 2021, 119-125.

[2] Jim Wallis, *America's Original Sin: Racism, White Privilege, and the Bridge to a New America.* Grand Rapids, MI: Baker Publishing Group, 2016, or Jemar Tysby, *The Color of Compromise: The Truth about the American Church's Complicity in Racism.* Grand Rapids, MI: Zondervan, 2020.

Such one-dimensional assumptions disregard an individual's discrete qualities because it is easier to generalize about the entire group and relieve the messy work of looking for appropriate cues for them.

The ideas, for example, that all black people are morally deficient, and all black men exhibit a higher sexual appetite are historical stereotypes that, repeatedly, have proven inaccurate. Stereotypes may have little consequence for those who hold them. Yet, they brand individuals as consistently acting in a certain manner since they are members of their group. White people often assume that black people, as a group, are either good or bad, intelligent or intellectually limited, reasonable or unreasonable, and valuable or worthless based on that identity.

The intellectual laziness of stereotyping fails to adjust attitudes and behaviors toward the individual. It is unnecessary to spend the mental energy to know them since the stereotype explains everything significant about them. We mentally dismiss them, without acquainting ourselves with them as equally deserving of our attention or elevating them to an unreachable status. Though inaccurate, stereotyping can be good or bad—benign or negative—in that we overestimate or downplay moral virtues, physical power, or the intellectual acumen of an entire group. Either extreme leads to miscues in our interactions, robbing us of opportunities to appreciate the individual. Yet stereotyping is simply holding ideas about who people are.

Prejudicial attitudes suggest that such knowledge should guide our actions toward, and interactions with, the group or its members. Prejudice involves, primarily negative, stereotypes that assume the less admirable traits of the assessment of black people are true for all—or at least most. It may be inclusive or exclusive. Inclusive prejudice targets all individuals within the group with the negative stereotype while with exclusive prejudice, we summarily prevent anyone not specifically a part of our group from being considered. For example, racial profiling by police is inclusive prejudice, while attitudes that exclude black from carrying out certain tasks or holding particular positions, simply because they are not white, exemplify exclusive prejudice. Most white people hold some prejudice toward black people and see them as who they count us to be. No amount of truth changes that assessment, while circumstantial evidence fuels prejudice. As unfair as prejudice may be, however, it can be a hidden, internal attitude that mostly constrains us to avoid the other, robbing us of rich opportunities for interaction with those who are different—it does not, necessarily, materially harm the other.

Conversely, discrimination is the active working out of prejudicial attitudes—granting or withholding reward to others based primarily on prejudice. It results in actively denying or limiting material opportunities in ways that affect wellbeing. While a person can mask prejudice, at times, overcompensating for it, discrimination is the visible disclosure of deeply held attitudes. It occurs intentionally when attitudes lead us to believe that members of the other group deserve to be treated differently. No excuse is made for this behavior for, after all, blacks should know their place and expect to be treated in a certain manner when they step out of it. Throughout the Jim Crow era, discriminatory practices reminded black people of their second-class status and kept them from rising above it. Inferior educational resources, exclusionary employment practices, inadequate community infrastructure, and biased judicial systems, all stood to remind black people of "their place."

Yet, discrimination may also occur involuntarily, as the natural outworking of residual attitudes as indirect discrimination results from apparently neutral actions that disproportionately disadvantage or benefit one group and fail to bring equity to the disparate parties. Hidden prejudice is not so much targeted at preventing the other group from attaining status or resources. Rather it aims to protect those who fear they, or future generations of their group, may lose their way of life.

Practices that appear to be in the group's interest, can, in actuality, be patronizing, or, implicitly or openly, condescending while failing to accord full human capacity. Patronizing behavior ascribes intellectual, moral, or spiritual limitation that objectifies the other as needing our "care" while exacting psychic acquiescence and/or a sense of obligation. It expects the other to exhibit dependency and gratefulness for the little that is allotted to them.

Patronization can masquerade as offering helpful solutions to a situation in which the other finds him or herself. But this assistance requires relinquishing free moral agency; the aim is either placating the other's felt need to resist oppression or reducing them to child-like dependency that removes the opportunity to decide on their best course of action.

Paternalistic attitudes assume that without our help the subject could not possibly make it. These attitudes allow us to provide aid we determine they need without crediting what group members sense they require. For we assume that they are too mired in the situation, or otherwise too deficient to know what is good for themselves. We create programs and projects for them, based on our sense of their need or what we would desire were we in their place. Importantly, these projects fall short of securing total liberation for the other and allowing them equality with us. Paternalism, therefore, directs well-intentioned benevolence toward a person or group in ways that are, actually, intrusive.

Bigotry, as broad intolerance, expresses itself as supremacism—a generalized belief that one's group is superior to all other groups and/or deserves to be treated with deference by all other people. This mindset can show itself as blatant hostility, total avoidance, or psychic harassment. Most people hold stereotypes of other groups in one form or another, and there may be many who have prejudicial attitudes or discriminate in some way. Further, many well-meaning people—even Christians—who by failing to determine and fully consider the desires of the other can become patronizing. Yet, few Christians are consciously bigoted. Acts of bigotry, however, could be as small as labeling, name-calling, or ignoring people when they should have our attention. Or, they might include such large transgressions as joining organizations whose aim is to intimidate, demoralize, or disenfranchise others.

Bigoted people circle the wagons, closing themselves off from the possibility of meaningful or protracted engagement with others. For, ultimately the aim of bigotry is to avoid interaction with the other group—allowing them to inhabit their own space. For, at the least, the bigoted person desires to never have to transact meaningful commerce with the other as an equal.

Bigotry becomes vilification when we openly slander or publicly act in ways that encourage others to exhibit contempt toward a group. While, surprisingly, Bible-believing Christians have been part of or supported groups such as the Ku Klux Klan or have taken part in or looked the other way at lynchings, such seemingly innocuous act as vilifying comments on social or public media or giving a condemning speech can license others to become intolerant or, even, violence.

Individuals, groups, or societies are oppressive when their bigotry drives them to carry out systematic, sustained abuse, exploitation, and injustice that causes psychological, emotional, physical, or economic harm, or extract advantage for the perpetrator. Explicit oppression aims to render the other helpless in mounting a defense. Oppression is rarely carried out by a solitary individual. It is, generally, carried out by a powerful oligarchy or by an entire segment of society. They enacted laws, amass police and military resources, and establish tariffs and sanctions. Conditions are made so intolerable that they temper the will and spirit of the other to resist or provoke a radical attempt to eradicate the cause.

Systematic oppression does not come about as an unfortunate, unintended consequence of otherwise neutral practices. Rather it is calculatingly directed at those who, for some reason, cannot protect themselves. The Church can be complicit in oppression, then, not because of simple, benign neglect of the other; but when it intentionally decides not to intervene against harm to the black community. In making this decision, it gives tacit, moral support for an insinuated or explicit rationale. So, silence, itself, is oppressive.

Oppression exacts psychic or material loss from an individual or a group in ways that restrict full human flourishing. Someone must lose for someone else to gain. Someone or some group must surrender some portion of their full humanity for the other to sense that they are flourishing.

The most extreme outworking and the harshest manifestation of racism is the strategic attempt to completely, or substantially, eliminate any threat from the other by deliberately imposing conditions that lead to their physical, mental, or material destruction. While that destruction might be the immediate result of a targeted action or set of actions, it can involve gradual, sustained, or indirect attempts to destroy the other.

Genocide can be accomplished through many strategies. Like the difference between the immediate death of a heart attack or the slow, painful, increasingly debilitating death of cancer, it can be accomplished through measures that do not outrightly kill, yet render a community incapable of fully human functioning and, finally, lead to the death of significant numbers of its members. Since the end goal is destroying the legacy of the community, genocide involves any measure that cause it to eventually die. The most egregious examples include measures that prevent or disrupt the birth cycle such as forced birth control or isolating men from women through involuntary conscription or mass incarceration. But other measures include introducing or failing to address disease or other unbearable living conditions or promoting policies that encourage dysfunctional behavior to bring about the group's decline.

For Christians, outright genocide is unthinkable; it stands against every principle of the faith. Yet throughout history, genocidal acts have been justified (and sometimes celebrated) by otherwise decent men and women and the silence of many churches sometimes implicates Christians in processes we profess to condemn. For example, while the

Middle Passage was horrendous on all fronts, the level of violence enacted on the black community during was demonic and the journey did not involve a first-class ticket on a luxury liner. Instead, individuals created in the image of God were treated like animals, property, or mere "cargo." Extreme conditions during the arduous voyage where they were subjected to close quarters, insufficient ventilation, inadequate food, and lack of medical attention guaranteed that massive numbers of less abled captives would perish during the transit. Since sickly, or physically-challenged, slaves were of little service, but still required material resources, they were dispensable and the death of any individual was of no consequence, except to lessen the bottom line. An estimated fifteen percent of the two million potential slaves who left Africa died before reaching the New World. The protracted, history of lynching of African Americans and others over one hundred years of American history is another example that involved the loss over than 5000 African American men, women, and youth between 1882 and 1968.[3]

This is a vital conversation for the church, the black community, and the wider society. Further, in a politically tense, racially charged climate, the poisonous atmosphere makes a very uncomfortable conversation even more difficult. Yet, to move forward and bring any resolution, we must allow ourselves to be uncomfortable with authentic dialogue. Such conversations cannot be singular events but must be ongoing. Nor can they be superficial and politically correct; they must dig deep into the core of what ails us and follow with intentional actions.

At this critical point, which is both hopeful and challenging, some sincere white Christians may genuinely question the goal of such conversation. History has been hopeful in that members of the African diaspora have seen someone who looks like them elected first to the

---

[3] For a thorough discussion of these, see Estrelda Alexander, "Manifestations of the Will to Power" in *The Will to Power: Confronting Ideologies that Dismantle Christian Community*. Lanham, MD: Seymour Press, 2019.

highest office, and second to the next most powerful office in the, ostensibly, most powerful nation in the world. In fact, many white Christians might pose the inquiry, "you have had the presidency and have the vice presidency, what else do black people want?" And while, on the surface, that innocent-sounding question may seem reasonable, it misses the point that though we have had singularly important victories, entrenched racial disparity is part of the fabric of the Christian Church, this nation, and much of the global community.

Thus, a concise, salient answer to the query is that black people want what all God-imaged members of the human community desire—the opportunity not just to survive – or subsist, but to flourish, and live out our full God-given potential without fear of limitation. We want the opportunity to be in full communion with those who claim to represent what is fully human.

Indeed, many posing that question have little understanding of the emotional, mental, and spiritual toll of sustained racial discrimination, even among, seemingly, privileged minority persons. Such disparity has assured that through several generations, for a variety of reasons, all but the most fortunate people of color hang near the bottom rung of the socio-economic ladder with little genuine hope of ever reaching beyond its midpoint. Even among people of color who have— seemingly—made it, the nagging sense of somehow never being regarded as an equal lingers in the psyche as a debilitating reminder of "our place." Nineteenth century Holiness evangelist, Amanda Berry Smith, summed up the white Christian community's lack of perception of racial disparity when she asserted, "I think [white] people would understand the quintessence of sanctifying grace if they could be black about twenty-four hours."[4] Her poignant statement speaks to the reality of racial disparity that has continued to plague the African

---

[4] Amanda Berry Smith's An Autobiography: The Story of the Lord's Dealings with Mrs. Amanda Smith, the Colored Evangelist: Containing an Account of Her Life Work of Faith, and Her Travels in America, England, Ireland, Scotland, India, and Africa as an Independent Missionary. Chicago: Meyer & Brother Publishers, 1893.

American community since well before her time. Yet the apparent inability of both sides of the Christian community to face the racial issue head-on causes immeasurable angst for black Christians. It has created an unresolved discontent among the ranks, and though not discussing the issue might seem like a genuine effort to "keep the, perceived, "bond of peace," it goes little distance in maintaining genuine "unity of the Spirit."[5]

Pentecostal educator, Marilyn Abplanalp, offered the insightful critique that, within a specific branch of Pentecostalism, the subject of racism is the "undiscussed, undiscussed." Abplanalp articulated classical Pentecostalism's "don't ask, don't tell" policy dictates that we don't talk about the subject, and we don't talk about the fact that we don't talk about the subject.[6] This policy might go a long way in keeping people from being uncomfortable with a hard conversation, but it does nothing to keep black Pentecostal Christians from full participation in what the Spirit is doing in the church and the world.

Still, efforts for healing cannot accomplish anything substantial if they only involve talking. We must follow words, and good intentions, with action that recognizes the seriousness of the problem—the deep fissure—that runs throughout the body of Christ as it does through American society. We cannot dismiss it as an insignificant or imagined grievance by a few disgruntled persons within an unintentionally marginalized community.

The first step in Christians addressing racism is see the problem within the church as well as in the broader society. For, like an incurable disease with increasingly debilitating, yet often undetected symptoms, denying its existence accomplishes nothing and, in the end, proves harmful. As with those undiagnosed symptoms, we feel less than healthy without knowing exactly why. White and black Christians

---

[5] Ephesians 4:3

[6] Marilyn Abplanalp, Ethnic Inclusion in Pastoral Leadership in the Assemblies of God Fellowship from 1906-1999: A Case Study, Paper Presented to the 31st Annual Meeting of the Society for Pentecostal Studies, Southeastern University of the Assemblies of God, Lakeland, FL, March 14-16, 2002.

do not know, for example, why we distrust each other. All we know is that our parents did not like or completely trust them, and they taught us not to like them or trust them. We do not even remember what we dislike or distrust about them. Often, again, we have never held a substantial conversation with any group member. So, we could not explain what we have against them.

Within our cultural matrix, cues about how we are to experience and relate to other people continually bombarded us, and each one shapes attitudes about the community. The family into which we are born, the institutions that educate us, the religious traditions, denominations, and local congregations that inform and form us spiritually and ethically, our exposure to media messages, as well as individual experiences with the other, all shape our attitudes. Often these mindsets form with little effort, as we passively hear and observe the postures, conversations, and actions of our nurturers. Through repeated exposure to these cues, we imbibe and adopt a worldview that becomes a part of our embedded way of thinking about how to navigate interactions with them.

Nonetheless, as we mature, expose ourselves to other possibilities for engaging others, and more deeply reflect on our embedded positions, navigating relationships becomes more nuanced and complicated. Simple, habitual reactions become less spiritually satisfying and force us to recognize that we are, possibly wrong about, at least some of, them. We come to recognize that they, their point of view, and their cry for justice deserve more consideration than we have given. When we recognize glimpses of the full God-imaged createdness and humanity of every person regardless of race or ethnicity, we can accord them the dignity and respect such recognition demands. For we can never accord them the equality that authentic reconciliation demands if we envision them as anything less.

Yet, we must also develop the humility that allows us to see every positive attribute we possess, either as individuals or as members of a social or cultural group, as a gift from God. These are never something for which we can legitimately claim special privilege. Our cultural identity, race, gender, intellectual capacity, and "every good thing given and every perfect gift [that is in us] is from above and comes down from the Father..."[7] We, therefore, have no bragging rights. We own nothing that was not given to us and that investment is for service on behalf of the world that "God so loves."

It is easy to convince ourselves that we are okay; we are not racist. We can easily pride ourselves in our liberality in allowing black people their own space; in not bothering them—or allowing ourselves to be bothered by them. Our call to obedience, however, requires actively working to liberate those in whom we hold no personal stake, while recognizing that each of us is, in some way, a stakeholder in the other. We must adopt an attitude of repentance–turning away from toxic mindsets and engaging in tangible attempts to repair the breach created by centuries of racial disparity. We cannot accomplish change in our strength alone since genuine change relies on the Holy Spirit's empowerment to tackle entrenched prejudice in the soul and spirit of our nation and the Church.

How We Got Here

Christians share a common faith in a Christ who loves and died for all children—black, yellow, red, and white—of the world. Yet, fallen humanity constantly struggles to live out the gospel and none of us gets it one hundred percent right. Each of us is shortsighted and "fall short of the glory of God." One result of this shortsightedness is racism. Yet, Jesus' atoning blood is equally efficacious for all sin and not even the sin of racism is impervious to redress. There is no level of human disruption that can completely derail God's intended relational intimacy or render it totally resistant to its life-changing effects.

---

[7] Jas 1:17

The road to racial healing begins with white Christians deliberately and sensitively listening to the narrative of oppression that continues to affect the black community without off-handedly dismissing it as fabricated, revisionist history. It is a narrative that begins with being involuntarily torn from our homeland and relocated for the economic prospering of those who considered themselves our superiors. We did not come seeking freedom from persecution or political asylum, or a better life. Rather, our ancestors were wrenched from their families, communities, and culture and deposited in a strange and hostile place that did not value them as human.

In the tragic experience of slavery awaiting new arrivals, fully human men and women reflecting God's image, were counted as only 3/5 of a human being, considered the personal property of others, estimated to not have fully developed souls, and often accorded treatment not suitable for a dog. Slavery was more than an unfortunate blip on the radar screen of American history. Rather, the institution was intentionally a completely dehumanizing experience laced with unspeakable cruelties. Men and women were shackled like animals, beaten with whips, separated from their families, and killed for any social infraction deemed inappropriate. Women were raped, men were castrated, and both genders, including children, were beaten into submission. As they were stripped of their culture, no attention was paid to the slave's personal, familial, or communal welfare.

The horrendous experience that has unfolded over two centuries of chattel slavery, nearly a century of Jim Crow racial policies, and a half-century of symbolic racism has left a legacy of what Joy DeGruy calls "Post Traumatic Slave Syndrome."[8] When de jure or actual slavery was ended, Reconstruction and the Jim Crow Era de facto slavery remained solidly in place. Practices such as enforced housing

---

[8] Joy DeGruy, *Post Traumatic Slave Syndrome: America's Legacy of Enduring Injury and Healing.* Portland OR: Joy DeGruy Publications Inc., 2017.

segregation replaced slave cottages, inadequate health care ensured higher morbidity rates and susceptibility to preventable conditions, and inferior education replaced restrictions on teaching slaves to read. Abrogation of voting rights through legal, as well as, illicit interventions continued our disenfranchisement from the political system. The continuing threat of violence from the police, vigilante groups, and rogue individuals continues to lock entire segments of our communities in fear. These experiences only exacerbated the residual pain of slavery leaving indelible spiritual and psychic scars on the African American community that cannot be easily expunged and whose reality cannot be denied or explained away.

Jim Crow Era discriminatory practices reminded black people of their second-class status and kept them from rising above it. They were afforded inferior educational resources in segregated classrooms, excluded from many employment opportunities, and pushed into communities that lacked the adequate infrastructure to sustain a viable quality of life. A biased judicial system continuously failed to offer equal protection under the law and still ensures the mass incarceration of black men and women, and stiffer penalties for similar crimes committed by white people. And, an exclusionary political system that disenfranchised black people from voting, holding office, or improving living conditions within our communities. These measures were established to remind black people of "their place" as a permanent underclass.

During the Civil Rights Era, earlier targeted discrimination found its corollary in indirect inequity resulting from actions that appeared to equally impact all parties, but disproportionately disadvantaged blacks. Practices that appeared to be neutral and impartial and offer equal opportunity failed to bring about equity and left black people in a disadvantaged and often dangerous posture. The Insistence that "separate but equal" educational opportunities were available to all made no sense when the path to such education continued to be structured in ways that denied black people adequate resources. Even so, the revisionist history taught to many black and white students still ignores the significant contribution of the black community.

This period saw more assertive and vocal strategies by the African American community to avail themselves of those "inalienable rights" that had been inferred from the Declaration of Independence and Constitution. Their actions led to a protracted period of racial tension that pitted two versions of the American dream against each other. In one, the opportunities are endless. In the other, the most many can hope for is to get by. Yet, black people want the same future for our children that every good other parent wants, and we try to envision a future in which our children can thrive without fear of limitation.

In contemporary America, some make the myopic suggestion that racism has ceased to exist and are tempted to succumb to the "here we go again" attitude. But, racism is a real and ongoing experience in the everyday lives of black Americans and unless forced by the sovereign design of birth to live within the reality of people of color, it is almost impossible to understand how unsettled the issue is even within the Christian church. In personal, social, and professional encounters, assumptions are made that the black individual is somehow less intelligent, less capable, less industrious, less economically stable, less moral, and, more importantly, less deserving of common human respect and dignity than is the white brother or sister. Black people—including many deeply spiritual black Christians—who have suffered through this legacy of oppression are still hurting from ingrained trauma that needs to be recognized. Yet, throughout this unfortunate, sinful history some white Christian leaders as well as individual white Christians, especially within the Evangelical community, have ignored the plight of their black brothers and sisters and are silent regarding racial injustice.

This dark history needs a hearing and recognition for what it has been and, for many, still is. Then we can discuss the highly sensitive issues that divide us, fracture the church, and make us uncomfortable as well as address misinformation and misunderstandings about what and who black people are. And, we can shed light on the horrific reality of the black experience in America that began with the Middle Passage and has unfolded over their 400-hundred-year history in this country. Such a conversation must confront the reality that many—if not most—black Christians feel that many—if not most—white Christians have failed to faithfully live out biblical brotherhood. Many sense that the white church is implicated either by an attitude of indifference, silence in the face of their brothers' horrendous maltreatment, active participation in discriminatory practices, building and sustaining discriminatory structures and institution, and refusing to acknowledge that, even when they have not directly participated in racial division, they have benefitted from it.

Such a conversation starts with correcting misinformation about what and who black people are. First, there is only one species of humanity, and only one human family. And since the concept of race is a contemporary social construction, developed to bolster systems of oppression, we know that, though there are many ethnic groups, there is only one race—the human race! Black people are just that—people—who, like everyone else, are created in God's image with no ontological, genetic difference from any other group. They are not lesser beings, but share the same proportional distribution of intelligence, morality, emotional intelligence, and spirituality that exists among all other groups. Secondly, all of us are—white, black, Asian, Latino, are fallen and flawed. Each group carries the same proneness to sin and pathology as others. But it is untenable that many in the white church think that, before the Middle Passage, all Africans were heathen when the rest of the world was Christian. There were Christians in Africa before white missionaries arrived there and we cannot excuse slavery as God's way of rescuing the black African from pagan religion.

Further, many members of the white community fail to understand the deep psychic costs of sustained racial discrimination, even among, seemingly, privileged minority persons. The unfounded degree of force used in incidents of police violence against our community, for example, is felt by many African Americans as a new form of lynching. First, repeated unanswered occurrences in which perpetrators are either never charged with a crime, or are charged, tried, but ultimately set free to leave the African American community fearful and traumatized. This angst is echoed in remarks of a megachurch pastor that, "I used to pray that my teenage sons would not come home and tell me they had gotten a young woman pregnant. I now pray that they just come home alive." While that might sound exaggerated and trite, many black leaders attest to fear that their sons, grandsons, or other male members of their families, communities, or congregations may become victims. The entire black community is traumatized as it is perpetually tormented by the oppression woven into the fabric of this nation.

Repairing the breach requires discarding toxic attitudes that see racism as an unfortunate by-product of American economic, social, or political policy or and racist attitudes are personal preferences of a few misguided people. For black people, racism is a traumatizing, dehumanizing, morally debilitating, everyday reality. Our trauma is a culmination of a history of oppression in which we have been treated to the unspeakable cruelties of slavery, defined as less than a human reflection of God's image, confined to segregated neighborhoods, provided inferior education and other resources, targeted for violence, and effectively locked out of the political system. As Christians, it should see such disruption to God's intended intimate relationality as sin. Racism is sin, discrimination is ungodly, and prejudice is life-destroying evil.

Without correcting such attitudes, efforts at healing the church or society are unsustainable, nothing of substance is accomplished, and we are only talking. Yet, words and good intentions must be followed by three important steps. There is a deep fissure in the nation and body of Christ and reconciliation comes about when both sides acknowledge their complicity and live in a posture of genuine and perpetual repentance.

To claim to not see race–to be color blind–is not helpful. While color blindness purportedly disregards racial characteristics in social interaction between races, it ignores disparities that continue to exist within society. Such a claim negates the lived reality of genuine differences of experience–not a different or lower type of humanity— that has been part of African American's history of being oppressed and marginalized. Though this is not the intention of such a claim, it perpetuates patterns that produce racial inequity by normalizing the majority group's race.

For the black Christian community or individual, racial equality is more than a political issue. It is a biblical and spiritual issue. Scripture is replete with examples of God calling the community to be just and chides them for not being so. A racially divided church can never be a biblically effective church or an authentic reflection of the body of Christ. The church should be at the head of the push for justice— crying out like the Old Testament prophets and like Jesus. We must be willing to take on Jesus' proclamation at face value, that, "the Spirit of the Lord is upon each of us to preach good news to the poor. Justice is part of God's, nature and character and reflected in God's attitude and actions toward the created and so loved world. So, the church must not see advocates for justice as radically liberals subversives of the God-ordained social order.

For the white community, privilege—not as something actively signed on to—but as advantage that accrues because of birth—is not simply a matter of material wellbeing, though it involves access to material resources and power denied the black community. It is the absence of disenfranchisement, freedom from being judged by your racial identity, and lack of restriction to what you can become, where you can live, what positions you are deemed "qualified" or disqualified for. It is freedom from estimations of what you can achieve or should desire and the liberty of not continually having to think about these realities. And it is liberation from succumbing to the mental, emotional, and spiritual harm such continual wrestling presents. Whiteness—no matter one's economic or social standing—provides this opportunity, regardless of whether one is conscious of, or, uses it.[9]

Much of the media-exploited social disorder in the black community arises from a legacy of socialization to be dysfunctional. You cannot destroy a people's family structure or the support systems that allows them to be whole and expect them to have intact, functional families. You cannot rob a people of their economic viability or access to viable employment and expect them to be financially stable. You cannot rob a people of their dignity and expect that they will have a sense of worth. You cannot rob a people of adequate educational resources and opportunity and expect them to value and pursue knowledge. You cannot continue to withhold equal justice from a people and expect them to trust the justice system or act within the bounds of the law. You cannot impose definitions of spirituality on a people that negate and delegitimize their faith experience and expect to draw them to your churches. You cannot rob a people of knowledge of their role in history and expect them to thrive and have hope for the future.

If we are to make headway in repairing that breach, the white church must recognize that some specific practices and actions have not been helpful, and others have only served to widen the breach. Though recent pronouncements regarding justice point us forward, it is not beneficial to resist holding conversations about the reality of black Christian. Yet, the failure of the church and its leaders to speak prophetically about the issue is evidenced in the deafening silence through as centuries of atrocities–lynchings, bombings, imposition of unethical social and economic policies, and provision unhealthy

---

[9] For a deeper discussion of white privilege, see for example, Robin DiAngelo, *White Fragility: Why It's So Hard for White People to Talk about Racism*. Boston: Beacon Press, 2018 or Jim Wallis, *America's Original Sin: Racism, White Privilege, and the Bridge to a New America*. Grand Rapids, MI: Brazos Press, 2017.

housing and inadequate schools, were committed. The lack of a public voice from white Christian leadership has been particularly hard to hear since we are empowered by the Spirit to guide the church and help it gain a balanced perspective on these issues.

When the white church – especially those who hold Scripture in high regard as God's word—fails to defend the oppressed and redress injustice it is pouring acid into an open wound and wondering why the wound doesn't heal. Failing to acknowledge the ongoing pain of racism, labeling any protest as agitation, and encouraging black Christians to maintain silence about their experience in the supposed interest of unity and peace, achieves neither. Rather it drives the sense of disenfranchisement underground and forces the black community to internalize the hatred and turn it against itself leading to the spiral of dysfunction that white Christians so often decry.

Such silence can be interpreted in several ways or stem from a small number of causes. Some fear saying the wrong thing, so they say nothing. Some are simply disinterested in the plight of African Americans Christians since it is not their problem. But it is not enough that you don't hate any black people or you leave black people alone.

Some fear repercussion from colleagues who might sanction their efforts as radical or liberal. Yet Christians must question whether they have brought into a political agenda that, purportedly, upholds one set of biblical principles regarding personal, moral holiness while disregarding ethical concerns for the wellbeing of an entire community. Many in the black community wake up each morning knowing there are people, even within the Christian community, who know nothing about them but discard and make assumptions about them solely because of their skin color. The most disappointing aspect of racism is the white Church's failure to take the problem of racial disparity seriously and stand with black Christians in addressing the problem in any significant way. Many black Christians feel that segments of the white Church have failed to faithfully live up to the biblical standard of Christian brotherhood.

The church as the body of Christ, which should be at the front of confronting everything that disrupts God-intended relationality, showing the world how to live justly, too often has lagged behind more socially progressive elements of society in producing satisfying responses to injustice. Beginning with the complicity in the slave trade, black and other minorities have been betrayed by its inability to separate economic gain from ethical and spiritual concerns.

As with secular corporations and institution, various segments within church have segregated structures which lock black people out of the highest levels of leadership. Allegations that black against white racism is evidence by the fact that black people have often created separate bodies ignores the reality of their felt need for protection from the harshest outworking of racism in majority white bodies. No denomination whose constituency is less than 50% white should have a governing and administrative structure that is 90% white. Though the black constituency has grown exponentially, leadership remains solidly ensconced in hands of whites and attempts to question that paradigm taken as a threat.

Cries for just treatment often seem to fall on deaf ears. Pat statements such as "I don't see color," I love everyone," I don't hate anyone," "I never owned slaves," and "all lives matter" are not helpful. They provide no solace for the fractured black reality. Rather, black people read them as a negation of who they are and a refusal to see the very real grievances with which they are forced to contend. For, to not see color doesn't overlook a person's physical make up. It disregards the lived reality of every black person and fails to acknowledge their struggle for authentic existence. Love is an active word and negation rather than hatred, is its converse.

Sustained oppression causes lingering trauma within our community. It exhibits itself in nihilism – a sense of unrelenting hopelessness, higher rates of physical, emotional, and mental illness. If not managed, the lingering effects of racism will destroy the Church as well as the society. Lessening the effects of entrenched racism, to any degree, involves deliberate, but necessary steps. The start is recognizing its real and powerful existence followed by acknowledgement any role in perpetuating racism by either actively supporting it or failing to call it out when we see it. And, finally, there must be a commitment to living in a state of perpetual repentance that resists the temptation to render that support and that allows room for seeking authentic relationship with the other. For only then, can we effectively oppose racism. To miss any of these steps or attempt to put one before the other is to derail the entire project.

Acknowledgment

Coming to terms with the reality that innate racism can never be cured is sobering. However, its most debilitating symptoms can be restrained, so that the black community is spared its uglies consequences. Such an urgent endeavor is a never-ending project, requiring diligence. As we confess that is not merely their negative attributes, way of life, or lack of Christian faith that deters intimate human relationship we can become serious about the prospect of weakening racist tendencies. And at the end, if we are serious, we must concede that, we have found the enemy and, at least in part, "it is us."

For despite protestations to the contrary, racism's deep-seated nature does not allow the white church to neatly divide itself into good and bad camps. While some white Christians have stood in solidarity with black brothers and sisters and others have been explicitly guilty, no one can completely resist the innate urge of the privileged to perceive oneself as better – and more representative of the image of God – than, at least, one other person. No one has been fully able to, completely, avoid this common frailty. For, in its essence, it is inescapable.

From that simple acknowledgement, the possibility of genuine reconciliation, though tentative at best, comes into view. Still, we must also concede that the road to our goal is continually fraught with opportunities for missteps and faux pas that endanger the project. In some instances, we will misunderstand each other. We will misspeak or be misheard. And, here, humility becomes enormously important. For we must always be ready to ask forgiveness rather than assert or pretend that the misstep is the other's fault. Only then, can we make progress and fend off the painful game of face-off we play with each other.

Admitting that this is the best that we can do allows us to grant others grace when they fall short. It helps us understand that their powering – like ours – is not always deliberate or malicious. Yet, none of us can, too easily, excuse ourselves for attitudes and actions that come about as the consequence of our Will to Power. As brothers and sisters, we must struggle together daily – moment by moment – to overcome an invincible disposition that can only be humbly acknowledged, recognized for what it is and repented of.

Repentance

Again, the ultimate antidote is living in a perpetual posture of repentance as the only means of restraining racist attitudes and agendas. The imperative of repentance for our lack of love is not immediately apparent since we do not hate black people. Still, our inclination to disregard them and deny their full humanity has caused harm. Genuine repentance is most visibly represented in mature, agape love. The Apostle Paul inserts a seeming incongruous intrusion into one of his most often quoted passage when he inserts,

> *[w]hen I was a child, I used to speak like a child, think like a child, reason like a child; when I became a man, I did away with childish things.*[10]

Walking in uninterrupted penitence requires growing up spiritually by continually renewing of our mind to reflect on the other's lived reality until a change of attitude wards off the sin that "so easily besets" each of us. For the temptation to boast of our innocence

---

[10] I Corinthians 13:11

246

always lodges within us, ready to overtake us and cause us to, again, give in to the Will to Power.

Paul's words, however, highlight the difference between immature and mature love or disingenuous and genuine charity. Immature, childish love seeks a return benefit for the one extending it. We love them for who they are – and what they provide – to us, whether it be the support and sustenance provided by a parent, the benefit of friendship offered by a playmate, the assistance given by a colleague, or the emotional support and sexual gratification of a lover. They are there to aid, affirm, and comfort us and we love them for doing just that. When they no longer deliver these things, our love wanes.

Mature love is extended for the benefit of the other, and esteems him or her as a worthy recipient, regardless! As the Apostle insists, authentic love does not seek benefit for itself[11] and, as Jesus contends, is extended even to our enemy.[12] For such love "does not take into account a wrong [that has been] suffered."[13] This love is deliberate, and is constantly vigilant in confronting the isms that creep into our minds and spirits. It determinately resists the temptation to base interactions on childish notions of what love is.

The Christian mandate for mutual servanthood and "submitting [our]selves one to another is a serious obligation. [14] Only mutual submission within the bounds of mature love allows us to move the conversation from one of counter demands to one that hears what the other is authentically saying. and discerning their legitimate claims and grievances. Repentance, however, is more than a confession of guilt on being caught in the act or a fleeting sense of general remorse for the situation in which we find ourselves. Genuine repentance concedes that our attitudes and actions toward have, and continue to, implicate us in working out the Will to Power. It agrees that we partake in

---

[11] I Corinthians 13:5
[12] Matthew 5:44
[13] Ibid.
[14] Eph 5:21

systems that have caused injury and leads us to assist in the remedy. Only such a posture represents the true repentance that acknowledges and owns the history of racial wrong that has been committed. It involves our becoming, not simply non-racist, but antiracist; undertaking deliberate acts to repair the harmed black community.

Living intentionally, as if every person and every injustice mattered, is a call to be deliberate about what we do and say. It involves us in conversation with those who because of physical and cultural identity are unlike us. Again, it involves us in intentionally hearing—and not offhandedly dismissing their humanity, journey, or pain. It is to purposely reach across barriers to establish formerly untenable relationships. It is to resist using privilege at the expense of others, while initiating processes that accrue privilege to ourselves. When we deliberately exchange our racist tendency for these, seemingly unnatural, attitudes and actions, we move toward conquering our inclination to just be who we are, and to allow others to go on as they are, to the detriment of both.

For this project to be successful, repentance and forgiveness must go hand in hand. While we repent of what we have done to them, we must forgive them for what they have done to us. For the latter is no good without the former. The willingness to pardon is one of the surest signs of involvement in the Kingdom of God. For Jesus challenged us that unless we can forgive, we have no claim as part of that Kingdom.[15]

The ability to forgive and still hold accountable is possibly one of the most difficult tasks we can be asked to take on. Forgiving does not mean holding the offender harmless or pretending no harm has been done. That is foolish naivete. Neither is it dismissing or downplaying the extent of real damage that has been caused. That is self-delusion.

Forgiveness is not a free pass to intimate relationality. It does not require us to irresponsibly trust the offender to never again act unjustly. Nor does it relieve the other's responsibility for owning and attempting to redress the harm they have caused. Though biblical

---

[15]Mark 11:26

forgiveness does not stop short when this acknowledgment is not forthcoming, the most authentic mode of forgiveness is reciprocal. We can only have genuine reconciliation and cease to be convinced that their overtures are disingenuous, after mutually embracing forgiveness. The imperative remains acknowledging deep-seated wounds their bigotry has caused and not dismissing claims of injury, while at the same time, accepting their overtures of genuine repentance.

It begins with intentionally entering into dialogue with others. Not just casual discussion, but quality conversation that allows us to comprehend each other's viewpoint and concedes the right to hold completely opposing convictions. We, in turn, have a responsibility to speak those convictions with passion–to speak their truth in love. We must speak with—not at—others about what we perceive as their problem, but about our common human experience. As we let down our guard about who we are, we allow them to do the same. Hopefully, this, in turn, allows both sides to approach the point where we share hopes, aspirations, struggles and victories. As we, repeatedly, do this, we gradually become comfortable with each other and come to view each other as equal participants in our God-imaged createdness. Only after that can the conversation move to the issues that continue to separate us.

It has been difficult for the church to speak a hard truth on the issue of racial justice. For we find ourselves in either of two unacceptable, and unhelpful, positions. When we reach a point of ultimate disquiet, we speak a hard truth that seemingly falls on deaf ears. Or we are so careful to appear loving, that our words fail to convey truth. But we must hear the truth in love. To listen with openness to the heart cry of brothers and sisters who are forced to live in situations that privilege will not allow us to imagine. And, it equally important to act in truth and love and to work for a just church and society.

For Christians, deepening conversation calls for community democratization that creates safe, affirming spaces where each person, regardless of race, is equally valued for their gift and allowed contribute, and power, authority, and responsibility for cultivating a Kingdom paradigm is shared, and each person is accorded equal worth in the Kingdom building project. Since faith without works is dead, again, repentance involves intentional action aimed at change. The onus is on the white church to become dissatisfied with simple, though supposedly heartfelt, lament over the situation, but to fortify itself to fight along with black brothers and sisters to destroy the demon of racism. Such actions start with calling it out wherever we see it in our ranks and educating colleagues about its existence. Yet it also requires confronting the powers within our own systems that perpetuate its existence. Then, there must be a willingness to speak to an unjust society and stand in solidarity to demand just treatment for people of color.

Contributors

Estrelda Alexander

Dr. Estrelda Alexander, a sociologist, political theologian and educator, is president of William Joseph Seymour Foundation, an institution she founded in 2010. She also serves as the executive director of the Pan-African Pentecostal Archive and executive publisher of Seymour Press. In 1998, she was called to be Associate Dean of Community Life at Wesley Theological Seminary and served in that capacity until 2002. She left Wesley to serve on the theology faculty of Regent University School of Divinity until 2013, rising to the rank of full professor. She received her B.A. in sociology from Howard University, her M.A in sociology from Columbia University, where she was a Ford Foundation fellow, her M.Div. from Wesley Theological Seminary, and her Ph.D. in political theology from The Catholic University of America. She has authored eight books and more than thirty essays and journal articles on Pentecostal history, theology, race, gender, and social justice. Her latest work, *The Spirit of the Lord: The Holy Spirit, Social Justice and the Prophetic Witness of the Church* is set for release later this Summer.

Kimberly Ervin Alexander

Kimberly Ervin Alexander is Director on RSM Online at the Ramp School of Ministry in Hamilton, Alabama. Previously, she served as Associate Professor of the History of Christianity at Regent University School of Divinity and, at the Pentecostal Theological Seminary, as Associate Professor of Historical Theology and Assistant Vice-President for Academics. She is an Honorary Research Fellow at the Manchester Wesley Research Centre in Manchester, England. Alexander is a past president of the Society for Pentecostal Studies. In addition to numerous articles and book chapters, she is the author of *Pentecostal Healing: Models of Theology and Practice*, and, with R. Hollis Gause, *Women in Leadership: A Pentecostal Perspective*. With James

Philemon Bowers, she co-authored *What Women Want: Pentecostal Women Ministers Speak for Themselves.* Her current research examines early Pentecostal experience and the experiences and contributions of women in Pentecostalism, including the work Church of God missionary Margaret Gaines among persons of Arabic descent in Tunisia and Palestine.

Carver Anderson

Cofounder and Executive Director of the Bringing Hope Charity in Birmingham, England. A social scientist and practical theologian, Anderson has over 35 years' experience at practitioner and senior management levels, working with individuals, families and communities plagued by multiple and complex challenges. Ordained Bishop in the New Testament Church of God, taught, lectured, and presented at seminars, conferences, workshops, and retreats across Great Britain and throughout Europe, Africa, Jamaica, and the United States.

James Philemon Bowers

James Bowers holds a BA in Biblical-Historical Studies from Lee University, MA from Pentecostal Theological Seminary, M.Div. from Louisville Presbyterian Seminary, and the Ph.D. in Christian Education and Historical Theology from the Southern Baptist Theological Seminary. He is an ordained Elder in the United Methodist Church and a pastor. He is also Professor of Practical Theology and Formation and DMIN Director at Virginia Bible College. Previously, he was Vice President of Pentecostal Theological Seminary. He has written successful grant proposals for Lilly Endowment and the Templeton Foundation and developed and directed the highly impactful *Pastoral Covenant Group Initiative* for 10 years in the Church of God. His published works include *Portrait and Prospect: Church of God Pastors Face the 21st Century, You Can Have What You Say: A Pastoral Response to the*

Prosperity Gospel, and he co-authored with Kimberly Alexander *What Women Want: Pentecostal Women Ministers Speak for Themselves.* He has also written various chapters on pastoral excellence, Spirit baptism, and theological education and his research interests include issues in Christian Formation, Pentecostalism, and Wesleyan/Methodist theology.

Clifton R. Clarke

Dr. Clarke gained his bachelor's degree from the University of Nottingham (UK), his master's degree from the University of Derby (UK) in Religious Pluralism and his Ph.D. from the University of Birmingham (UK). He taught theology at the University of Nottingham for five years before moving to Ghana as a Professor of theology teaching in various theological institutions. Dr. Clarke was also a part of the founding team that built Pan African Christian University College in Accra Ghana where he served as a Professor and Dean from 2002 – 2007. He served as Associate Professor of Intercultural Studies at Regent University, Virginia from 2008 until 2017, when he accepted the position as the Associate Dean of the William E. Pannell Center for African American Church Studies and professor of Black Church Studies at Fuller Theological Semin44ary. Currently Dr. Clarke is the Senior Pastor of New Beginnings Church in Simi Valley California. He is the author of six books the most recent being the *"The Love Remedy: The Cure for a Racial Divided World"*

Marcia F. Clarke

Before assuming her position as Affiliate Assistant Professor of Practical Theology at Fuller Theological Seminary, scholar and preacher, Dr. Marcia Clarke served as Assistant of Director of Careers and Alumni Services, Regent University School of Law. Prior to that, she served for ten years as a missionary in Ghana, alongside her husband with whom she currently served in pastoral ministry. She completed her Ph.D. in Practical Theology as the University of Birmingham University and holds a M Ed. from the University of Nottingham, a M.A. in Theology from Fuller Theological Seminary, and a Bachelor of Education from Nottingham Trent University.

Trevor L. Grizzle

A native of Jamaica, Dr. Grizzle is both founder and lead pastor of Hope International Ministries. He was a Church of God missionary to Ghana, West Africa. He is a graduate of Lee University (B.A.), and Southwestern Baptist Theological Seminary in Fort Worth, Texas (M.Div. and Ph.D.) An Ordained Bishop in the Church of God, he has been a professor of New Testament and Greek for thirty-five years at Oral Roberts University Graduate School of Theology and Ministry, Tulsa, Oklahoma, and author of *Church Aflame* , a commentary on Acts 1-12 and *The Epistle of Paul to the Ephesians* (Deo Publishing, UK, 2013). In addition, he is a contributor to the *Spirit-filled Life Bible* and *The African Cultural Heritage Topical Bible*. Dr. Grizzle is a popular speaker at conventions and conferences nationally and internationally.

Patrick L. Kelly

Patrick L. Kelly, an ordained Church of God Bishop. Kelly is a pastor and author who has led churches in Canada and the U.S. He holds a B.A. and an M.A. in Theology and was conferred with a D.Div degree. He currently serves as Lead Pastor of Cathedral Church of God in Deerfield Beach, Florida.

Bradley Ramsey

Serves as pastor of Lake Worth Church Of God in Lake Worth Beach, Florida was first licensed as a minister in the Church of God at the age of 15. He attended Lee University where he completed a B.A. in Bible and Theology and the Pentecostal Theological Seminary in Cleveland, TN where he earned an M.Div. with and emphasis in Biblical Studies. He earned an additional M.Phil. at the University of Birmingham, where he later completed doctoral studies. Ramsey has preached around the world including at the William Carey School of World Missions in South Africa. Ramsey is currently pastoring the Lake Worth Church of God, in Lake Worth Beach, Florida.

David G. Roebuck

David G. Roebuck, Ph.D., directs the Hal Bernard Dixon Jr. Pentecostal Research Centre. He is an assistant professor of religion at Lee University and an adjunct faculty member of the Pentecostal Theological Seminary. In 2004, Dr. Roebuck was appointed Church Historian of the Church of God. Dr. Roebuck earned his Ph.D. in Religion at Vanderbilt University (1997). His major was the history of Christianity, and his dissertation was "Limiting Liberty: The Church of God and Women Ministers, 1886-1996." His educational experience also includes a B.A. in Christian Education from West Coast Christian College (1981), a M.Div. from the Church of God Theological Seminary (1984), and a M.A. from Vanderbilt University

Phyllis Thompson

Phyllis Thompson is a Pentecostal educator. She has a background in development education and Pastoral ministry in the UK. She served as the National Education Director for the New Testament Church of God in England and Wales from 2007-2018. She is the pioneer and coordinator of the New Testament Church of God Heritage Centre and the Oliver Lyseight Lectures. Phyllis is currently a member of the leadership team of her local Church in Northampton, England, a member of the European Pentecostal Theological Association [EPTA]Executive Committee. She sits on the Church of God International Education Board and is a member of the Church of God International Historical Commission. She has written on topics to do with Black Majority Churches, and women in Christian leadership. Recent publications include her contribution to *Faith of our Fathers* (Pathway Press 2009), *Challenges of Black Pentecostal Leadership in the 21st Century* (SPCK 2013) and *Challenges of Pentecostal Theology in the 21st Century* (SPCK 2020) the latter two for which she is the editor.

Wayne C. Solomon

Wayne Solomon is Pastor of Transformed Life Ministries in Clermont Florida. Formerly the Church of God Administrative Bishop of the Great Lakes Region and Florida. Solomon is Adjunct Professor of Sociology and Religion at Lee University, and Adjunct Professor of Practical Theology at Pentecostal Theological Seminary. He is a highly motivated, international leader and conference speaker whose work has positively impacted thousands of lives worldwide. Dr. Solomon is author and co-author of twenty-one booklets and three books. Bishop Solomon holds a D.Min, an M.A. a B.A. and associate degrees, Certificates and Diplomas in Leadership, Sociology, Theology, Management and Human Services. He obtained his education at the Pentecostal Theological Seminary, Brown University, Harvard University, the University of the West Indies, Lee University, Rhode Island College, Quinebaug Valley Community College and the New Testament Church of God Bible Institute of Trinidad and Tobago.

Bibliography

"Dr Selwyn E Arnold, New Testament Church of God." https://ntcg.org.uk/ about/history/dr-selwyn-arnold/, accessed January 11, 2021.

"Selwyn Arnold Obituary (2013), *The (Trenton, NJ) Times,* https://obits.nj.com/amp/obituaries/trenton/167941744.

Abplanalp, Marilyn. "Ethnic Inclusion in Pastoral Leadership in the Assemblies of God Fellowship from 1906-1999: A Case Study", Paper Presented to the 31st Annual Meeting of the Society for Pentecostal Studies, Southeastern University of the Assemblies of God, Lakeland, FL, March 14-16, 2002.

Adedibu, Babatunde. *Coat of Many Colours: The Origin, Growth, Distinctiveness and Contributions of Black Majority Churches to British Christianity.* (Gloucester, UK: Wisdom Summit, 2012).

Aldred, Joe. Respect: *Understanding Caribbean British Christianity.* (Peterborough: Epworth Publication, 2005).

Alexander, Estrelda Y. *Black Fire: One Hundred Years of African American Pentecosta*lism (Downers Grove, IL: InterVarsity Press, 2011).

_____.*Limited Liberty: The Legacy of Four Pentecostal Women* (Cleveland, OH: Pilgrim Press, 2008).

_____.*The Will to Power: Confronting Ideologies that Dismantle Christian Community.* (Lanham, MD: Seymour Press, 2019).

_____.*The Women of Azusa Street.* (Cleveland, OH: Pilgrim Press, 2005).

_____. "Seymour, William Joseph 1871-1922." in *The Dictionary of Pan-African Pentecostalism*, Volume One: North America. (La Vergne: Wipf and Stock Publishers, 2018).

Alexander, Kimberly Ervin and R. Hollis Gause. *Women in Leadership: A Pentecostal Perspective.* (Cleveland, TN: Center for Pentecostal Leadership and Care, 2006).

Alexander, Valentina. "Breaking Every Fetter: To What Extent has the Black Led Church in Britain Developed a Theology of Liberation?" PhD Thesis, University of Warwick, 1996.

Amo, Antonius Guilielmus. "On the Apathy of the Human Mind or the Absence of Sense and of the Faculty of Sensing in the Human Mind and the

Presence of These in our Organic and Living Body," University of Wittenburg, Schlomach, April 1734.

Anderson, Allan. *An Introduction to Pentecostalism: Global Charismatic Christianity.* (Cambridge UK: Cambridge University Press, 2004).

Anderson, Carver. "Black Young Men: Problematisation, Humanisation and Effective Engagement" in Julie M. Parsons and Anne Chappell, ed. *The Palgrave Handbook of Auto/Biography,* (London: Palgrave MacMillan, 2020).

_____. *Commission on Gangs and Violence: Uniting to Improve Safety.* (Birmingham, UK: Office of West Midlands Police and Crime Commissioner, 2017).

_____. "Towards a Practical Theology for Effective Responses to Black Young Men Associated with Crime for Black Majority Churches" PhD thesis, Birmingham University, 2015.

Anselm. *Cur Deus Homo* (New York: Magisterium Press, 2015).

Aquinas, Thomas. *Summa Theologica,* trans. Fathers of the English Dominican Province (New York: Benziger Brothers, 1911–1925).

Arnold, Selwyn E. *From Scepticism to Hope: One Black-Led Church's Response to Social Responsibility.* Bramcote. (Nottingham, UK: Grove Books Ltd., 1992).

Asante, Molefi Kete. *The Egyptian Philosophers: Ancient African Voices From Imhotep to Akhenaten* (Chicago: African American Images, 2000).

Athanasius of Alexandria, *On the Incarnation* (Salt Lake City, UT: Pantianos Classic, 1944).

Aulen, Gustaf. *Christus Victor* (London: SPC, 2010); Kelly Brown Douglas, *The Black Christ* (Maryknoll, NY: Orbis Books, 1993).

Austin-Broos, Diane. *Jamaica* Genesis: Religion and the Politics of Moral Orders (Chicago: University of Chicago Press, 1997).

Baker-Fletcher, Karen. *Dancing with God: The Trinity from a Womanist Perspective* (St Louis, MO: Chalice Press, 2006).

Bantu, Vince L. *Gospel Haymanot: A Constructive Theology and Critical Reflection on African and Diasporic Christianity* (Downers Grove, IL: InterVarsity Press, 2020).

Barclay, William. *The Mind of St. Paul* (New York: Harper & Row, 1975).

Bartleman, Frank. *How Pentecost Came to Los Angeles*. (Los Angeles: Frank
   Bartleman, 1925).

Beckford, Robert. *Dread and Pentecostal: A Political Theology for the Black Church in
   Britain*. (London: SPCK, 2000).

_____. *God and the Gangs: An Urban Toolkit for Those who Won't be Sold Out,
   Bought Out Or Scared Out*. (London: Darton, Longman and Todd Ltd, 2004).

Berkhof, Louis. *Systematic Theology*. (Edinburgh: Banner of Truth Trust, 1981).

Berry, Mary Frances. *Black Resistance/White Law A History of Constitutional Racism
   in America*. (New York: Penguin Books, 1994).

Black, Allen. *The Book of Mark*. (Joplin, MO: College Press, 1995).

Blum, Edward J. and Paul Harvey. *The Color of Christ: The Son of God and the Saga of
   Race in America* (Chapel Hill, NC: University of North Carolina Press, 2012).

Boff, Leonard. and Clodovis Boff. *Introducing Liberation Theology* (Tunbridge Wells,
   Kent: Burns & Oates, 1987).

Breasted, James Henry. *Development of Religion and Thought in Ancient Egypt*.
   (Philadelphia PA: Pennsylvania University Press, 1972.)

Bright, C. F. "Stick to the Church of God," *Church of God Evangel*, (29 March
   1924).

Brogdon, Lewis. *Hope on the Brink: Understanding the Emergence of Nihilism in Black
   America* (Eugene OR: Wipf and Stock Publishers, 2013).

Brooks, Ira. *Where do We go from Here: A History of 25 Years of the New Testament
   Church of God in the United Kingdom – 1955-1980*. (London: Charles Raper,
   1982).

Brown, A. Elaine Crawford. *Hope in the Holler: A Womanist Theology*. (Louisville,
   KY: Westminster John Knox, 2002).

Bruce, F. F. *New Testament History*. (North Kingston, RI: Kingsley Books 1980).

Bryan, Beverley, Stella Dadzie and Suzanne Scafe. *The Heart of the Race: Black
   Women's Lives in Britain*. (London: Virago Press, 1986).

Buber, Martin. *I and Thou* (Mahwah, NJ: Paulist Press, 2003).

Bulmer, Martin and John Solomos. *Racism*. (New York: Oxford University Press,
   1999).

Burke, Daniel. "Black Christians are bracing for a Whitelash." CNN, July 21, 2020. https://www.cnn.com/2020/07/10/us/white-black-christians-racism-burke.

Butler, Cheryl Nelson. 'The Racial Roots of Human Trafficking", September 1, 2015, https://www.uclalawreview.org/racial-roots-human-trafficking/

Butt, Kyle. "Jesus, the Syrophoenician Woman, and Little Dogs" http://www.apologeticspress.org/. APContent.aspx?category=22&article=317. Accessed 9/28/2020.

Byfield, Cheron. *Black Boys Can Make It: How They Overcome the Obstacles to University in the UK and USA*. (Stoke on Trent, UK: Trentam Books Limited, 2008).

C. E. B. Cranfield. "St Mark," *The Cambridge Greek Testament Commentary* (London: Cambridge University Press, 1959).

C. F. Bright. "Stick to the Church of God," *Church of God Evangel*, 29 March 1924, 2.

Cannon, Katie and Anthony Pinn. *The Oxford Handbook of African American Theology* (Oxford, UK: Oxford University Press, 2014).

Cappel, Cecilia. "'From Whence Cometh My Help'? Domestic Abuse and Black-Led Churches in Britain" PhD thesis, University of Surrey, 2009.

Carter, J. Kameron. *Race: A Theological Account*, 1st edition. (New York: Oxford University Press, 2008).

Cartledge, Mark J. *Encountering the Spirit: The Charismatic Tradition*. Traditions of Christian Spirituality Series. (Maryknoll, NY: Orbis Books, 2007).

_____.*Practical Theology: Charismatic and Empirical Perspectives* (Carlisle, Cumbria: Paternoster Press, 2003).

Charles W. Conn. *Like A Mighty Army: A History of the Church of God, 1886-1996* [Tribute Edition] (Cleveland, TN: Pathway Press, 2008).

Church of God. *Echoes from the General Assembly*, (Cleveland, Tenn.: n.p., 1912), 7.

Church of God, *Minutes of the Eleventh Annual Assembly of the Churches of God*. (Cleveland, TN: n.p., 1915).

_____. *Minutes of the Thirteenth Annual Assembly of the Churches of God* (Cleveland, TN: Church of God Publishing House, 1917).

_____., *Minutes of the Fourteenth Annual Assembly of the Churches of God*. (Cleveland, TN.: Church of God Publishing House, 1919.

_____. *Minutes of the Fifteenth General Assembly of the Churches of God*. (Cleveland, TN: Church of God Publishing House, 1920).

_____. *Minutes of the Seventeenth Annual Assembly of the Churches of God*. (Cleveland, TN: Church of God Publishing House, 1922).

_____. *Minutes of the Eighteenth Annual Assembly of the Churches of God*. (Cleveland, TN: Church of God Publishing House, 1923).

Church of God Colored *Work*. *Minutes of the 30th Annual Assembly of the Church of God Colored Work*. (Jacksonville: Church of God Colored Work, 1954)

Clifton Clarke R. *The Reason Why We Sing: Introducing Black Pentecostal Spirituality*. (Cambridge, UK: Grove Books).

Coard, Bernard. *How the West Indian Child is Made Educationally Sub-Normal in the British School System* (London: New Beacon Books, 1971).

Cone, Cecil. *The Identity Crisis in Black Theology* (New York: African Methodist Episcopal Church, 1975).

Cone, James H. *Black Theology and Black Power* (New York: Seabury Press, 1969).

_____.*God of the Oppressed* (Maryknoll, NY: Orbis Books, 2012).

_____.*Martin & Malcolm and America*. (Maryknoll, NY: Orbis Books, 2002).

_____.*Speaking the Truth – Ecumenism, Liberation, and Black Theology* (Grand Rapids, MI: William B. Eerdmans Publishing Company, 1986).

_____.*The Cross and the Lynching*. (Maryknoll, NY: Orbis Books, 2011).

Conn, Charles W. *Like A Mighty Army: A History of the Church of God, 1886-1996*. [Tribute Edition] (Cleveland, Tenn.: Pathway Press, 2008).

Conn, J. Stephen. *Growing up Pentecostal*. (Longwood, TX: Xulon Press, 2006).

Cossey, James E. R. M. *The First of His Kind*. (Cleveland, TN: Pathway Press, n.d.).

Crawford, A. Elaine. Brown *Hope in the Holler: A Womanist Theology*. (Louisville, KY: Westminster John Knox, 2002).

Crews, Mickey. *The Church of God: A Social History*. (Knoxville, TN: The University of Tennessee Press, 1990).

Crockatt, Richard. "American Liberalism and the Atlantic World, 1916-17," *Journal of American Studies* 11:1 (Apr 1977).

De Wolfe, Thomas. *Norman, Inheriting the Trade: A Northern Family Confronts Its Legacy as the Largest Slave-Trading Dynasty in U.S. History.* (Boston: Beacon Press 2008).

DeGruy, Joy. *Post Traumatic Slave Syndrome: America's Legacy of Enduring Injury and Healing.* (Portland OR: Joy DeGruy Publications Inc., 2017).

Deutscher, Guy. *Through the Language Glass: Why the World Looks Different in Other Languages.* (London: Arrow Books, 2010).

Deweese, Charles W. "Baptist Women Deacons and Deaconesses: Key Developments and Trends, 1609-2005." *Baptist History and Heritage.* (Summer 2005).

DeYmaz, Mark. *Building a Healthy Multi-Ethnic Church: Mandate, Commitments, and Practices of a Diverse Congregation.* (San Francisco, CA: Jossey-Bass/John Wiley, 2007).

DiAngelo, Robin. *White Fragility: Why It's So Hard for White People to Talk about Racism.* (Boston: Beacon Press, 2018).

Dixon, Thomas F. Jr. *The Clansman: An Historical Romance of the Ku Klux Klan.* (New York, Doubleday, 1905).

Du Bois, W. E. B. "Does the Negro Need Separate Schools?" *Journal of Negro Education* 4:3 (July 1935).

_____. *The Souls of Black Folk.* (Chicago: A.C. McClurg & Co, 1903).

Dulles, Avery. *Models of the Church.* (London: Image Books, 2002).

Durham, William H. "The Great Revival at Azusa St.: How It Began and How It Ended," *Pentecostal Testimony* 1:8 (1911), 3.

Ehrenspreger, Kathy. "Paul, his People and Racial Terminology," *Journal of Early Christian History,* 3:1 (2013), 17-32.

Ely, Peter and David Denny, *Social Work in a Multi-Racial Society.* (Aldershot, England: Gower Pub Co., 1987).

Emerson, Michael and Christian Smith. *Divided by Faith: Evangelical Religion and the Problem of Race in America.* (Oxford, UK: Oxford University Press, 2001).

Evans, James. *We Have Been Believers: An African American Systematic Theology.* (Minneapolis, MN: Fortress, Press 2012).

Felder, Cain Hope. *Troubling Biblical Waters: Race, Class, and Family*. (Maryknoll, NY: Orbis Books, 1989).

_____, ed. *Stoney the Road We Trod: American Biblical Interpretations*. (Minneapolis, MN: Augsburg Fortress, 1991).

Freire, Paulo. *Pedagogy of the Oppressed*. (London: Penguin Education, 1972).

Frenk, Julio. "Racism and Public Health." *Harvard T.H. Chan School of Public Health News*, December 17, 2014. https://www.hsph.harvard.edu/news/features/racism-and-public-health-statement-from-dean-julio-frenk/.

Fretheim, Terrence E. *The Suffering of God*. (Minneapolis, MN: Fortress Press, 1984).

Fryer, Peter. *Staying Power: The History of Black People in Britain*. (London: Pluto Press, 1984).

Gayraud, Wilmore. and James H. Cone. *Black Theology: A Documentary History 1966-1979*. (Maryknoll, NY: Orbis Books, 1979).

Glynn, Black. *Men, Invisibility, and Crime: Towards a Critical Race Theory of Desistance*. (London: Routledge, 2014).

Goff, Phillip Atiba and Hilary Rau. "Predicting Bad Policing: Theorizing Burdensome and Racially Disparate Policing through the Lenses of Social Psychology and Routine Activities." https://journals.sagepub. com/doi/full/10.1177/0002716220901349.

Gramlich, John. "Black Imprisonment Rate in the U.S. has Fallen by a Third Since 2006." Pew Research Center, *FactTank* https://www.pewresearch. org/ fact-tank/2020/05/06/black-imprisonment-rate-in-the-u-s-has-fallen-by-a-third-since-2006/.

Grant, Jacquelyn. *White Women's Christ and Black Women's Jesus: Feminist Christology and Womanist Response*. (Atlanta: Scholars Press, 2012).

Green, Hilary. *Educational Reconstruction: African American Schools in the Urban South, 1865–1890*. (New York: Fordham University Press, 2016).

Grenz, Stanley. *Theology for the Community of God*. (Grand Rapids, MI: William B. Eerdmans Publishing Co., 2000).

Griffin, Michael and Jennie Block W. eds. *In The Company of The Poor: Conversations with Dr. Paul Farmer and Fr. Gustavo Gutierrez*. (Maryknoll, NY: Orbis Books, 2013).

Grizzle, Trevor. *Church Aflame: An Exposition of Acts 1-12.* (Cleveland, TN: Pathway Press, 2000).

Grudem, Wayne. *Systematic Theology.* (Grand Rapids, MI: Zondervan, 1994).

Gushee, David. *The Righteous Gentiles of the Holocaust: A Christian Interpretation.* (Minneapolis: Fortress Press, 1994).

Herbjørnsrud, Dag. "The African Enlightenment." *AEON.* Dec. 13, 2017. https://aeon.co/essays/yacob-and-amo-africas-precursors-to-locke-hume-and-kant.

Hickson, Peter C. *"History of the Church of God Colored Work" in Minutes of the 30th Annual Assembly of the Church of God Colored Work.* (Jacksonville, FL: Church of God Colored Work, 1954).

Hill, Timothy. "Racism is Sin-God Despises It." *Faith News*, 27 May 2020, https://vacog.org/blog/hill-condemns-racist-acts.

Hoffman, Kelly M., et al. "Racial Bias in Pain Assessment and Treatment Recommendations, and False Beliefs about Biological Differences between Blacks and Whites," Proceedings of the National Academy of Sciences, https://www.pnas.org/content/early/2016/03/30/1516047113.abstract.

Hollenweger, Walter J. *Pentecostalism: Origins and Developments Worldwide.* (Peabody, MA: Hendrickson Publishers, 1997).

Hopkins, Dwight. *Introducing Black Theology of Liberation.* (Maryknoll, NY: Orbis Books, 1999).

Howell, R. B. C. *The Deaconship: Its Nature, Qualifications, Relations, Duties.* (King of Prussia, PA: Judson Press 1946).

Hudson, Andrew S. "An African Reading of an Appalachian Church: An Intentional Reconstructive Ethnohistory of the Church of God." M.Div. thesis. Princeton Theological Seminary, 2011.

Hunter, Harold D. "A Journey Toward Racial Reconciliation: Race Mixing in the Church of God of Prophecy," in Cecil M. Robeck Jr. and Harold D. Hunter, eds. *The Azusa Street Revival and Its Legacy.* (Cleveland, TN: Pathway Press, 2006).

Isaac, Benjamin. *The Invention of Racism in Classical Antiquity.* (Princeton, NJ: Princeton University Press, 2004).

Jackson, Joseph E. *Reclaiming Our Heritage: The Search for Black History in the Church of God.* (Cleveland, TN: Church of God Black Ministries, 1993).

James, George G.M. *Stolen Legacy: Greek Philosophy is Stolen Egyptians Philosophy.* (Trenton, NJ: Africa World Press, 1992).

James, Marcy, et al. "Public Health Policy for Preventing Violence," *Health Affairs*,12, no 2(1993):7-29, http://content.healthaffairs.org/content/12/4/7.

Jenkins, Richard and John Solomos. *Racism and Equal Opportunity Policies in the 1980s,* 2nd ed. (Cambridge, UK: Cambridge University Press,1989).

Jennings, Willie James. *After Whitness: An Education in Belonging.* (Grand Rapids, MI: William B. Eerdmans Publishing Co., 2020).

_____. *The Christian Imagination: Theology and the Origins of Race.* (New Haven, CT: Yale University Press, 2011).

Jones, Major J. *The Color of God: The Concept of God in Afro-American Thought.* (Macon, GA: Mercer University Press, 2000).

Jones, William. *Is God a White Racist.* (Boston: Beacon Press, 1997).

Kane, Margaret. *What Kind of God: Reflections on Working with People and Church in North-East England.* (London: SCM Press, 1986).

Kant, Immanuel. *Critique of Pure Reason.* (Boston: St. Martin's Press, 1929).

Kay, William K. *Pentecostalism: A Very Short Introduction* (Oxford: Oxford University Press, 2011).

Kendi, Ibram X. *How to Be an Antiracist.* (New York, NY: One World, 2019).

King, Martin Luther, Jr. *"I Have a Dream." In A Testament of Hope: The Essential Writings of Martin Luther King, Jr*, 1st ed. (San Francisco: Harper & Row, 1986).

_____. *"I See the Promised Land." In A Testament of Hope: The Essential Writings of Martin Luther King, Jr,* 1st ed. (San Francisco: Harper & Row, 1986).

_____. *Strength to Love.* 1st Fortress Press ed. (Philadelphia: Fortress Press, 1981).

_____. "The UnChristian Christian." *Ebony*, (August 1965).

_____. 'What is Your Life's Blueprint,' Speech delivered to Barrett Junior High School, October 26, 1967. https://1ccaxf2hhhbh1jcwiktlicz7-

wpengine.netdna-ssl.com/wp-content/uploads/2017/01/MLK-Lifes-Blueprint.pdf.

King, Martin Luther, Jr. and James Melvin Washington. *A Testament of Hope: The Essential Writings of Martin Luther King, Jr.* 1st ed. (San Francisco: Harper & Row, 1986).

Kirk, John Andrew. "Race, Class, Caste and the Bible," *Themelios*, 10:2 (Jan 1985).

Kozol, Jonathan. *Savage Inequalities: Children in American Schools.* (New York: Broadway Paperback, 1991).

Land, Steven J. *Pentecostal Spirituality: A Passion for the Kingdom.* (Sheffield: Sheffield, 1993).

Lane, William. *The Gospel of Mark: The English Text With Introduction, Exposition, and Notes,* (The New International Commentary on the New Testament). (Grand Rapids, MI: William B. Eerdmans Publishing Co., 1974).

Lee, Hak Joon. "Church and State in Kings Ethics." Lecture 6 presented at the Theology and Ethics of Martin Luther King Jr. Conference, Fuller Theological Seminary, Summer 2020.

_____. *The Great World House: Martin Luther King, Jr., and Global Ethics.* (Cleveland, OH: Pilgrim Press, 2011).

Lee, Hak Joon and Peter J. Paris. *We Will Get to the Promised Land: Martin Luther King, Jr.'s Communal-Political Spirituality.* (Eugene, OR: Wipf & Stock Publishers, 2017).

Lee, Matthew T. and Margaret M. Poloma. *A Sociological Study of the Great Commandment in Pentecostalism: The Practice of Godly Love as Benevolent Service.* (Lewiston, NY: Edwin Mellen Press, 2009).

Lemons, M. S. *Questions Answered.* (Cleveland, TN: Church of God (Cleveland, TN, n.d.).

Lindsay, Ben. *We Need to Talk about Race: Understanding the Black Experience in White Majority Churches.* (London: SPCK, 2019).

Long, Charles H. "African American Religion in the United States of America: An Interpretative Essay," *Nova Religio: The Journal of Alternative and Emergent Religion* 7:1 (July 2003).

Lugo, Esteban. "A Theology of Ethnic Diversity: God's Mosaic," *Center for Economic Justice Online*, April 30, 2013. https://www.cejonline.com/ article/ a-theology-of-ethnic-diversity-gods-mosaic.

Lundskow, George N. *The Sociology of Religion A Substantive and Transdisciplinary Approach*. (London: SAGE, 2008).

Lynn, Marvin and Adrienne Dixon. *Handbook on Critical Race Theory in Education*, 2nd ed. (New York: Routledge, 2015).

Lyseight, Oliver. *Forward March: An Autobiography*. (Sedgley, West Midlands: George S Garwood, 1995).

Macchia, Frank D. *Baptized in the Spirit: A Global Pentecostal Theology*. (Grand Rapids, MI: Zondervan, 2006).

MacRobert, Iain. *The Black Roots and White Racism of Early Pentecostalism in the USA*. (Eugene, OR: Wipf and Stock, 2003).

Marcy, James, et al. "Public Health Policy for Preventing Violence," *Health Affairs*, 12:2 (1993):7-29.

Mason, Eric. *Woke Church: An Urgent Call for Christians in America to Confront Racism and Injustice*. (Chicago, IL: Moody Publishers, 2018).

Mays, Benjamin E. *The Negro's God as Reflected in his Literature*. (Eugene, OR: Wipf and Stock, 2010).

Mbiti, John. *African Religion and Philosophy*. (New York: Anchor Books, 1970).

Michel, David. *Telling the Story of Black Pentecostals in the Church of God*. (Cleveland, TN: Pathway Press, 2000).

Middleton, Richard. *The Liberating Image: The Imago Dei in Genesis 1*. (Grand Rapids, MI: Brazos Press, 2005).

Mitchem, Stephanie Y. "Embodiment," in *The Oxford Handbook of African American Theology*, ed. Katie Cannon and Anthony Pinn. (Oxford, UK: Oxford University Press, 2014).

Montgomery, Carrie Judd. "The Work in Los Angeles." *Triumphs of Faith* 27:1 (January 1907).

Moore, Rosetta Austin. *The Impact of Slavery on the Education of Blacks in Orange County, North Carolina: 1619–1970* (Morrisville, NC: Lulu Publishing Services, 2015).

Morgan, Louis F. "Bishop J.H. Curry: An Eminent Church Leader," *Church of God History and Heritage*, (Winter/Spring 2003).

Muir, R. David. "Black Theology, Pentecostalism, and Racial Struggles in the Church of God" (PhD. Dissertation University of London: King's College, 2003).

Mutowa, Cosmos. 'Cosmos' Story', *The Link* (Autumn 2020): 12–14.

Niebuhr, Reinhold. *The Nature and Destiny of Man* (Louisville, KY: Westminster John Knox, 1996).

Noll, Mark A. *God and Race in American Politics: A Short History.* (Princeton, NJ: Princeton University Press, 2008).

Nolland, John. *The Gospel of Matthew* (Grand Rapids, MI: William B. Eerdmans Publishing Co., 2005).

Oden, Thomas C. *How Africa Shaped the Christian Mind: Rediscovering the African Seedbed of Western Christianity.* (Downers Grove, IL: InterVarsity Press, 2007).

Oltman, Adele. *Sacred Mission, Worldly Ambition: Black Christian Nationalism in the Age of Jim Crow.* (Athens, GA: University of Georgia Press, 2008).

Olusoga, David. *Black and British: A Forgotten History.* (London: Pan Books, 2017).

Patten, Eileen. "Racial, Gender Wage Gaps Persist in U.S. Despite Some Progress," Pew Research Center, July 01, 2016 https://www.pewresearch.org/ fact-tank/2016/07/01/racial-gender-wage-gaps-persist-in-u-s-despite-some-progress.

Pattison, Stephen. *The Challenges of Practical Theology: Selected Essays.* (London: Jessica Kingsley, 2007).

Paul Ballard and John Pritchard. *Practical Theology in Action: Christian Thinking in the Service of Church and Society*, 2nd ed. (London: SPCK, 2006).

Paul, Kathleen. *Whitewashing Britain: Race and Citizenship in the Post-War Era.* (Ithaca, NY: Cornell University Press, 1997).

Paveley, Rebecca. "Churches Together in England Presidents Call for Action to End Racism", *Church Times* (31 July 2020), 3.

Pearson, Roger. *Shockley on Eugenics and Race.* (Washington, DC: Scott Townsend Publishers, 1992).

Perdue, Leo G., ed. *Families in Ancient Israel. 1st ed. The Family, Religion, and Culture.* (Louisville, KY: Westminster John Knox Press, 1997).

Phillips, Mike and Trevor Phillips. *Windrush: The Irresistible Rise of Multi-Racial Britain.* (London: HarperCollins, 1998).

Pieterse, Jan Nederveen. *White in Black: Images of African and Blacks in Western Popular Culture.* (New Haven, CT: Yale University Press, 1992).

Pinn, Anthony. *Terror and Triumph.* (Minneapolis, MN: Augsburg Fortress, 2003).

_____. *The Black Church in the Post–Civil Rights Era. (*Maryknoll, NY: Orbis Books, 2002).

Pitirim A. Sorokin. *The Ways and Power of Love: Types, Factors, and Techniques of Moral Transformation.* (Philadelphia, PA: Templeton Foundation Press, 2002).

Plantinga, Richard J., Matthew D. Lundberg, and Thomas R. Thompson. *Introduction to Christian Theology.* (Cambridge, UK: Cambridge University Press, 2010).

Pratt, Trudy A. "Building the Kingdom: Memories of Bishop Crawford F. Bright," *Church of God History and Heritage,* (Winter/Spring 2003).

Raboteau, Albert J. *Slave Religion the "Invisible Institution" in the Antebellum South.* (Oxford, UK: Oxford University Press. 2004).

Reddie, Anthony. *Black Theology in Transatlantic Dialogue.* (New York: Palgrave Macmillan, 2006).

Ricoeur, Paul. *Freud and Philosophy: An Essay on Interpretation.* (New Haven: Yale University Press, 1970).

Robeck, Cecil M. *The Azusa Street Revival and Mission: The Birth of the Global Pentecostal Movement.* (Nashville: Nelson Publications, 2006).

Robins, R. G. *A. J. Tomlinson: Plainfolk Modernist.* (New York: Oxford University Press, 2004).

Robinson, Elaine. A. *Race and Theology.* (Nashville, TN: Abingdon Press, 2012).

Robinson, Jo Ann Gibson, and David J. Garrow. *The Montgomery Bus Boycott and the Women Who Started It: The Memoir of Jo Ann Gibson Robinson.* (Knoxville, TN: University of Tennessee Press, 1987).

Rodgers, Darrin J. *Northern Harvest: Pentecostalism in North Dakota.* (Bismarck, ND: North Dakota District Council of the Assemblies of God, 2003).

Roebuck, David G. "Faithful Pilgrims: Establishing the Church of God," in Andrea Johnson, ed., *Servants of the Spirit: Portraits of Pentecostal/Charismatic Pioneers.* (Des Moines, IA: OBC Publishing, 2010).

271

_____. "Restorationism and a Vision for a World Harvest: A Brief History of the Church of God." https://fliphtml5.com/jjnr/qodq/basic, 1999.

_____. "Unraveling the Cords that Divide: Cultural Challenges and Race Relations in the Church of God (Cleveland, TN)." Paper presented at the annual meeting for the Society for Pentecostal Studies, Memphis, TN, March 10-12, 5.

Rothenberg, Paula S. *White Privilege: Essential Readings on the Other Side of Racism.* (New York: Worth Publishers, 2005).

Schleiermacher, Friedrich. *The Christian Faith.* (London: T&T Clark, 2003).

Sheldrake, Phillip. *Encountering the Spirit: The Charismatic Tradition.* Traditions of Christian Spirituality Series. (Maryknoll, NY: Orbis Books, 2007).

Simmons, E. L. *History of the Church of God.* (Cleveland, TN: Church of God Publishing House, 1938).

Smith, Amanda Berry. *An Autobiography: The Story of the Lord's Dealings with Mrs. Amanda Smith, the Colored Evangelist: Containing an Account of Her Life Work of Faith, and Her Travels in America, England, Ireland, Scotland, India, and Africa as an Independent Missionary.* (Chicago: Meyer & Brother Publishers, 1893).

Smith, Joseph E. H. "The Enlightenment's Race Problem and Ours." *The New York Times,* (February 11, 2014).

Sölle, Dorothee. *Theology for Sceptics.* (Minneapolis MN: Fortress Press, 1995).

Span, Christopher M. *From Cotton Field to Schoolhouse: African American Education in Mississippi, 1862–1875.* (Chapel Hill, NC: University of North Carolina Press, 2009).

Spurling, R. G. *The Lost Link.* (Turtletown, TN: R. G. Spurling, 1920).

Stifler, J. M. *An Introduction to the Study of the Acts of the Apostles.* (New York: Fleming & Revell, 1892).

Stott, John. *Issues Facing Christians Today: A Major Appraisal of Contemporary Social and Moral Questions.* (Basingstoke, UK: Marshalls, 1984).

_____. *The Spirit, the Church, and the World: The Message of Acts.* (Downers Grove, IL: InterVarsity Press, 1990).

Sturge, Mark. *Look What the Lord Has Done: An Exploration of Black Christian Faith in Britain.* (Bletchley, UK: Scripture Union, 2005).

Swann, Michael S. *The Holy Jumpers: A Concise History of the Church of God of Prophecy in the Bahamas (190-1974).* (Maitland, FL: Xulon Press, 2018).

Sweet, Leonard L. *Black Images of America, 1784–1870.* (New York: Norton, 1976).

Terrell, JoAnne Marie. *Power in the Blood? The Cross in the African Experience.* (Eugene, OR: Wipf & Stock, 1997).

Thompson, H. Paul Jr. "'On Account of Conditions that Seem Unalterable:' A Proposal about Race Relations in the Church of God. (Cleveland, TN) 1909-1929," *Pneuma: The Journal of the Society for Pentecostal Studies,* 25: 2 (Fall 2003).

Thompson, Phyllis, ed. *Challenges of Pentecostal Theology in the 21st Century.* (London: SPCK, 2020).

Thompson, Sydney. *Unfolding Destiny: An Autobiography. (*Birmingham, UK: Majesty Design and Print, 2004).

Thuesen, Sarah Caroline. *Greater than Equal: African American Struggles for Schools and Citizenship in North Carolina, 1919–1965.* (Chapel Hill, NC: University of North Carolina Press, 2013).

Tomlinson, A. J. *Diary,* 2, Nov. 26, 1908.

_____. *The Last Great Conflict.* (Cleveland, TN: Walter E. Rodgers, 1913).

Tomlinson, Homer. A. *Book of Doctrines: Issued in the Interest of the Church of God.* (Cleveland, TN: Church of God Publishing House, 1922).

Toulis, Nicole Rodriguez. *Believing Identity: Pentecostalism and the Mediation of Jamaican Ethnicity and Gender in England. Explorations in Anthropology.* (Oxford, UK, Berg Publishers, 1997).

Tysby, Jemar. *The Color of Compromise: The Truth about the American Church's Complicity in Racism.* (Grand Rapids, MI: Zondervan, 2020).

Villafane, Eldin. *The Liberating Spirit.* (Grand Rapids MI: William B. Eerdmans Publishing Co., 1993).

Wade, Nicholas. *A Troublesome Inheritance: Genes, Race, and Human History.* (New York: Penguin Books, 2014).

Wallis, Jim. *America's Original Sin: Racism, White Privilege, and the Bridge to a New America.* (Grand Rapids, MI: Baker Publishing Group, 2016).

273

Ware, Frederick. *African American Theology: An Introduction*. (Louisville, KY: Westminster John Knox Press, 2018).

Warren, Mervyn A. *King Came Preaching: The Pulpit Power of Dr. Martin Luther King, Jr.* (Downers Grove, IL: InterVarsity Press, 2001).

Wesley, Arun Kumar. "Sacralisation and Secularisation: An Analysis of a Few Biblical Passages for Possible Racial Overtones and Ethnocentrism," *The Asia Journal of Theology*, 16:2 (Oct 2002).

West, Cornel. *Race Matters*. (Boston: Beacon Press, 1993).

West, Cornel. *The Cornel West Reader*. (New York: Basic Books, 1999).

William Barclay. *The Mind of St. Paul*. (New York: Harper & Row, 1975).

Williams, Heather Andrea, Waldo E. Martin Jr., and Patricia Sullivan. *Self-Taught: African American Education in Slavery and Freedom*. (Chapel Hill, NC: University of North Carolina Press, 2005).

Wills, Charles W. "Global White Supremacy," in Paula S. Rothenberg, ed., *White Privilege: Essential Readings on the Other Side of Racism*. (New York: Worth Publishers, Inc., 2021).

Wills, Richard W. *Martin Luther King Jr. and the Image of God*. (Oxford, UK: Oxford University Press, 2009).

Wilmore, Gayraud and James H. Cone. *Black Theology: A Documentary History 1966-1979*. (Maryknoll, NY: Orbis Books, 1979).

Wilmore, Gayraud S. *Black Religion and Black Radicalism: An Interpretation of the Religious History of African Americans,* 3rd ed., rev. (Maryknoll, NY: Orbis Books, 1998).

_____. *Last Things First*. (Louisville, KY: Westminster John Knox Press, 1982).

Wimbush, Vincent L. *MisReading America: Scriptures and Difference*. (New Brunswick, NJ: Rutgers University Press, 2008).

_____. *Scripturalectics: The Management of Meaning*. (New York: Oxford University Press, 2017).

_____., ed., *Theorizing Scriptures*. (New Jersey: Rutgers University Press, 2008).

Woodson, Carter C. G. *The Education of Negroes Prior to 1861*. (New York: Arno Press, 1968).

Wright, Christopher J.H. *The Mission of God's People: A Biblical Theology of the Church's Mission.* (Grand Rapids, MI: Zondervan Academic, 2010).

Yancy, George. *Christology and Whiteness.* (London: Routledge, 2012).

Index

www.ingramcontent.com/pod-product-compliance
Lightning Source LLC
Chambersburg PA
CBHW070057030426

42335CB00016B/1926